Confronting Security Challenges on the Korean Peninsula

Edited by
Bruce E. Bechtol Jr.

Marine Corps University Press
Quantico, Virginia

The views expressed in this book are solely those of the authors. They do not necessarily reflect the opinions of the organizations for which they work, Marine Corps University, the U.S. Marine Corps, the Department of the Navy, or the U.S. government.

Contents

Introduction 1
    Bruce E. Bechtol Jr.

Chapter One
    Transfer of Wartime Command—Some Personal Thoughts 7
    Raymond P. Ayres Jr., Lieutenant General, USMC (Retired)

Chapter Two
    North Korea's Strategy of Compellence, Provocations, and the
    Northern Limit Line 13
    Robert M. Collins

Chapter Three
    The ROK–U.S. Military Alliance: Transformation and Change 37
    Cheon Seongwhun

Chapter Four
    The Lee Administration and Changes in ROK Strategic Culture ... 75
    Doug Joong Kim

Chapter Five
    The North Korean Military Threat 99
    Joseph S. Bermudez Jr.

Chapter Six
    Irregular Warfare on the Korean Peninsula 137
    David Maxwell, Colonel, USA

Chapter Seven
    Understanding North Korea's Human Rights Abuses 151
    Chuck Downs

Chapter Eight
    Breaking Barriers: The Media War for North Korea 167
    Donald Kirk

Chapter Nine
    The "Faminist" State 189
    George Alan Hutchinson

Symposium Participants 219

Introduction

by Bruce E. Bechtol Jr.

On September 1, 2010, the Marine Corps University, the Korea Economic Institute, and the Marine Corps University Foundation co-hosted an academic symposium dealing with the Korean Peninsula. Entitled "Confronting Security Challenges on the Korean Peninsula," the conference brought together scholars, practitioners, policy officials, and university students to address several challenging and ongoing questions dealing with the peninsula. The impressive list of speakers and panelists included retired general officers and ambassadors who have years of experience in Korea and the region, scholars from top universities and research institutes in both the United States and Korea, and practitioners—from both the military and policy communities—again from both countries.

There was a variety of diverse perspectives presented at the symposium, and as the reader will see in the book, they were often both relevant and compelling. If there was one thing that all conference participants agreed on, it was that the Korean Peninsula was and is in a state of flux. This is easily demonstrated if one simply considers that since the symposium convened during the summer of 2010, North Korea has launched an artillery attack against South Korean islands near the west coast of the peninsula, shown the world that it now has a highly enriched uranium processing facility (probably to be used for nuclear weaponization), and formally declared Kim Jong-il's third son as the next leader of the Democratic People's Republic of Korea (DPRK). Meanwhile, Pyongyang continues to engage in what are probably the worst human rights practices on the planet. The content of all of the papers presented at the recent symposium was relevant to all of these issues, and there were also many other points discussed that the reader is likely to find interesting.

There were three panels at the symposium, as well as two keynote speakers. Ambassador Charles "Jack" Pritchard, president of the Korea Economic Institute, gave an excellent speech addressing Northeast Asian regional issues before more than 150 people at the symposium luncheon.

The other keynote speaker, retired Marine Corps Lieutenant General Raymond P. Ayres, presented an outstanding speech to open the symposium, and graciously presented us with a copy. The general's speech, in its entirety, is presented in chapter 1. It addresses the issue of changing wartime operational control of Republic of Korea (ROK) and U.S. military forces—an issue that is highly relevant today—and offers important perspectives for those who will continue to deal with military issues on the Korean Peninsula as the United States and the Republic of Korea transition their command and control structure between now and 2015.

The panels addressed important issues relevant for both the present and future of the Korean Peninsula that remain important for the analysis and planning of future military operations and diplomatic relationships. The peninsula is also an important security pivot in U.S. foreign policy and military planning in the region—and one that will continue to be the focus of attention for Washington because of the importance of the ROK–U.S. alliance, and the unpredictable instability of the North Korean regime.

On the first panel, "Strategic Challenges on the Korean Peninsula," all three of the papers presented are included as chapters in this book. All of the individuals who were kind enough to contribute their chapters to this volume are former active duty U.S. or South Korean military personnel who continue to contribute to the scholarship relating to Korea through their work with the government and policy communities.

In chapter 2, "North Korea's Strategy of Compellence, Provocations, and the Northern Limit Line," Robert M. Collins discusses the discernible patterns of security policy that North Korea has displayed in recent years. To do this, he addresses many recent and important issues, such as the sinking of the ROK Navy corvette *Cheonan*, North Korea's brinkmanship and provocations, and possible actions that the ROK–U.S. alliance can take to deter these actions.

In the second paper (chapter 3) from the first panel, "The ROK–U.S. Military Alliance: Transformation and Change," Cheon Seongwhun suggests a unique and comprehensive approach to strengthening the alliance in light of the complex relationships and history that has existed between these two great nations. He offers policy recommendations and important perspectives that provide balance and shed light on the political, military, and cultural issues that play a role in giving us all a better understanding of what many consider to be Washington's most important security relationship in East Asia.

Doug Joong Kim, in the third paper from the first panel (chapter 4), discusses how South Korean policy has changed dramatically since the election of President Lee Myung-bak. Kim makes a compelling case for the school of thought that since President Lee's inauguration, South Korea has been far more capable of containing North Korean aggression, of moving closer to its key ally the United States, and improving its stature and operational readiness as a force for security and stability in Northeast Asia.

The second panel of the symposium was important because it addressed an issue that has come to the forefront since the revelations of Kim Jong-il's poor health—"Planning for Contingencies on the Korean Peninsula." It has now become apparent from recent events in the North, that present and future planning must involve not only experts from the military, but also the international and geo-political arenas, regional specialists, and various national and international agencies from both the United States and our allies. It was in the spirit of this important "whole of government approach" and doctrine that the second panel was convened.

In chapter 5, Joseph S. Bermudez Jr. of *Jane's Defence Weekly* addresses both the conventional and unconventional military threat that North Korea poses in his composition. Bermudez has written a simply brilliant essay that—by the numbers—destroys many fallacies and rumors about North Korea's true military capabilities. Those who have an interest in the North Korean order of battle, combat capabilities, and strategic military agenda, will find this chapter to be both interesting, and quite compelling.

U.S. Army Colonel David Maxwell, a member of the faculty at the National Defense University and one of the other presenters on the second panel, has contributed the chapter entitled, "Irregular Warfare on the Korean Peninsula." In his essay, Colonel Maxwell, an expert and experienced military planner and Special Forces officer, seeks to "explore some of the potential outcomes on the Korean Peninsula following either collapse of the Kim family regime or following conventional and unconventional conflict with North Korea as well as to examine some of the possible ways to prepare for and deal with those outcomes."

The third and final panel of the symposium was important because it provided interesting analysis regarding an issue that is not often discussed at military conferences—human rights. Entitled, "Human Rights and the Future of North Korea," the panel presents three papers that address this issue from distinctly different perspectives. Our contributors provide chapters that address human rights in North Korea from the diverse perspectives of a human rights activist and scholar, an expert logistician, and a broadly experienced and highly respected journalist.

In chapter 7, entitled "Understanding North Korea's Human Rights Abuses," Chuck Downs, the executive director of the Committee for Human Rights in North Korea, states in part:

> Basic freedoms, even those guaranteed by international agreements the North Korean regime has signed, are routinely denied to North Korea's citizens. The regime's food distribution policy and its political caste system predetermine that large segments of the North Korean population receive none of the food provided by international relief agencies and other countries. North Korea's political prison camps operate with an unmatched level of brutality. Its human rights crisis has serious regional and international consequences; it has caused a flow of refugees who often end up as victims of exploitation, violence, or crime when they cross into neighbouring countries, and China's approach to this humanitarian crisis is to send the refugees back to the North where they face certain persecution.

This essay provides a conceptual framework for understanding North Korea's human rights violations—and gives the reader extremely important insights.

Don Kirk, a widely respected journalist on East Asian affairs, provides us interesting and insightful analysis in chapter 8, entitled, "Breaking Barriers: The Media War for North Korea." He gives us the unique perspective of one who understands the media—particularly in East Asia—better than almost anyone. His insights will offer the reader ideas and important facts that will shed new light on how the press influences outside views North Korea—and the regime itself.

The final chapter addresses an issue that will be very important for both military planners and non-governmental organizations with a stake in North Korean human rights. In his essay entitled, "The 'Faminist' State," George Hutchinson addresses up-to-date data that provides important information regarding North Korea's constant fight to keep millions of its people from being malnourished. He states in part:

> Similar to the cycle that started in 1989, the period beginning in 2005 is characterized by increased international isolation, elevated status of the military, and the murkiness associated with North Korean political succession. However, unlike 1989, when the nation failed to adapt to a world shifting under its feet, it is North Korea that has systematically chosen to shift away from the world since 2005.

In this volume, our authors have given us several important theoretical frameworks, new concepts, and diverse perspectives regarding the security challenges that Washington and its allies now confront on the Korean Peninsula. Through their research and writing, our distinguished scholars, military officers, diplomats, and practitioners have made valuable contributions to the scholarship relating to the security and the stability of the Korean Peninsula, and the threats and challenges that are imminent for the future. In addition to our contributing authors, I would like to thank the gifted designer for this volume, Vincent J. Martinez. It is the hope of the Marine Corps University, the Korea Economic Institute, and the Marine Corps University Foundation—as well as all of the participants from the symposium—that this book will inspire continued interest and motivate further analysis within the military and policy communities regarding the security issues now confronting the Korean Peninsula.

Chapter 1

Transfer of Wartime Command—Some Personal Thoughts

by Lieutenant General Raymond P. Ayres Jr.
U.S. Marine Corps (Retired)

I was here [in Quantico, Virginia,] four years ago and made some remarks about wartime operational control in Korea because the big topic at that time was the transition to ROK [Republic of Korea] government operational control of its forces during war. With the recent shift in the effective date of the transfer of wartime command from April 2012 to December 2015, it is in the headlines again—especially in Korea.

I want to share some of my personal thoughts about this. What I have to say has nothing to do with any government position, ROK or U.S. It has nothing to do with any military position. This is just Ayres' point of view.

As designated in United Nations Security Council Resolution 86 of July 7, 1950, the United States is the executive agent for the United Nations for all matters related to the armistice on the Korean Peninsula, to include the resumption of hostilities. That's an important point. We're not at peace in Korea. We're at armistice in Korea. People forget that we're still technically at war. This responsibility is executed through the United Nations Command or UNC.

The UNC is not a warfighting command. The warfighting would be done by the Combined Forces Command (CFC)—at least while CFC still continues to exist. CFC is a bilateral command formed between the Republic of Korea and the United States. It is led by a binational system where the national command authorities of both nations make the decisions. The United States runs the war in Korea if it resumes. That gets lost in the translation sometimes because a U.S. Army general commands both the United Nations Command and the Combined Forces Command. It appears that the United States is running the war, but he's taking direction from both national command authorities.

CFC has its basis in the treaty between the two nations for the defense of Korea in the event of another attack by the North. The commander has always been an American Army general—dual-hatted as the commander of both UNC and CFC. This dual-hatting makes perfect sense for the purpose of ensuring consistency of focus. There is no divergence between how the United Nations Command and Combined Forces Command look at things—the same commander is in charge.

The U.S. force contribution is the United States Forces, Korea—USFK. The ROK contribution is almost the entire armed forces of Korea. Each nation commands its own forces on a day-to-day basis during armistice, and the Commander CFC exercises operational control of designated ROK and U.S. forces during hostilities. This follows the principle of war known as "Unity of Command." We only have 11 principles of war. We've had them for a long time. Nobody disputes them. And they are valid as the fundamental basis for how we conduct military operations.

The CFC organization for combat includes six major Combined Component Commands: Ground, Navy, Air, Marine, Special Operations, and Psychological Operations. Three of these are commanded by Americans with ROK deputy commanders. The other three have ROK commanders with U.S. deputies. There are numerous units below these levels provided by both the ROK and the United States.

Many aspects of operational control of combat units have been resolved satisfactorily years ago. For example, an entire U.S. Army corps would fall under the operational control of a ROK field army commander for combat operations. The current issue of transfer of wartime command deals with the ROK Joint Chiefs of Staff, CFC, and component levels, not at the levels below that.

The United States has a firm national policy that U.S. forces will only engage in combat under a U.S. commander. I agree with that policy wholeheartedly. This does not mean that there must there be an American commander at every level in the chain of command, however. If the United States can take this position wouldn't an identical policy be equally reasonable for other nations to apply? More specifically, if the war is taking place in the Republic of Korea, a sovereign nation, why should their forces operate under the operational control of a U.S. commander? It is not automatically a bad idea that they might want to have wartime operational control of their forces.

I'm sure that this last question was the driving force behind former President Roh Moo-hyun's initiative for a "self-reliant defense" and "wartime OPCON" of ROK forces.

Movement toward ROK lead in the defense of the ROK is a welcome development. What would not be welcome would be the premature assumption of responsibility. That is why the shift to December 2015 has occurred.

I don't believe that we'll see another shift in the effective date, and I am convinced that the transition is going to happen. We're not going back, no matter how many people in the United States or the ROK—whether they're military or otherwise—think this is a bad idea. We're going to do it.

Four years ago I said that we would do this as well as it can be done. Now I think we're going to do it even better with the additional time. The last thing we would want to do is shift this responsibility before we're really ready to do it. That is exactly why it's been postponed to December 2015 from April 2012.

Real experts have spent countless hours over many years working through the details of bi-lateral command relationships during deliberate planning and in exercises and wargames. It will ultimately be up to those experts, who actually understand the challenges, to educate those who don't—if they will listen!

There are no details that can't be worked out once the right conditions have been attained. In an ideal world the ROK would be totally self-sufficient with regard to its own national security. Up to the present time it has not been ready for such self-sufficiency. The ROK government has prioritized national economic development and social programs over national defense for decades. To be blunt—the *desire* for full sovereignty over its own defense, by itself, will not change the current capabilities of the ROK for national security. What makes the ROK defense issue so unique is the "tyranny of proximity" where a large portion of more than a million-man military is within artillery range of the ROK capital of Seoul. The deterrence and defense challenges in this situation are extreme. No other nation faces such challenges.

There are areas where it has been mutually agreed that the ROK side was ready to assume responsibility. The special operations forces are commanded by a ROK general. Rear area security is the responsibility of a ROK Army commander. The psychological operations effort is led by a ROK general. The counter–fire fight was assumed by the ROK side in 2005.

There are other areas where the United States remains best able to command and control, particularly air and sea operations. No nation in the world comes close to the U.S. capabilities in these areas—and it would be foolhardy to weaken our combined capabilities in these areas in particular.

This brings us to ground operations. Despite being surrounded on three sides by the sea, and notwithstanding the critical importance of airpower, Korea remains a predominantly ground theater of operations. The Army is dominant among the ROK services. The next Korean war will be won on the ground.

More than 15 years ago the ROK four-star deputy CFC commander was designated as the commander of the Ground Component Command, or GCC. Prior to that, the CFC Commander functioned as his own GCC commander. No separate staff was formed to be the GCC HQ. The CFC staff continued to function as the GCC staff. In my opinion, when this arrangement was originally agreed to, it was more cosmetic than actual. That was probably fair enough in the beginning, however, the time has long passed for this to be turned into reality. In recent years a small staff for the GCC commander has been carved out of the ROK officers assigned to CFC. This has been a step in the right direction, but it is not sufficient.

There needs to be a separate commander and a robust combined GCC staff consisting of both ROK and U.S. officers established to support this most critical component of CFC. Had we done this 10 years ago—when we should have—all the necessary lessons would have already been learned, and the doubts would have been relegated to history. Perhaps the issue of "wartime OPCON" might never have been raised.

The new concept calls for wartime operational command of ROK forces by the ROK CJCS [Chairman of the Joint Chiefs of Staff]. The new U.S. contribution will be the U.S. Korea Command or KORCOM. There will be no Combined Forces Command. The ROK side will be in the lead, and KORCOM will be in support. This is known as a "supported-supporting" relationship, and it is well understood by both the ROK and U.S. militaries.

The most significant sacrifice the ROK–U.S. alliance is making is the disestablishment of CFC. CFC was created to establish unity of command in the face of a million-man-plus military, which is now armed with significant WMD [weapons of mass destruction] and asymmetric capabilities within artillery range of Seoul. However perfectly we work out the details of the supported–supporting relationship, it will never completely replicate unity of command.

The day will come when the ROK is totally responsible for its own national security and for its own defense. I have no idea when the conditions will be right for that to occur. I suspect it will be decades. In the meantime we have a new target date for the ROK side to assume responsibility for taking the lead for the alliance in the defense of the ROK.

There is actually a lot of good news associated with this. The delay in the transfer of wartime command from April 2012 until December 2015 is not just pushing the effective date down the road. We will not simply pick up the same plans three-and-a-half years later. It is an opportunity to synchronize all major alliance initiatives starting immediately. To quote the ROK Minister of National Defense Kim Tae-young, it is an "opportunity to remodel the alliance for the next generation." He is wrong only in one regard. It is an opportunity to contribute to many generations to come.

The extra three-and-a-half years will allow us to fully develop, train for, and implement a robust ROK command and control capability and to establish a fully capable ROK ground operations command among other things.

The shame will be on us if we fail to make the very most of this opportunity.

Chapter 2

North Korea's Strategy of Compellence,[1] Provocations, and the Northern Limit Line

by Robert M. Collins

After fighting a war that ended not in peace but in an unsteady ceasefire established by the July 27, 1953 Armistice Agreement, the Republic of Korea–United States alliance has successfully deterred war on the Korean Peninsula for 57 years. Yet, in the face of a relentless North Korean regime determined to undermine the legitimacy and stability of the South Korean government, the alliance has not been able to deter a steady stream of North Korean military provocations, including those associated with Pyongyang's weapons of mass destruction and missile programs. North Korea has been able to set the pace and level of political and military tensions on the Korean Peninsula through the employment of a strategy of compellence using well-timed military provocations and other shows of force, supported by provocative strategic communication initiatives, and modified by an aggressive negotiation strategy and conciliatory diplomatic initiatives designed to shape alliance responses—both unilateral and bilateral—and garner political and economic concessions that support the survival of the Kim family regime.

Clausewitz taught us that a state might use military force to achieve political objectives. The use of the military is but one tool of a state to gain that objective,[2] and North Korea has employed the military tool as well as any other over the last half century in the conduct of its coercive diplomacy and compellence strategy. This strategy enables the attainment of otherwise unattainable goals, considering North Korea's moribund economy and their provocative political and diplomatic tactics. We are all familiar with North Korea's steady stream of coercive actions over the decades since the end of

---

[1] The term "compellence" was coined by Thomas Shelling in his book, *Arms and Influence* (New Haven, CT:Yale University Press, 1966) to describe the counterpoint of deterrence.

[2] Carl von Clausewitz, *On War* (translated by J. J. Graham) http://www.clausewitz.com/readings/OnWar1873/BK1ch01.html.

the Korean War, and the sinking of the Republic of Korea (ROK) Navy corvette *Cheonan* on March 26, 2010 is but the latest in a long history of provocations.

I will attempt to put the sinking of the *Cheonan* in the context of North Korea's compellence strategy and examine what may be next on North Korea's provocation agenda.

Pyongyang's Compellence Strategy

North and South Korea have been locked politically in a zero-sum game even before the inception of both states in 1948. Their politically antithetical stances of communism versus anti-communism have since morphed over the last 25 years into a classic confrontation between a totalitarian regime and a full-blown democracy. While there has been on-again, off-again progress on economic and social cooperation, the zero-sum approach in government-to-government meetings remains a central characteristic in inter-Korean relations, though rarely directly addressed as anything but some formula of North-South unification. Fearing the superior diplomatic-economic advances of the ROK, North Korea has chosen to develop a coercive diplomacy to counter considerable ROK strengths.

As noted political scientist Alexander L. George has taught us, "coercive diplomacy is a strategy that combines threats of force, and, if necessary, the limited and selective use of force."[3] North Korea's use of force to shape the alliance has certainly not been limited, and it has been selective. Whether to deter the United States, gain international acceptance of its nuclear and long-range missile programs, demonstrate its own deterrence capabilities, gain the withdrawal of U.S. Forces–Korea, eliminate the Northern Limit Line, undermine the South Korean government, or gain concessions contributing to survival of the Kim regime, North Korea's provocations can be and should be directly tied by analysts to the North's political-military objectives of its compellence strategy. Thus, Pyongyang's compellence strategy serves the regime effectively in terms of gains versus losses in the zero-sum game with South Korea.

A leading figure in developing the concepts of coercion, Thomas

---

[3] Alexander L. George, *Forceful Persuasion: Coercive Diplomacy As An Alternative to War* (Washington: U.S. Institute for Peace Press, 1991), 5–12.

Schelling, emphasizes that compellence is active and "induces his (target of coercion) withdrawal, or his acquiescence, or his collaboration by an action that threatens to hurt."[4] He further explains that compellence "requires that the punishment be administered *until* the other acts rather than *if* he acts."[5] (For the alliance, deterrence and defense focuses on *if* he acts.) Apparently, North Korea is an excellent student of Schelling's, as it has consistently "punished" the alliance through the aforementioned well-timed provocations. Complementing these aggressive actions, North Korea employs threatening themes and messages in its strategic communication and information operations to imply that further force is forthcoming if compliance by the alliance does not take place. The North targets not only ROK and U.S. leaders, but also their regional counterparts, the international media, and the ROK public as well.

North Korea's threats of war are nearly legendary. North Korean compellence creates conditions favorable to further provocation over those of deterrence and can create an imbalance of willingness to escalate, particularly if domestic political debate and public opinion in the ROK favors non-response by the alliance. Hyping tensions and threatening war or retaliation serves to accentuate the perception that tensions are at an intolerable level for those not accustomed to it. The North Korean leadership has proven that they are and has arguably shaped the ROK public by inducing fear of war and creating by-products in political decision-making in the ROK. North Korea has shown it is more motivated than the ROK to use force and this is likely because the North demonstrates little competence in other forms of national power compared to the South.

Laying in direct contrast to the alliance's strategy of deterrence and defense, North Korea's compellence strategy has used a variety of provocations to gain specific political, economic, and military concessions. Due to Pyongyang's consistent employment of provocations, the Korean Peninsula has 57 years of experiencing crisis after crisis of varying intensity, suffered nearly 600 ROK and U.S. military deaths, and has been to the brink of war twice—in 1976 and 1994. While alliance deterrence depends upon posture, vigilance, readiness, and capabilities to demonstrate strength, North Korea chooses to initiate action strong enough to draw political and economic responses but not so strong as to draw military retaliation.

---

[4] Schelling, *Arms and Influence*, 67–80.
[5] Ibid.

Besides the sobering strategic provocations of two nuclear tests and continued development and launching of long-range ballistic missiles, by 2003, North Korea had conducted 1,439 major provocations, primarily against the ROK, but also against U.S. personnel and assets.[6] North Korea has attacked and destroyed several U.S. aircraft, hijacked a U.S. naval ship and ROK civilian aircraft, and murdered scores of South Korean citizens. It has planned and attempted to assassinate the ROK president in 1968, 1970, 1974, 1981, and 1983. It has conducted naval skirmishes along the Northern Limit Line (NLL) where the North Korean Navy sunk several ROK ships in the 1960s, 1970s, 1990s, and this decade as well. It has hijacked hundreds of ROK fishing boats for the purpose of training captured fishermen as sleeper agents when returned to the South. Furthermore, from 1960 through 2007, North Korea has conducted 1,243 known infiltrations by 3,718 personnel. From 1973 through 2007 (not counting 1981–88), the North has crossed the Northern Limit Line a total 4,166 times.[7]

On occasion, North Korea has gone beyond alliance thresholds such as in the case of artillery exchanges in the 1960s[8] and the 1976 axe murders in the Joint Security Area. In the latter, the alliance executed a major show of force by going to DEFCON 3 for three weeks, deploying the aircraft carrier USS *Midway* (CVA 41) to Korean waters, and flying B-52 and F-111 missions along the DMZ for weeks. This led to the only known "statement of regret" from North Korean leader Kim Il-sung within hours of the alliance response.[9]

Furthermore, I personally heard former Secretary of Defense William Perry state twice that during the nuclear crisis of 1994, he was within two days of recommending to then–President William J. Clinton an attack on North Korea's Yongbyon nuclear plant to stop Pyongyang's plutonium program. Escalation from there is anybody's guess, but the alliance most assuredly would have received some form of major kinetic response.

---

[6] Andrew Scobell and John M. Sanford, *North Korea's Military Threat: Pyongyang's Conventional Forces, Weapons of Mass Destruction, and Ballistic Missiles*, Strategic Studies Institute Monograph, (Carlisle, PA: US Army War College, April 2007), 27.
[7] Narushige Michishita, *North Korea's Military-Diplomatic Campaigns, 1966-2008* (London: Routledge, 2010), 202–3.
[8] Interview data with USFK staff officer from the 1960s.
[9] Richard A. Mobley, "Revisiting the Korean Tree-Trimming Incident," *Joint Forces Quarterly*, Summer 2003, http://findarticles.com/p/articles/mi_m0KNN/is_35/ai_n8563325/pg_7/?tag=content;col1.

North Korea has demonstrated that it recognizes some limits in their compellence strategy and use of provocations. Even in the *Cheonan* sinking the North has vigorously denied responsibility, presumably to limit alliance justification for retaliation. Alliance credibility, particularly U.S. credibility in terms of resolve to use force, no doubt lies in North Korean motivations to limit its actions. The North Korean perspective of U.S. credibility has been shaped over the decades by the United States' use of force to coerce a number of international antagonists to its will. With deep involvement in Vietnam, North Korea found during the 1960s it could be very aggressive in the Korean Theater of Operations as the United States showed restraint in serious provocations against U.S. aircraft and ships and the alliance found it difficult to stop North Korean guerilla infiltrations. However, subsequent U.S. use of force in Grenada, Panama, Bosnia-Herzegovina, Kosovo, Somalia, two wars against Iraq, and Afghanistan—not to mention the Korean War—have clearly demonstrated American resolve to use force. U.S. forward deployment of ground, air, and naval forces in the ROK and Japan, and treaty alliances with those two nations carry no small self-perceived threat to the Kim family regime, particularly should Pyongyang find the motivation or miscalculation to initiate hostilities against South Korea. Despite North Korea's read of this U.S. threat and regional commitment, the question remains—is North Korea "deterrable?" The answer would be "apparently so," given that North Korea has not executed a general attack in the last 57 years. As is not so commonly understood, the ROK–U.S. alliance's most effective strategic communication lies in the military intelligence collected by the Korean People's Army's own ISR—that is: intelligence, surveillance, and reconnaissance—against alliance capabilities and readiness activities.

But when it comes to provocation, North Korea appears to be "undeterrable." To paraphrase a noted economist, "strategy is not concerned with the efficient application of force, but with the exploitation of potential force."[10] North Korea's strategy of compellence exploits North Korea's capabilities and most recently, that exploitation has centered in those areas where North Korea has invested its capital in the military—in the asymmetric areas of their nuclear and missile programs, as well as in the world's largest special operations force.[11]

---

[10] Thomas Schelling, *The Strategy of Conflict*, (Cambridge, MA: Harvard University Press, 1960, 1980), 5.
[11] For a comprehensive analysis of North Korea's asymmetric military capabilities, see Bruce E. Bechtol Jr., *Defiant Failed State: The North Korean Threat to International Security* (Dulles, VA: Potomac Books, 2010).

Tyranny of Proximity

The single greatest enabler of this compellence strategy is the forward deployment of the 1.2 million–man Korean People's Army (KPA). The KPA is the fifth largest armed force in the world and about 70 percent of it is deployed south of Pyongyang.[12] This emplacement has evolved incrementally over the decades and can be characterized as "creeping normalcy." (See Figure 2.1) Most of the KPA is located within 43.5 miles of the Demilitarized Zone which separates North Korea from South Korea, and much of the KPA's combat power—including long-range artillery and short-range ballistic missiles—is located within 40 miles of the ROK capital of Seoul. This "tyranny of proximity" enables North Korea to attack with little tactical warning.

The KPA is comprised of 153 divisions and brigades. This includes 20 corps commands that lead "60 infantry divisions/brigades, 25 mechanized infantry brigades, 13 tank brigades, 25 special forces brigades, and 30 artillery brigades.[13] North Korea maintains the world's largest special operations force of approximately 100,000 troops.[14] Other estimates range from 88,000 to 120,000,[15] and one recent estimate puts those forces at 180,000.[16] Approximately 250 systems of 170mm Koksan guns and 240mm multiple-rocket launchers are deployed within range of Seoul.[17]

The forward deployment of KPA forces and its associated long-range artillery and missile arsenal threatens extensive damage to Seoul in any future conflict in a limited or general attack, or provocation leading to escalation of artillery exchanges. This would destroy one the world's 15 largest economies as Seoul is the economic as well as political and cultural center of South Korea. Some estimates insist that the casualties from a

---

[12] Statement of Gen Leon J. Laporte, Commander, United Nations Command, Commander, Republic Of Korea–United States Combined Forces Command, and Commander, United States Forces Korea; before The Senate Armed Services Committee, 1 April 2004, http://www.dod.gov/dodgc/olc/testimony_old/108_second.html.

[13] Andrew Scobell and John M. Sanford, 22.

[14] Statement of Gen B. B. Bell, Commander, United Nations Command; Commander, Republic Of Korea–United States Combined Forces Command; and Commander, United States Forces Korea, before the Senate Armed Services Committee; 7 March 2006.

[15] Andrew Scobell and John M. Sanford. See ch4, n38.

[16] *Chosun Ilbo*, "N. Korea 'Has 180,000 Special Forces Ready to Cross into South,'" 16 June 2010, http://english.chosun.com/site/data/html_dir/2010/06/16/2010061601318.html.

[17] Statement of Gen B. B. Bell, 2006.

missile and artillery attack on the South could end up in the hundreds of thousands. The 170mm guns and 240mm rocket launchers are chemical round–capable and could fire up to 10,000 rounds per minute on the capital and surrounding areas. The number of rounds the KPA could deliver across the entire front is significantly higher and would be devastating to the ROK and its population.

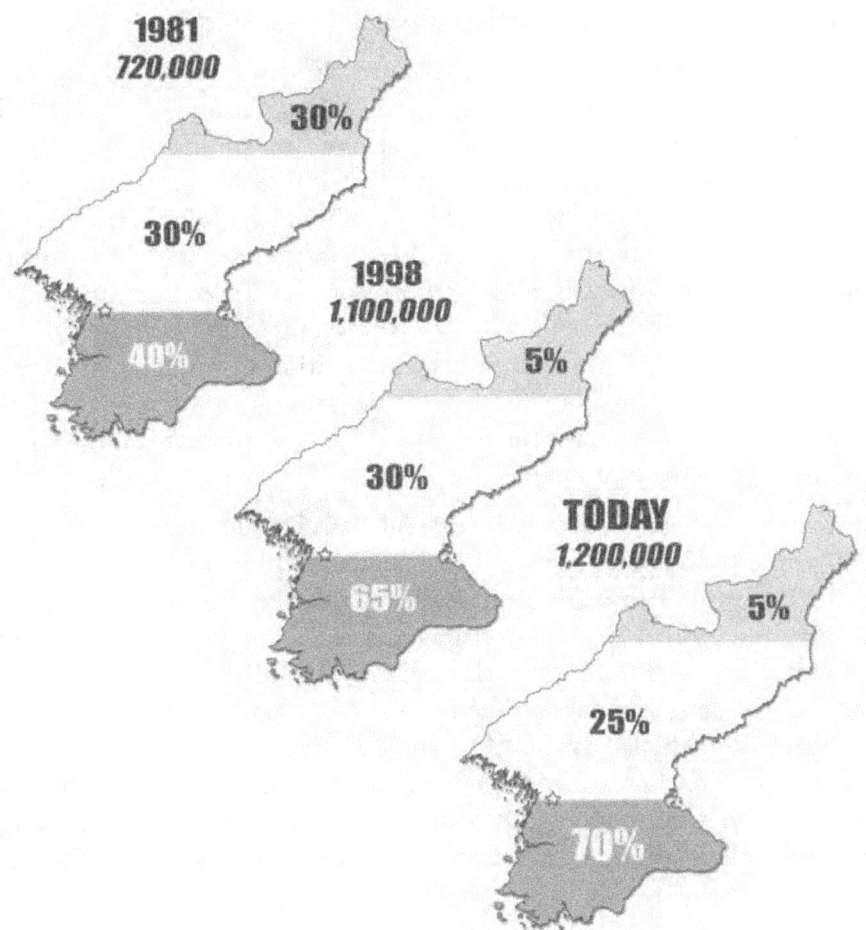

Figure 2.1 - Korean People's Army Forward Deployment.

Source: USFK Story Brief, 2005, and Andrew Scobell and John Sanford, *North Korea's Military Threat: Pyongyang's Conventional Forces, Weapons of Mass Destruction, and Ballistic Missiles*, Strategic Studies Institute Monograph (Carlisle, PA: U.S. Army War College, April 2007), http://www.strategicstudiesinstitute.army.mil/pdffiles/PUB771.pdf, 66.

The chemical round capability of these systems would significantly increase casualties, particularly against an unprotected civilian populace of one of the world's largest cities. One former U.S. commander of ROK–U.S. Combined Forces Command stationed in Seoul estimated that another all-out war on the Korean Peninsula would result in a million casualties, roughly 52,000 American dead or wounded in the first 90 days, more than $100 billion in costs to the United States, and a trillion dollars in economic damages and lost business.[18]

Through manipulation of this "tyranny of proximity" Pyongyang has been able to raise and lower political and military tensions almost at will to achieve tactical and strategic goals of weakening or reversing international and/or unilateral sanctions, influencing South Korea's public, and South Korea to pay the North about $2.2 billion in cash and other support during the Kim Dae-jung and Roh Moo-hyun administrations. This was paid in return for North-South engagement topped by a summit meeting with Kim Jong-il by each president. Another major achievement was the acquisition of millions of metric tons of heavy fuel oil from a U.S.-led consortium as a result of shutting down the North's Yongbyon nuclear plant in accordance with the Agreed Framework of October 21, 1994.[19]

In my own subjective thinking, and I am certainly not alone, there is no other military theater in the world where tactical actions *so quickly* take on major strategic implications. North Korea's proximity-dominated force posture creates an environment where local provocations set in motion actions and decisions that quickly impact national leaders, immediately feed the security fears of the ROK public, and are eagerly hyped by the ROK and international media. The history of North Korea's provocations demonstrates that manipulation of this proximity has become institutionalized within its leadership thinking as the primary component of their compellence strategy.

---

[18] Vernon Loeb and Peter Slevin, "Overcoming North Korea's 'Tyranny of Proximity'" *Washington Post*, 20 January 2003, http://www.washingtonpost.com/ac2/wp-dyn/A15466-2003Jan19?language=printer.

[19] See Korean Peninsula Energy Development Organization—Executive Director's Statement, 31 December 2004, http://www.kedo.org/pdfs/KEDO_AR_2004.pdf.

North Korean Negotiation Strategy

Complementing Pyongyang's compellence strategy is the North's negotiation strategy.[20] Once its provocations lead to the negotiation table, the North exploits the desired de-escalation in tensions to obtain the desired concessions. It employs both bilateral and multilateral negotiations to shape the diplomatic environment, frequently pitting ROK interests against those of the United States to gain the most from its interlocutor.

There is a detectable pattern in the North's negotiation strategy. One of the best assessments of this process is the eight-step strategy explained below by a U.S. Army officer with more than 150 negotiation sessions with the North Koreans at the Joint Security Area in Panmunjom.

1. Cause the "appearance" of tension.
2. Blame the UNC, ROK, and United States for the tense situation.
3. Quickly agree "in principle" to a major improvement in relations and publicize the "breakthrough."
4. Set artificial deadlines to pressure the other side.
5. Politicize and draw out negotiations front-loading the agenda and demanding preconditions (which are often the true objectives).
6. Blame the UNC, ROK, and United States for the protracted talks.
7. Demand compensation or a major concession, before attending future meetings.
8. Go back to step 1.[21]

---

[20] For more information on North Korean negotiation strategies, see: Chuck Downs, *Over the Line: North Korea's Negotiating Strategy* (Washington: AEI Press, 1999); Richard Saccone, *To the Brink and Back: Negotiating with North Korea* (Elizabeth, NJ: Hollym International, 2003); Scott Snyder, *Negotiating on the Edge: North Korean Negotiating Behavior* (Washington: United States Institute of Peace Press, 1999); and C. Turner Joy, *How Communists Negotiate* (Santa Monica, CA: Fidelis Publishers, 1970).

[21] Interview with retired U.S. Army LtCol Stephen M. Tharp who developed these steps for the United Nations Command in the late 1990s. He spent more than six years with the UNC Military Armistice Commission and met with the North Korean People's Army delegations at Panmunjom on more than 150 occasions. He was the last UNC Officer to meet with the Chinese representative, a total of 12 meetings.

Confronting Security Challenges on the Korean Peninsula

This strategy is employed quite successfully because the North can fall back on provocations, kinetic or non-kinetic, at any time it perceives that negotiations have failed from their perspective.

Pyongyang's Shaping of the Northern Limit Line

The sinking of the *Cheonan* was just the latest in Pyongyang's efforts to shape the confrontation over the Northern Limit Line in the Yellow Sea (sometimes called the West Sea in Korea). The NLL was established unilaterally in August 1953 by General Mark Clark, Commander, United Nations Command (UNC), for the purpose of separating forces under the conditions of an armistice. The NLL became the maritime line in the water whereby ROK and U.S. ships would not cross beyond into the North. This line took into account the security of the five Northwest Islands under UNC control as designated in the Armistice. Though legally not a maritime border, the NLL has served as a geographical point of contention since its

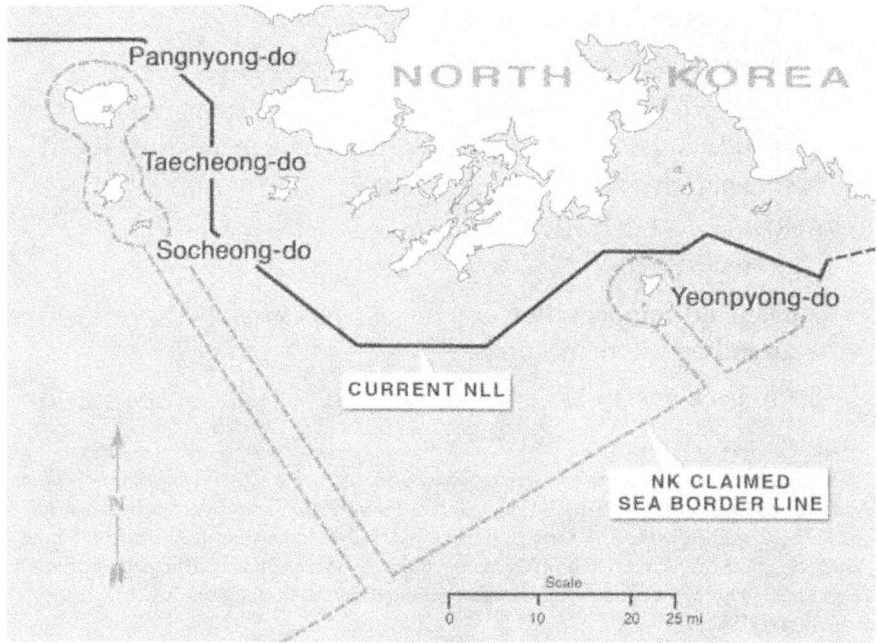

Figure 2.2 North Korea's Sea Border Line Claim.

Source: ROK Ministry of Unification 2007, as reported in Bruce Bechtol, "The *Cheonan* Incident and North Korea's Northern Limit Line Strategy," http://www.defensestudies.org/?p=2575#more-2575.

establishment—North Korea trying to change the status quo in the Yellow Sea, and South Korea steadfastly defending the NLL as a defense line on its western maritime flank.

North Korea originally demanded 12-mile territorial waters at the time of armistice talks. In March 1955, through a cabinet resolution, the nation decided its territorial waters would be 12 miles, although such an action was never propagated to the outside world.[22] Indeed, at the time, North Korea did not maintain a navy of any credibility to enforce such a claim. At a plenary meeting of the Military Armistice Commission in December 1973, the North claimed that the entire area lying southeast of U-Do as being their coastal waters, based on Article 13 of the Armistice Agreement. It made the same claim during negotiations on the South–North Basic Agreement in 1992.[23] In July 1977, the DPRK declared a 200-mile exclusive economic zone (EEZ) based on median lines. It then declared that the EEZ boundary line was the sea military demarcation line in August 1997.[24] At the Panmunjom General Officers Talks of July 21, 1999, North Korea declared that the line connecting the equidistant points between South and North Korea and China was the new sea demarcation line and that the area north of that line would be North Korea's Sea Military Control Zone.[25] (See Figure 2.2)

After the Korean People's Army–Navy suffered losses in an engagement with South Korean naval forces in November 2009, North Korea continued to shape the Yellow Sea environment politically and militarily. The DPRK, in another attempt at abrogating the NLL, designated a "peace-time firing zone" around it that December. In the following two months, KPA artillery fired numerous volleys into the zone for the first time, claiming that these firings were routine exercises.[26]

To demonstrate how important the Kim regime regards the conflict over the NLL, one can look at the reassignment of General Kim Kyok-sik from the senior KPA active-duty position of Chief of the KPA General

---

[22] Republic Of Korea Ministry of National Defense, "The Republic Of Korea Position Regarding The Northern Limit Line," August 2002, http://www.military.co.kr/english/NLL/NLL.htm.
[23] Ibid.
[24] Ibid.
[25] Ibid.
[26] Sun-won Park, Strategic Posture Review: South Korea, Brookings Institution, http://www.brookings.edu/articles/2010/0317_korea_park.aspx.

Staff—roughly the equivalent of the U.S. Chairman of the Joint Chiefs of Staff—to the position of KPA 4th Corps commander. On the surface this appears to be a demotion after serving for two years as the chief and then being relegated to the seemingly second tier of a frontline commander. That is odd to be sure. But a closer look at General Kim's career shows that he was the KPA 2d Corps commander for at least ten years from before 1997 to February 2007. The 2d Corps is deployed directly north of Seoul astride the primary avenue of approach from North to South crossing the DMZ. During that time, he would have studied the ROK–U.S. Combined Forces Command and their operational plans more than anyone in the North as it was his responsibility to lead the defeat of the alliance's combined forces should another Korean War break out. Also during that time, the KPA deployed hundreds of long-range artillery systems comprised of 170mm Koksan guns and 240mm multiple-rocket launchers, most of which can range Seoul. As the 2d Corps commander, Kim would have been intimately involved in the artillery's deployment and related employment strategies and plans. It is hard to imagine that any other KPA general understands as well as Kim Kyok-sik the use of artillery as a "show of force" tool supporting North Korea's coercive diplomacy and compellence strategy. Upon reassignment to the 4th Corps, General Kim completely redid the coastal artillery deployment so as to provide maximum coastal ground support to any KPA actions in the vicinity of the NLL and the Northwest Islands.

One report, quoting ROK intelligence sources, states that Kim strengthened KPA guerilla training in the Yellow Sea area and that this was detected several times by ROK ISR. The same report went on to say that "Kim Jong-il told Kim Kyok-sik that his mission was complete and that he should come back"[27] (presumably to Pyongyang).

Sinking of the *Cheonan* and the Alliance's Response

On May 20, 2010, the ROK president-appointed Joint Civilian–Military Investigation Group (JIP) held a news conference and publicly announced on Korean television the results of their eight-week investigation into the sinking of the *Cheonan*. The group was composed of experts from

---

[27] Yonhap News, (Military Intelligence Report On KPA Actions Directly After The *Cheonan* Sinking), in Korean, 4 April 2010, http://news.naver.com/main/read.nhn?mode=LPOD&mid=tvh&oid=001&aid=0003238455.

Australia, Sweden, the United Kingdom, and the United States. Their findings were supported and confirmed by a separate Multinational Combined Intelligence Task Force that included the ROK, United States, Australia, Canada, and the United Kingdom and was comprised of 25 experts from 10 ROK agencies, 22 military experts, and 24 foreign experts.[28] The two findings concluded that "of North Korea's fleet of 70 submarines, a 'few small submarines, along with a mother ship' left a North Korean naval base on the West (Yellow) Sea two to three days prior to the attack. When the *Cheonan* sank on 26 March, a North Korea-made, wake-homing CHT-02D torpedo created a shock wave and bubble effect that caused the corvette to split apart and sink, leaving 46 ROK sailors dead, not to mention others who died in salvage efforts."[29] The conclusion was that North Korea was responsible.

These findings have not gone undisputed, including differing opinions from within the ROK cabinet. Conspiracy theories include U.S. Navy SEALs sinking the *Cheonan* so that the United States could scare the Japanese into letting the U.S. Marine bases remain on Okinawa, or that a ROK Navy submarine fired a previously-captured CHT-02D torpedo at the warship to artificially create a crisis, or that the United States created this incident to simulate a "Gulf of Tonkin incident" whereby it could justify subsequent offensive actions against North Korea, or, according to one ROK government official, the *Cheonan* sunk when hit by an old mine.[30]

Consequently, ROK President Lee announced that he was abrogating the Inter-Korean Agreement on Maritime Transportation and North Korea would no longer be able to sail its merchant ships through the Cheju Strait. He also stated he was suspending inter-Korean trade and exchanges and would continue anti–North Korean propaganda broadcasts along the DMZ. In a turn of ROK military strategy, he stated that "if our territorial waters,

---

[28] Park In-kook, "Letter dated 4 June 2010 from the Permanent Representative of the Republic of Korea to the United Nations addressed to the President of the Security Council," *United Nations Security Council*, S/2010/281, 4 June 2010, http://www.securitycouncilreport.org/atf/cf/%7B65BFCF9B-6D27-4E9C-8CD3-CF6E4FF96FF9%7D/DPRK%20S%202010%20281%20SKorea%20Letter%20and%20Cheonan%20Report.pdf.

[29] The Joint Civilian-Military Investigation Group, *"Investigation Result on the Sinking of ROKS* Cheonan." 20 May 2010, news.bbc.co.uk/nol/shared/bsp/hi/pdfs/20_05_10jigreport.pdf.

[30] Peter Foster, "*Cheonan* Sinking: Top Ten Conspiracy Theories" *The Telegraph*. http://blogs.telegraph.co.uk/news/peterfoster/100042229/cheonan-sinking-top-ten-conspiracy-theories/.

airspace, or territory are militarily violated, we will immediately exercise our right of self-defense."[31]

North Korea's Counter-response

In the 26 months leading up to the *Cheonan* attack, North Korea had grown frustrated with South Korea's Lee Myung-bak administration over the discontinuation of the very generous non-reciprocal "sunshine" policies of former Presidents Kim Dae-jung and Roh Moo-hyun. Thus North Korea cut off most ties with the South and declared all inter-Korean agreements as being "dead documents."[32] Subsequent to that, the DPRK navy suffered an embarrassing loss of face during the November 2009 naval firefight along the NLL. The *Cheonan* sinking came just five months later. This repeats a similar "deadly defeat–recover face" exchange in 1999 and 2002, also along the NLL. Soon after the November defeat, Kim Jong-il visited the North Korean naval station at Nampo (directly north of and the closest naval base to the NLL) and called upon the sailors there to become more advanced in the navy's weaponry and strategy. He also called for them to form suicide squads so as to become heroes.[33]

Unsurprisingly, North Korea denied attacking the *Cheonan*, instead claiming that the conservative Lee Myung-bak administration was manufacturing a crisis to raise peninsular tensions and create domestic support for his ruling party in the South's June local elections.[34] On May 28, 2010, Pyongyang televised a first-ever news conference by the Kim Jong-il–chaired National Defense Commission that rebutted Seoul's evidence point by point.[35] A North Korean Foreign Ministry spokesman laid out why

---

[31] Gus Lubin, "South Korea Threatens War If North Korea Makes One More Provocation," Business Insider, 23 May 2010, http://www.businessinsider.com/south-korea-threatens-war-if-north-korea-makes-one-more-provocation-2010-5#ixzz0xU0bFaqx.

[32] David Eimer, "North Korea Cuts All Links with South Korea." *The Telegraph*, http://www.telegraph.co.uk/news/worldnews/asia/northkorea/4394455/North-Korea-cuts-all-links-with-South-Korea.html.

[33] *Chosun Ilbo*, "Kim Jong-il Called for Stronger Navy After Defeat in Skirmish," 6 May 2010, http://english.chosun.com/site/data/html_dir/2010/05/06/2010050601362.html.

[34] Miyoung Kim, "North Korea denies it sank South's navy ship," Reuters, 17 April 2010, http://www.reuters.com/article/idUSTRE63G0CN20100417.

[35] Pyongyang Korean Central Television, "NDC News Conference on *Cheonan* Incident," 28 May 2010, in Korean.

Seoul's evidence on the *Cheonan* is flawed, reiterating a May 20 proposal to send an "inspection team" to review the South's case (June 4).[36]

Only hours after U.S. President Barack H. Obama asked PRC President Hu Jin-tao to take a stronger stance against North Korea on the *Cheonan* sinking incident, Pyongyang announced that it would "bolster its nuclear deterrent."[37] Whether that "bolstering" is weaponization of a plutonium weapon mounted on a competent delivery system or a new highly-enriched uranium device remains to be seen. One month later in July, North Korea threatened to use nuclear weapons in a "retaliatory sacred war" in response to alliance naval exercises.[38]

Perhaps, North Korea's most significant gain from the attack on the *Cheonan* was on the diplomatic front: China and Russia refused to accept the JIP findings and thus, for the most part, defused alliance justification for retaliation.

International Responses

The ROK and United States took the findings and reported them directly to the U.S. Security Council on June 4, 2010.[39] The ROK sought a United Nations Security Council resolution condemning North Korea for the attack, as well as seeking an apology and compensation from Pyongyang. However, China blocked these demands, instead agreeing to a formal statement that did not require a vote, but certainly of far less impact. Nor would China refer to the attack directly, instead calling it a "sinking."[40]

The UNSC's president for the month of July, Nigeria's U Joy Ogwu, read a president's statement in lieu of a Security Council resolution condemning North Korea. His statement acknowledged the JIP findings

---

[36] Pyongyang Korean Central Broadcasting Station, "DPRK FM Spokesman on US, ROK Attempting To Refer *Cheonan* Incident to UNSC," 4 June 2010.

[37] BBC, "North Korea Threatens 'New' Nuclear Deterrent" 28 June 2010, http://www.bbc.co.uk/news/10430574.

[38] Park Chan-Kyong, "N. Korea Threatens Nuclear Response To Naval War Games," *Sydney World Herald*, 24 July 2010, http://news.smh.com.au/breaking-news-world/nkorea-threatens-nuclear-response-to-naval-war-games-20100724-10pg2.html.

[39] See Park In-kook letter.

[40] Joe Lauria, "China Stalls U.N. Efforts Against North Korea," *Wall Street Journal*, 8 July 2010, http://online.wsj.com/article/na_wsj_pub:sb10001424052748703636404575352962809339090.html.

blaming the DPRK for the attack and condemned the attack itself, but fell short of directly condemning the North.[41]

This led to public condemnation of North Korea by leaders of influential nations such as Japan, United Kingdom, and Australia, not to mention the alliance.

For China, the attack on the *Cheonan* immediately became a no-win situation. By acknowledging that North Korea was responsible for the ship's sinking, China would be giving tacit approval for any ROK or U.S. retaliatory response. Beijing lacks influence over Kim Jong-il's decisions unless they are willing to withhold aid such as food and fuel, less they create instability inside North Korea. That is counter to their desire for a stable buffer state. Kim Jong-il met with PRC leader Hu Jin-tao in his visit to Beijing May 3–6,[42] shortly after attacking the *Cheonan*. This put President Hu in a difficult position at best. China needs North Korea as a strategic and operational buffer from the United States and its influence in the ROK and Japan. Consequently, the stability of North Korea is vital to this position and the threat of escalating military tensions on the Korean Peninsula is something Beijing must avoid from the outset—and they successfully did so. By not supporting any UNSC resolution condemning North Korea, ROK and U.S. justification for retaliation was essentially squashed.

Furthermore, when the alliance decided to conduct a major show of force with an antisubmarine exercise—including the deployment of the aircraft carrier USS *George Washington* (CVN 73)—in the Yellow Sea as a less-than-kinetic response to North Korea's sinking of the *Cheonan*, China successfully pressured the deployment of the carrier to the other side of the Korean Peninsula. This kept major U.S. power out of waters adjacent to China, and thereby de-escalated tensions.

The crux of China's position, however, is more accurately reflected in the statement by PLA Major General Luo Yuan in which he stated, "It is like your mother-in-law . . . you just can't get rid of her. You have to find a way to manage her." He was discussing China–North Korean ties.

---

[41] Security Council Condemns Attack On Republic Of Korea Naval Ship '*Cheonan*', Stresses Need To Prevent Further Attacks, Other Hostilities In Region. Security Council SC/9975, Meeting 6235, 9 July 2010, http://www.un.org/News/Press/docs/2010/sc9975.doc.htm.

[42] CBSNews.com, "Kim Jong Il Ends Secret Trip To China." 6 May 2010, http://www.cbsnews.com/stories/2010/05/06/world/main6464954.shtml.

Representative of China's position on the United States is Admiral Yang Yi, a former director of the Institute for Strategic Studies at the People's Liberation Army National Defense University. He wrote in the August 13 edition of the *China Daily* newspaper that the U.S. decision to use a nuclear-powered aircraft carrier in ROK-U.S. naval drills in the Yellow Sea would provoke China. He went on to threaten that the United States would "pay a costly price" for its "muddled decision," and its adherence to the "Cold War mentality."[43]

Russia's response had some significant parallels in terms of interest in limiting U.S. influence within the region. Unlike a recently "leaked" Russian Foreign Ministry policy document that gives an impression of being more friendly to the West, Russia's military doctrine document released last February clearly has an anti-Western tone. According to the doctrine, "dangers to Russia include deployment of foreign (i.e., American) troops in states bordering Russia and strategic missile defense."[44] We should assume that this applies to Russia's view of the Korean Peninsula also. There is no love lost between Russia and North Korea but their common anti-U.S. stance gives them common ground. Most Russian analysts see limiting the influence of the United States in Northeast Asia as being far more important than Russian–North Korean relations. This fits quite well into the international political aspect of Kim Jong-il's survival strategy whereby he can leverage major regional powers' anti-U.S. stance to his advantage.

On the technical approach, Russia sent a team of four submarine and torpedo experts from its navy to Seoul to evaluate the ROK JIP's evidence and concluded that there was insufficient evidence to find North Korea guilty, insisting that the evidence was "not weighty enough."[45] The Russian team disputed the findings by focusing on timing issues, presence of fishing nets on the *Cheonan* screws, and the assumption of sea mines in the area.[46]

---

[43] Bloomberg, "Chinese Admiral Says U.S., South Korea Drills 'Fresh Provocation' to China," 13 August 2010, http://www.bloomberg.com/news/2010-08-13/chinese-admiral-says-u-s-south-korea-drills-fresh-provocation-to-china.html.

[44] David J. Kramer, "Russia's 'new' stance remains anti-West," *Washington Post*, June 22, 2010, http://www.washingtonpost.com/wp-dyn/content/article/2010/06/21/AR2010062103696.html.

[45] Vladimir Radyuhin, "Russian Probe Undercuts *Cheonan* Sinking Theory," *The Hindu*, 9 June 2010, http://thehindu.com/news/international/article450117.ece.

[46] Leonid Petrov, "Russia Navy Expert Team's Analysis on the *Cheonan* Incident" *WordPress*, 28 July 2010, http://leonidpetrov.wordpress.com/2010/07/28/russian-navy-expert-team%E2%80%99s-analysis-on-the-cheonan-incident/.

The bottom line is that Chinese and Russian responses seem to be designed to keep the alliance from justifying a retaliatory response, and thus a potential escalation of military tensions.

North Korea's Next Steps

Further development of North Korea's nuclear and missile programs have given the alliance new challenges in developing deterrence strategies. Pyongyang has begun to tout their "nuclear deterrent" and the realization of that will eventually undermine the relative stability of alliance deterrence on the Korean Peninsula.

The most dramatic recent change for the Kim regime is the realization that Kim Jong-il will not be around forever. As the regime attempts a second dynastic succession to Kim Il-song's grandson, North Korea will have to continue to focus on strategies that both gain concessions because they are needed in their overall strategy—to include negating the NLL—and applying credit to the succession process. From the North Korean perspective, their NLL claims are legitimate. Therefore the North's compellence strategy's implementation will continue, regardless of whether there is a succession issue or not.

The development of missile systems and artillery tactics will continue to increase the North's capability along the NLL. Improvements in the interoperability of the North Korean navy, air force, special operations forces, and the adjacent coastal artillery will become evident in future shows of force or direct provocations.

North Korea's success in the Yellow Sea and along the NLL is critical to establishing a flanking posture to Seoul's west. Success here leaves Seoul vulnerable to envelopment during a general or limited attack. But more immediately, it would enable Pyongyang to launch provocations much closer to Seoul's western flank and provide the North with more coercion at the negotiation table.

However, the most important development out of this tragedy, for Pyongyang at least, was gaining tacit approval from China and Russia for bad behavior that embarrassed both of them. Manipulation of Beijing's and Moscow's preferred anti-U.S. position on security matters in Northeast Asia will be invaluable in the years ahead as the Kim regime goes through another uncertain succession process.

Deterring Further North Korean Provocations

During a crisis on the Korean Peninsula that evolves into a road to war, efforts at de-escalation become critical to all parties and regional actors interested in avoiding conflict. As a potential crisis grows and expands, and miscalculations develop—apparent or not—all parties will endeavor to avoid war, both through deterrence measures and de-escalation efforts. North Korea will walk a fine line in conducting provocations to gain concessions supporting succession while simultaneously managing that succession, and war is the last thing needed during transition.

Given how adept the Kim regime is in orchestrating the implementation of its compellence strategy, deterring North Korean provocations is difficult at best. However, there are further steps that the alliance can take to increase their deterrence capability. A comprehensive political-military deterrence strategy that leverages alliance diplomatic, economic, and strategic communication capabilities to compliment the significant military capabilities of the combined ROK and U.S. forces would improve the deterrence posture of the alliance. Realistically, that posture is very effective politically and militarily now, particularly in terms of deterring a general or even limited attack. I propose implementing some concepts for consideration in limiting provocations.

First, political leaders in both the ROK and United States must recognize the North Korean regime for what it is. Many Korean analysts make this trite statement without explaining what it means. North Korea is a totalitarian political system that focuses not only on the continued survival of its leadership at the expense of its people and everything else, but also the prioritization of those values, procedures, and assets—particularly the military and the security apparatus—that enable their survival. The aforementioned values are institutionalized not only within the Korean Workers' Party, military, and government, but most important, they are inculcated at the individual level for every North Korean citizen—from common laborer to five-star general and government minister—who is evaluated and personally tested on their personal loyalty to Kim Jong-il and the survival of the Kim family regime. The institutionalization of these values was hardened during and after the transition from Kim Il-song to Kim Jong-il and we should expect the same during any successful transition from Kim Jong-il to his son, likely Kim Jong-un. Expectations that the regime will change to conform to international norms—other than as an operational pause to gain time for regime asset consolidation and/or major concession acquisition such as during the Agreed Framework—is wishful thinking. North Korean obstinacy is demonstrated by its continued provocations in the midst of very generous ROK engagement and U.S. focus on the North's denuclearization via the Six-Party Talks.

Second, the alliance must narrow the political seams within ROK security that the North so frequently seeks to exploit. There is a need to institutionalize the situational awareness of the alliance's national authorities and their supporting government and military analysts relative to the reality of tactical actions in the Korean Theater of Operations quickly leading to strategic consequences. This is not well understood within Washington, DC's beltway and it is overly politicized in the ROK. Neither is it completely understood how well North Korea manipulates the tyranny of proximity to maximize their ability to escalate and de-escalate political-military tensions to their tactical, operational, and strategic advantage. North Korean tactical provocations should not be interpreted as just "North Korea being North Korea" or "Kim Jong-il merely demanding attention."

The institutionalization of the alliance's "two-plus-two" meeting format should be a starting point for this process. Historically, this meeting was attended by the ROK Minister of Foreign Affairs and Minister of National Defense, as well as the U.S. Ambassador to the ROK and the Commander, United Nations Command–Combined Forces Command–United States Forces Korea on the U.S. side. However, to ensure complete alliance situational awareness at the most senior levels, the ROK Blue House National Security Advisor's presence should be considered, even above that of the Minister of Foreign Affairs. That could make it a three-plus-two meeting. The institutionalization of this forum, which was marginalized during the first decade of this century, could go a long way in developing a strategic common operating picture that includes anticipation of North Korean coercive actions, including provocations. This forum will be even more important after transition of wartime operational control of designated ROK forces in December 2015.

Third, formulation and implementation of an alliance strategic influence plan whereby the alliance gains through diplomatic, informational, military, and economic skills the cooperation and support of the international community, including China and Russia, to dissuade the Kim regime from coercive diplomacy and military provocations. Along these lines, Commander, ROK–U.S. Combined Forces Command, General Walter Sharp stated recently that "Kim Jong-il has said that North Korea will be a great and powerful nation by 2012, and the only way he has to get to that point is through military provocations and threatening the neighbors."[47] He also stated that, "the Republic of Korea–U.S. alliance needs more from the entire international community and all countries in the region, in particular China. We believe all countries in the region and China need to work in cooperation in addressing North Korean aggressive behavior. In particular we will welcome Chinese action even behind the scenes."[48]

Fourth, increasing the political impact of the ROK–U.S. Security Consultative Meeting and the ROK–U.S. Military Committee Meeting would improve the overall deterrence effect of those forums. Today, they stand as a major communication vehicle to the Kim regime that the alliance stands with great resolve in defending the ROK. However, bi-national presidential and legislative public support for those meetings would improve the message delivered to Pyongyang.

Fifth, the ROK side needs to spend more money on its defense. In particular, the National Assembly needs to assume responsibility for funding those capabilities that will improve deterrence. The priority for that funding should be the acquisition of a C4I—command, control, communication, computers, and intelligence—system that vastly improves the responsiveness of the ROK military communications. Such responsiveness was deemed lacking by the ROK government's Board of Audit and Inspection whose examination of the *Cheonan* tragedy resulted in the recommendation of relieving 27 leading military officers from their high-level positions of responsibility.

The Lee Myung-bak administration has taken notice of the need for change. Recently, a 14-member presidential committee urged President Lee to prepare operational plans for preemptive strikes against KPA bases by the ROK military if North Korean provocations were evident. Committee members stated that the *Cheonan* sinking had transformed their thinking

---

[47] Song Sang-ho, "U.S. Expects More N.K. Provocations," *Korea Herald*, 13 July 2010, http://www.koreaherald.com/national/Detail.jsp?newsMLId=20100709000706.
[48] Ibid.

on national defense and that the previous strategy of merely building capability was insufficient as a deterrent.[49] Rather than unilateral action, the alliance must be prepared to hit North Korea proportionately where it hurts—planned targets approved bilaterally—in the event of another provocation that results in death and destruction in South Korea.

---

[49] *Korea Herald*, "President Lee Urged to Switch to Active Deterrence," 15 August 2010, http://www.koreatimes.co.kr/www/news/nation/nation_view.asp?newsIdx=71433&categoryCode=113.

Chapter 3

The ROK–U.S. Military Alliance: Transformation and Change

by Cheon Seongwhun

The Era of Transformation and Change

It is natural that a military alliance adapts itself to changing security environments. Whether such changes are originated from internal needs of each alliance partner, overall bilateral relationship, or regional/international security dynamics, a stable and sustainable alliance must predict likely challenges, prevent potential risks, and take on them in a nimble and resolute way if they arise. Transformation and change often generates strategic challenges or invites resistance from vested interests or force of habit that must be overcome for the benefit of mutual alliance. Going through several stages of transformation and change during the last six decades, the ROK–U.S. alliance has grown mature, continued to build strong partnership, and face ongoing challenges as well.

The end of the Cold War provided the alliance with the first major challenge since the signing of the mutual defense treaty on October 1, 1953. The political and military changes occurred in the Soviet Union and the Eastern Europe were indeed transformational. The United States reacted swiftly to change the long-held alliance structure by taking such steps as— withdrawing all tactical nuclear weapons from the Korean peninsula, trying to reduce the U.S. conventional military presence on the peninsula according to the East Asian Security Initiative, agreeing to South Korean request of transition of the operational control (OPCON) during peace time, and letting a South Korean general lead the armistice talks with North Korea. Some of the steps were put into practice and others not. For example, realignment of the U.S. conventional forces in Korea was stopped because of the emergence of North Korea's nuclear weapons program, while the North flatly rejected a South Korean general as head of the United Nations Command delegation.

The tragic terror attacks on September 11, 2001 was another event that brought about transformational changes affecting security environments of the bilateral alliance. The United States has waged war on terror on two fronts—Afghanistan and Iraq. Without guaranteeing triumphal successes, these have affected U.S. domestic politics, its international relations, strategic thinking, and defense postures. Most of all, based on the realization that American power is not unlimited, U.S. policy makers have put that awareness into both diplomatic and military practice.

During the 2008 presidential campaign, for example, foreign and security policy planners in the Democratic camp proposed strategic leadership as a new kind of American leadership. Strategic leadership is based on the assumption that the 21st century is "an era of increasingly diffuse power, spreading to many different states and from states to non-state actors of many different kinds."[1] Considering that America cannot take global leadership for granted, nor can it revert to what worked in previous eras, strategic leadership requires "making wise and deliberate choices about how, when, and with whom to lead." It further says that "At times, our interests are best served when others lead with us, or even taken our place at the helm." In conclusion, "a doctrine of strategic leadership seeks effective action rather than American leadership for its own sake."[2]

In the military area, the Obama administration's Quadrennial Defense Review (QDR) introduces a concept of a cooperative and tailored posture for the U.S. defense role. This new concept is based on the recognition that while the United States will seek to strengthen or add cooperative measures to address shared regional and global security concerns, "such an approach recognizes that the United States cannot effectively manage these security challenges on its own, nor should it attempt to do so."[3] The QDR points out that "The United States will work with our allies and partners to effectively use limited resources by generating efficiencies and synergies from each other's portfolios of military capabilities, thereby enhancing our collective abilities to solve global security problems."[4] About reforming security assistance, it also emphasizes that "America's efforts remain constrained by

---

[1] Anne-Marie Slaughter, et al., *Strategic Leadership: Framework for a 21st Century National Security Strategy* (Washington, DC: Center for a New American Security, July 2008), 5.
[2] Ibid.
[3] *Quadrennial Defense Review Report* (Washington, DC: Department of Defense, February 2010), 63.
[4] Ibid.

a complex patchwork of authorities, persistent shortfalls in resources, unwieldy processes, and a limited ability to sustain such undertakings beyond a short period."[5]

The U.S. concept of strategic flexibility is also an element that can cause changes in the security environments of the ROK–U.S. alliance. While the United States seeks to optimize the use of its limited military resources worldwide by strategic flexibility, South Korea is concerned about its possible repercussions on the bilateral alliance. These concerns include: "the possible reduction of combined deterrent and defense capabilities on the Korean Peninsula and the risk of unwanted ROK involvement in a U.S. conflict with a third party if U.S. forces in South Korea are temporarily deployed to a military contingency elsewhere."[6] The two sides reached the following compromise in 2006 at the foreign minister–level talks:

> The ROK, as an ally, fully understands the rationale for the transformation of the U.S. global military strategy, and respects the necessity for strategic flexibility of the U.S. forces in the ROK. In the implementation of strategic flexibility, the U.S. respects the ROK position that it shall not be involved in a regional conflict in Northeast Asia against the will of the Korean people.[7]

Strategic flexibility could deepen the dilemma South Korea faces in relation to a rising and vociferous China. Since the diplomatic normalization in 1992, South Korea has expanded its ties with China across the board. As the bilateral relationship matures, its national interests increasingly depend upon the relationship with China. For example, China is placed as South Korea's number one trade partner, it accommodates the largest number of South Korean students studying abroad, and plays a key role to resolve the North Korean nuclear crisis as the host of the Six-Party Talks and the most influential country vis-à-vis North Korea. As rising China's influences are growing in Northeast Asia as well as worldwide, South Korea will become increasingly sensitive to what China says and does. In short, China is a critical regional/international factor that can bring about changes in the security environments on the Korean peninsula and the wider region.

---

[5] Ibid., 73.
[6] "New Beginnings—in the U.S.–ROK Alliance: Recommendations to the Obama Administration," The Korea Society and APARC at Stanford University, May 2010, 15.
[7] U.S. Department of State, "U.S.-South Korea Relationship Enters New Era, State Says" January 19, 2006, www.america.gov/st/washfile-english/2006/January/ 20060120134614ajesrom0.8530542.html.

China's outright opposition to ROK–U.S. naval exercise in the wake of the *Cheonan* incident and the U.S. decision not to let the aircraft carrier USS *George Washington* (CVN 73) enter the West (Yellow) Sea is a visible hint that the ROK–U.S. alliance comes to be affected by China.

Unchanging Realities on the Korean Peninsula

In this era of transformation and change, there are unchanging realities on the Korean Peninsula that are often ignored but are very significant in the context of the ROK–U.S. military alliance. First, the Korean Peninsula is still at war, and the armistice agreement remains as valid today as it has been over the last six decades. Second, the constitutional struggle between North and South Korea, that is, ideological competition and political rivalry between communism and parliamentarianism have never lessened, and in fact, seem to be intensified just before another power succession in North Korea. Third, North Korea's military threat has not weakened despite South Korean governments' engagement policy which was first declared by President Park Chung-hee in the early 1970s, intending to promote reconciliation, exchanges, and cooperation. In fact, during the Kim Dae-jung and Roh Moo-hyun administrations, South Korea was reckless by providing unconditional assistance to the North Korean regime and ignoring the harsh security realities on the peninsula.

In particular, North Korea's increasing threat of asymmetrical capabilities must be noted. According to a new strategic assessment by the U.S. Forces in Korea (USFK), North Korea has spent dwindling coffers to build a surprise attack capability "with little or no warning," specifically designed for affecting economic and political stability in South Korea.[8] The danger of overlooking North Korea's asymmetrical capabilities has been warned by several experts both in South Korea and the United States.[9] One American expert pointed out that "The North Korean military threat of 2010 is not the same as that of

---

[8] Thom Shanker and David Sanger, "U.S. to aid South Korea with naval defense plan," *New York Times*, May 30, 2010.

[9] Park Chang-hee, "A theoretical analysis of asymmetrical strategies," *Quarterly Journal of Defense Policy Studies*, Vol. 24, No. 1, Spring 2008, 179–205; Park Chang-kwon, "North Korea's asymmetrical strategies and South Korea's response," *North Korea*, March 2006, 121–32; Bruce Bechtol Jr., *Defiant Failed State: The North Korean Threat to International Society* (Washington, DC: Potomac Books, 2010); Andrew Scobell and John Sanford, *North Korea's Military Threat: Pyongyang's Conventional Forces, Weapons of Mass Destruction, and Ballistic Missiles*, Strategic Studies Institute, U.S. Army War College, April 2007.

1990 against which South Korea has been so well prepared to defend."[10] According to him, North Korea's military threat has not subsided in spite of the overwhelming resource constraints, and by focusing limited resources on asymmetric forces, "North Korea has maintained its capability to threaten the South, and has also continued to maintain its belligerent and uncooperative foreign policy."[11] In this context, he proposed to delay the timing of the wartime OPCON which had been agreed to transition on April 17, 2012 between progressive President Roh Moo-hyun and President George W. Bush in 2007. At the "Two-plus-Two" meeting of foreign and defense ministers of the two countries in July 2010, the ROK and the United States agreed to delay the transition to December 2015.[12]

The *Cheonan* sinking that occurred in March 2010 is a vivid manifestation of the unchanging realities on the Korean Peninsula despite worldwide propensity to change and transformation and the relaxed "Cold War is over" mentality. The incident was the DPRK's bold reaction to South Korean President Lee Myung-bak's principled North Korea policy based on his realization of the unchanging realities regarding the North. That is, the *Cheonan* incident is the North Korean regime's deliberate resistance to the South's prudent North Korea policy based on clear-headed awareness of constant security parameters on the Korean Peninsula. In this respect, it was a reminder of continuing North Korean threats that had often been overlooked by South Korea and the United States.

The *Cheonan* incident may be a harbinger of renewed North Korean provocations during that nation's tricky period of power succession. On August 12, 2010, U.S. Secretary of Defense Robert Gates voiced suspicion that the succession struggle could explain the attack on the South Korean naval vessel and Kim Jong-il's son "has to earn his stripes with the North Korean military." He also said that until the succession process is settled, this may not be the only provocation from North Korea.[13] According to

---

[10] Bruce Bechtol Jr., "The U.S. and South Korea: challenges and remedies for wartime operation control," Washington, DC, Center for U.S.–Korea Policy, March 2010.

[11] Ibid.

[12] Joint Statement of ROK–U.S. Foreign and Defense Ministers' Meeting on the Occasion of the 60th Anniversary of the Outbreak of the Korean War, Office of the Spokesman, U.S. Department of State, July 21, 2012, http://www.state.gov/r/pa/prs/ps/2010/07/144974.htm.

[13] David Sanger and Thom Shanker, "U.S. sees North Korea as rattling sabers for heir," *New York Times*, August 13, 2010.

retired U.S. Air Force Lieutenant General James R. Clapper Jr., then nominee as director of National Intelligence, the most important lesson from the *Cheonan* incident is "to realize that we may be entering a dangerous new period when North Korea will once again attempt to advance its internal and external political goals through direct attacks on our allies in the Republic of Korea. Coupled with this is a renewed realization that North Korea's military forces still pose a threat that cannot be taken lightly."[14] Clapper ranks the *Cheonan* incident as analogous to North Korea's bombing of Korean Airlines Flight 858 on November 29, 1987, which killed all 115 persons on board, or the recent unsuccessful dispatch of an assassination team to South Korea to kill senior North Korean defector Hwang Jang-yop.

The *Cheonan* Incident: Reminder of Overlooked Threats

Since Lee Myung-bak was sworn in as the 18th president of the Republic of Korea in 2008, North Korea has launched an ever-increasing hostile campaign against the South Korean government and the leading conservative Grand National Party. Unlike previous progressive presidents, Kim Dae-jung and Roh Moo-hyun, who were supportive of the Kim Jong-il regime, President Lee has taken principled and rigid approaches in dealing with North Korea. In return, the North has taken more belligerent actions against the South, which have created concerns about current and future security of the Korean Peninsula.

On January 17, 2009, the spokesman of the Joint Chief of Staff of the Korean People's Army (KPA) announced that the army would enter an all-out confrontational stage against South Korea and counter any attempt to nullify North Korea's self-designated demarcation line on the West Sea.[15] On February 2, just two weeks after the statement, the spokesman demanded that the United States and South Korea dismantle their own nuclear weapons and that denuclearization of the Korean peninsula be realized by mutual nuclear disarmament rather than by unilateral

---

[14] Additional Prehearing Questions for James R. Clapper Jr., Upon his nomination to be Director of National Intelligence, Select Committee on Intelligence United States Senate, July 20, 2010, 18, http://www.intelligence.senate.gov/100720/clapperpre.pdf.

[15] Korean Central News Agency, January 17, 2009.

dismantlement of North Korea's nuclear arsenal.[16] With hindsight, such antagonistic statements from the highest military command authorities in North Korea were a signal that the inter-Korean relations entered a military confrontation stage, moving beyond just a political dispute.

On April 5, 2009, North Korea conducted its third long-range ballistic missile test. The next month, on May 25, it conducted its second nuclear test. On March 26, 2010, the South Korean Navy corvette *Cheonan* was sunk in the West Sea. It was at 2122 Friday evening when the warship sank just south of the Northern Limit Line (NLL) near Baekryongdo Island. A sudden underwater explosion ripped the ship in two, killing 46 of 108 sailors on board.

International Joint Investigation

Amid rumors and speculations of North Korean involvement in this tragic incident, the South Korean government decided to launch a scientific, objective, and thorough investigation without hasty prejudgment. To increase the objectivity and fairness of the investigation, experts from the United States, the United Kingdom, Australia, Sweden, and later Canada were invited to join and assist the investigation. Within South Korea, a group of national experts in various fields were called from both military and civilian sectors. The Joint Civilian–Military Investigation Group (JIG) was formed with 25 experts from 10 South Korean institutions (22 military personnel and 3 civilian specialists recommended by the national parliament) and 24 foreign experts. The JIG was composed of four task forces—Scientific Investigation Team, Explosive Analysis Team, Ship Structure Management Team, and Intelligence Analysis Team.

After the nearly two-month-long intensive investigation, on May 20, the JIG reported the results of its investigation. The essence of the report is summarized as follows:[17]

- The JIG assesses that a strong underwater explosion generated by the detonation of a homing torpedo below and to the left of the gas turbine room caused Republic of Korea Ship (ROKS) *Cheonan* to split apart and sink.

---

[16] Korean Central News Agency, February 2, 2009.
[17] The Joint Civilian–Military Investigation Group, Investigation Result on the Sinking of ROKS *Cheonan*, (Seoul: The Ministry of National Defense, May 20, 2010).

- ROKS *Cheonan* was split apart and sunk due to a shockwave and bubble effect produced by an underwater torpedo explosion. The explosion occurred approximately 3 m left of the center of the gas turbine room, at a depth of about 6–9 m. The weapon system used is confirmed to be a high explosive torpedo with a net explosive weight of about 250 kilograms, manufactured by North Korea.

- The Multinational Combined Intelligence Task Force, comprised of five states including Canada confirmed that a few small submarines and a mother ship supporting them left a North Korean naval base in the West Sea two to three days prior to the attack and returned to port two to three days after the attack. It also confirmed that all submarines from neighboring countries were either in or near their respective home bases at the time of the incident.

- The torpedo parts recovered at the site of the explosion by a dredging ship on May 15, which include the five-blade contra-rotating propellers, propulsion motor and a steering section, perfectly match the schematics of the CHT-02D torpedo included in introductory brochures provided to foreign countries by North Korea for export purposes. The markings in Korean characters is consistent with the marking of a previously obtained North Korean torpedo. Russian and Chinese torpedoes are marked in their respective languages.

- The CHT-02D torpedo manufactured by North Korea utilizes acoustic/wake homing and passive acoustic tracking methods. It is a heavyweight torpedo with a diameter of 21 inches, a weight of 1.7 tons and a net explosive weight of up to 250 kilograms.

With these findings the group concluded:

> Based on all such relevant facts and classified analysis, we have reached the clear conclusion that ROKS *Cheonan* was sunk as the result of an external underwater explosion caused by a torpedo

made in North Korea. The evidence points overwhelmingly to the conclusion that the torpedo was fired by a North Korean submarine. There is no other plausible explanation.[18]

North Korea's Reactions

Barely thirty minutes after the JIG reported its findings, the spokesman of the National Defense Commission (NDC), the highest decision-making apparatus in North Korea, issued a statement criticizing the joint investigation. Defining the *Cheonan* incident as "a conspiratorial farce and charade by the group of traitors in a deliberate and brigandish manner to achieve certain political and military aims," the statement declared the following three points:

- The NDC will dispatch an inspection group to South Korea to verify material evidence proving that the sinking of the warship is linked with North Korea.

- North Korea will promptly react to any "punishment" and "retaliation" and to any "sanctions" infringing upon our state interests with various forms of tough measures including an all-out war. The all-out war to be undertaken by us will be a sacred war involving the whole nation.

- North Korea will brand any small incident that occurs in the territorial waters, air and land where its sovereignty is exercised including the West Sea as a provocation of confrontation maniacs and react to it with unlimited retaliatory blow, merciless strong physical blow.[19]

Following the position set by the NDC, North Korea launched an extensive domestic and international campaign of denying its involvement and blaming South Korea and the United States. At the time, Kim Jong-il appeared to bet his regime's fortune by ratcheting up tension on the Korean Peninsula, using his asymmetrical advantages vis-à-vis South Korea.

---

[18] Ibid.
[19] "Spokesman for the DPRK National Defense Commission Issues Statement," Korean Central News Agency, May 24, 2010, http://www.globalsecurity.org.

South Korea's Responses

Four days after the investigation result was released in public, on May 24, President Lee Myung-bak made a nationwide address. He defined the nature of the incident as "The *Cheonan* was sunk by a surprise North Korean torpedo attack. Again, the perpetrator was North Korea." He said that "their attack came at a time when the people of the Republic of Korea were enjoying their well-earned rest after a hard day's work. Once again, North Korea violently shattered our peace." Referring to the JIG's findings, President Lee insisted that "With the release of the final report, no responsible country in the international community will be able to deny the fact that the *Cheonan* was sunk by North Korea."[20]

Promising to take stern postures to hold North Korea accountable, President Lee announced seven major policy measures including "proactive deterrence" as a new national security concept vis-à-vis North Korea.[21]

1. Regarding inter-Korean relations, South Korea will not permit North Korean ships to make passage through any of the shipping lanes in the waters under South Korea's control, which has been allowed by the Inter-Korean Agreement on Maritime Transportation. South Korea will suspend the inter-Korean trade and exchanges except providing assistance for infants and children. Matters pertaining to the Kaesong Industrial Complex will be duly considered, taking its unique characteristics into consideration.

2. Regarding South Korea's military posture, it will not tolerate any provocative act by North Korea and maintain the principle of proactive deterrence. If South Korea's territorial waters, airspace or territory are violated, it will immediately exercise its right of self-defense.

3. As an international response, South Korea will refer this matter to the UN Security Council, so that the international community can join it in holding North Korea

---

[20] South Korean President Lee's National Address, May 24, 2010, http://www.cfr.org/publication/22199.
[21] Ibid.

accountable. North Korea violated the Charter of the United Nations and contravened the existing agreements reached for the sake of peace and stability on the Korean Peninsula, including the Korean War Armistice Agreement and the Basic Agreement between South and North Korea.

4. Toward the North Korean authorities, President Lee demands immediate apology to South Korea and the international community and calls to immediately punish those who are responsible for and those who are involved in the incident.

5. Despite the tragic incident, President Lee reconfirms that the overriding goal of South Korea is not military confrontation but the attainment of real peace, stability, and prosperity for all Koreans. He reiterates the South Korean vision of realizing the peaceful reunification of the Korean Peninsula.

6. President Lee expresses his regret that North Korea is a country still holding onto an empty ambition of forcefully reuniting the Korean Peninsula under the banner of communism and a country that still believes in making threats and committing terrorist activities. He sends a firm message to the North Korean regime that it is time to change and to start thinking about what is truly good for the regime itself and its people.

7. For the South Korean public, President Lee sends an awakening message. He acknowledges that South Koreans had been forgetting the reality that the nation faces the most belligerent regime in the world and that the ROK military made mistakes as well. He promises to solidify the national security readiness, reestablish the discipline, and reinforce combat capabilities of the ROK. He asks the South Korean public to strengthen its awareness of the importance of national security and not to waver in the face of threats, provocations, and divisive schemes by North Korea.

Invincible Spirit: A Reincarnation of Team Spirit of the ROK–U.S. Alliance

From the beginning, the Barack H. Obama administration has put prime importance on restoring the damaged alliance relationship with South Korea. The new U.S. administration has carefully listened to the ROK government and public in the process of formulating its North Korea strategy. After the U.S. presidential election in November 2008, some South Korean observers argued that the Lee Myung-bak government should revise its inflexible North Korea strategy in order not to be sidelined when the U.S.–Democratic People's Republic of Korea (DPRK) relations radically improve during the Obama presidency. However, such opinion proved to be groundless. The United States has been vigilant not to be trapped by Pyongyang's tactic of playing Washington off against Seoul.

At the same time, the United States has pursued denuclearization of North Korea through tough diplomacy—a U.S. version of a principled and prudent approach. The Obama administration thoroughly analyzed the process and the achievements of the Six-Party Talks during the past six years, and has promoted direct talks with North Korea as a supplementary means to facilitate denuclearization in the context of the six-party discussions. Bilateral contacts with Pyongyang have been made, based on realistic judgment and experience, not on wishful thinking. As Secretary of State Hillary Rodham Clinton remarked during her Senate confirmation hearing, the Obama administration does not have an illusion on negotiating with North Korea.[22] With the abrogation of the Geneva Agreed Framework, there are many people in the Democratic Party who believe that they should not let themselves be fooled by Pyongyang twice. Thus, the United States has exercised "strategic patience"—a resolve that North Korea has to make the first move to reengage and that it won't be granted any concessions.[23]

Such a stern position was manifested in the swift and rigid reaction to the *Cheonan* incident. From the beginning, the United States provided strong diplomatic and military support to South Korea. For instance, the U.S. military mobilized two destroyers, one salvor, a landing vessel, and 15

---

[22] "Senate confirmation hearing: Hillary Clinton," *New York Times*, January 13, 2009.
[23] Glenn Kessler, "Analysis: North Korea tests U.S. policy of 'strategic patience'," *Washington Post*, May 27, 2010, A12.

divers to join the search and rescue mission for missing sailors and the salvage operation of the wrecked ship. The U.S. experts actively participated in investigating the cause of the incident. The Obama administration also cooperated with the Lee Myung-bak government to hold North Korea accountable on the international stage. Such a firm position indirectly explains that the U.S. government is highly confident that sinking of *Cheonan* was perpetuated by the North Korean leadership.[24]

Right after the JIG reported the result of the investigation, the White House issued a statement to support the authenticity of the result and to give a warning to North Korea. In essence, the statement made these points:[25]

- The United States strongly condemns the act of aggression.

- The investigation report reflects an objective and scientific review of the evidence and points overwhelmingly to the conclusion that North Korea was responsible for this attack.

- This attack constitutes a challenge to international peace and security and is a violation of the Armistice Agreement.

- North Korea must understand that belligerence toward its neighbors and defiance of the international community are signs of weakness, not strength. Such unacceptable behavior only deepens North Korea's isolation.

Immediately after President Lee made his national address, the White House issued a supporting statement with four major points:[26]

- President Obama fully supports President Lee in his handling of the ROKS *Cheonan* incident and the objective investigation that followed. The measures that the government of the ROK announced today are called for and entirely appropriate.

- U.S. support for South Korea's defense is unequivocal, and the President has directed his military commanders to

---

[24] David Sanger, "U.S. implicates North Korean leader in attack," *New York Times*, May 22, 2010.
[25] Statement by the Press Secretary on the Republic of Korea Navy ship the *Cheonan*, Office of the Press Secretary, The White House, May 19, 2010.
[26] Statement by the Press Secretary on the Republic of Korea, Office of the Press Secretary, The White House, May 24, 2010.

- coordinate closely with their ROK counterparts to ensure readiness and to deter future aggression.
- The ROK intends to bring this issue to the United Nations Security Council and the United States supports this move.
- In response to the pattern of North Korean provocation and defiance of international law, the President has directed U.S. government agencies to review their existing authorities and policies related to the DPRK.

During her Asian tour on May 20 in Tokyo, Secretary of State Clinton remarked that South Korea's investigation of the sinking had been a "thorough and comprehensive scientific examination" and added that "[international responses] will not, and cannot, be business as usual." And she asserted that "It is important to send a clear message to North Korea that provocative actions have consequences."[27] During her briefing for the traveling press corps in Beijing on May 24, Secretary Clinton reiterated the four points of the White House statement issued on the same day.[28] At the first Two-plus-Two meeting of foreign and defense ministers of the two countries, both sides "committed to maintain a robust combined defense posture capable of deterring and defeating any and all North Korean threats."[29]

Such strong U.S. support was developed into joint military exercises around the Korean Peninsula. Most of all, "Invincible Spirit", the largest air and naval combined exercise in the history of the alliance, was held in the East Sea (Sea of Japan) during July 25–28, 2010. The exercise mobilized about 8,000 U.S. and ROK troops, 200 fighter jets, attack submarines, antisubmarine helicopters, and 20 vessels including the *Nimitz*-class USS *George Washington* (CVN 73) and the ROK Navy's 14,000-ton large-deck landing ship *Dokdo*. Four U.S. stealth fighters—the F-22 Raptor—were also deployed for the first time on the Korean Peninsula.[30] Several more joint exercises were planned to continue by the end of the year. The two sides

---

[27] Mark Landler, "Clinton condemns attack on South Korean ship," *New York Times*, May 21, 2010.
[28] Briefing on the Republic of Korea, Hillary Rodham Clinton, Secretary of State, May 24, 2010, http://www.state.gov.
[29] Joint Statement of ROK–U.S. Foreign and Defense Ministers' Meeting on the Occasion of the 60th Anniversary of the Outbreak of the Korean War.
[30] *Korea Times*, July 26, 2010, 1.

conducted their annual Ulchi Freedom Guardian exercise during August 16–26. Follow-up naval and air exercises were scheduled both in the East and West Seas until the end of December 2010.[31]

Invincible Spirit is a reincarnation of the "Team Spirit" military exercise which was held between 1976 and 1993. Usually held in late March, Team Spirit was a joint/combined exercise to evaluate and improve the interoperability of the ROK and U.S. forces. The ROK forces and USFK in South Korea were augmented by U.S. Army, Navy, Marine, and Air Force units from outside the country, totaling 200,000 individuals participated.[32] Because of the enormous scale of the exercise, Team Spirit was an effective deterrent to the North Korean leadership by reigning in its provocative and aggressive nature. It is well known that North Korean forces were fully alerted whenever the exercise was conducted. Team Spirit was halted from 1994 in a bid to denuclearize North Korea, and instead, much scaled-down mutations, most recently "Key Resolve," have continued. In view of the gravely worsened North Korean nuclear crisis, the decision to trade Team Spirit for dismantling North Korea's nuclear weapons development program became a stark policy failure.

Remarkable Chinese Reaction

The ROK–U.S. military cooperation in the wake of the *Cheonan* sinking incident resulted in outbursts of Chinese exasperation. China's reaction was regarded as "one element in what appears to be an attempt to turn the seas near it into a Chinese lake."[33] For instance, when it was reported that the ROK–U.S. joint naval exercise was scheduled in the West Sea near the eastern coastline of China, Foreign Ministry Spokesman Qin Gang remarked: "We have expressed our serious concern to the relevant parties, and will closely follow the development of the matter."[34] Two days later, on July 8, he elaborated China's opposition to the exercise:[35]

---

[31] *Korea Times*, July 29, 2010, 4.
[32] "Team Spirit," GlobalSecurity.org, http://www.globalsecurity.org/military/ops/team-spirit.htm.
[33] *The Economist*, July 31, 2010, 23.
[34] "China seriously concerned about US–ROK naval drill: spokesman," Xinhua News Agency, July 6, 2010.
[35] Foreign Ministry Spokesperson Qin Gang's Regular Press Conference on July 8, 2010, Beijing, Ministry of Foreign Affairs of the People's Republic of China, July 9, 2010.

> China has expressed grave concern to relevant parties over the issue. Our position is consistent and clear. We firmly oppose foreign military vessels and planes' conducting activities in the Yellow Sea and China's coastal waters that undermine China's security interests. We hope relevant parties exercise calmness and restraint and refrain from actions that might escalate tension in the region.

A week later, on July 15, Qin Gang reiterated Chinese opposition:[36]

> We firmly oppose any foreign military vessel or plane conducting activities in the Yellow Sea and China's coastal waters undermining China's security interests. Under the current circumstances, we hope relevant parties exercise calmness and restraint and refrain from activities that would escalate tension in the region . . . . This is a typical Cold-War thinking, dividing Northeast Asia and Asia-Pacific into different military blocs and viewing regional security from a confrontational even antagonistic perspective. Now, the situation has changed so much that no single country or military bloc can resolve regional security issues alone which ask for joint efforts of regional countries.

China intensified its campaign against the exercises by calling in high-ranking military officers as well. Major General Luo Yuan, deputy secretary general with the PLA Academy of Military Sciences, explained the reasons of Chinese opposition in an online discussion with citizens on *People's Daily Online*.[37] General Luo gave this rationale for China's opposition:

- Chairman Mao Zedong once said, "We will never allow others to keep snoring beside our beds." If the United States were in China's shoes, would it allow China to stage military exercises near its western and eastern coasts? Just like an old Chinese saying goes, "Do not do unto others what you do not want others to do unto you," if the United States does not wish to be treated in a specific way, it should not [force its] way [on] others.

---

[36] Foreign Ministry Spokesperson Qin Gang's Regular Press Conference on July 15, 2010, Beijing, Ministry of Foreign Affairs of the People's Republic of China, July 16, 2010.
[37] "Why China opposes U.S.–South Korean military exercises in the Yellow Sea," *People's Daily Online*, July 16, 2010.

- In terms of strategic thinking, China should take into account the worst possibility and strive to seek the best results. The bottom line of strategic thinking is to nip the evil in the bud. The ultimate level of strategic thinking is to subdue the enemy without fighting. Preventing crisis is the best way to resolve and overcome the crisis. China's current tough stance is part of preventive diplomacy.

- In terms of geopolitical strategy, the Yellow Sea [West Sea] is the gateway to China's capital region and a vital passage to the heartland of Beijing and Tianjin. In history, foreign invaders repeatedly took the Yellow Sea as an entrance to ... the heartland of Beijing and Tianjin. The drill area selected by the United States and South Korea is only 500 kilometers away from Beijing. China will be aware of the security pressure from military exercises conducted by any country in an area that is so close to China's heartland. The aircraft carrier USS *George Washington* has a combat radius of 600 kilometers and its aircraft [have] a combat radius as long as 1,000 kilometers. Therefore, the military exercise in the area has posed a direct security threat to China's heartland and the Bohai Rim Economic Circle.

- In a bid to safeguard security on the Korean Peninsula, the U.N. Security Council has just issued a presidential statement, requiring all parties to remain calm and restrained [with regard] to the so-called *Cheonan* naval ship incident, which had caused a major crisis on the Korean Peninsula. On the other hand, the joint military exercise by the United States and South Korea on the Yellow Sea has created a new crisis. This is another reason why China strongly opposes the military exercise on the Yellow Sea. In order to safeguard security on the Korean Peninsula, no country should create a new crisis, instead they should control and deal with the existing one.

- In terms of maintaining China–U.S. relations, especially the two parties' military relations, China must declare its solemn stance. China has been working to promote the healthy development of China–U.S. military relations. Therefore, China has clearly declared that it is willing to promote the development of the two parties' relations. Deputy Director of the General Staff General Ma Xiaotian has also expressed his welcome to U.S. Defense Secretary Robert Gates to visit China at a proper time.

According to South Korean daily *Hankook Ilbo*, a professor of China's National Defense University remarked on July 20, that the ROK–U.S. joint exercise's true purpose is to intimidate China.[38] As the Invincible Spirit exercise was carried out in the East Sea, China conducted a large-scale live-fire exercise including firing ground-to-air medium-range missiles in the West Sea. According to the China's state-run broadcasting service, CCTV, an artillery battalion of the PLA held the unusual exercise in an island area near the West Sea.[39] Citing Secretary of State Clinton's remark on July 27 at the Asian Regional Forum (ARF) held in Hanoi,[40] a newspaper in South Korea reported that new tension in Northeast Asia triggered by the *Cheonan* incident spread into the South China Sea and moved toward competition between the United States and China for hegemony in the entire East Asian region.[41] A similar observation was made by U.S. opinion makers, for example, that the Invincible Spirit exercise in South Korea and a diplomatic defense of the freedom of the South China Sea have shown an emerging conflict between America's renewed interests in Asia and Chinese resentment of influence by a distant power in the region.[42]

In response to fierce Chinese opposition to a big naval and air joint exercise involving the aircraft carrier *George Washington* in the West Sea, the United States maintained a fundamental position that every country has its own sovereign right to choose when and where to conduct military exercises. For example, at a breakfast meeting organized by the East Asian Institute

---

[38] *Hankook Ilbo*, July 21, 2010 (in Korean).
[39] *Korea Times*, July 28, 2010, 1.
[40] Secretary of State Hillary Clinton stated: "The United States, like every nation, has a national interest in freedom of navigation, open access to Asia's maritime commons, and respect for international law in the South China Sea. . . . The United States supports a collaborative diplomatic process by all claimants for resolving the various territorial disputes without coercion. We oppose the use or threat of force by any claimant." Remarks at Press Availability, National Convention Center, Hanoi, Vietnam, July 23, 2010, http://www.state.gov/secretary/rm/2010/07/145095.htm.
[41] *Maeil Business Newspaper*, August 3, 2010 (in Korean).
[42] Philip Bowring, "Washington shores up its strategic assets in Asia," *New York Times*, August 2, 2010.

on July 9, General Walter Sharp, commander of the USFK stated that "Every country has not only the right, but the obligation to train its forces against the type of threats they see and to do it within their international territory."[43] Pentagon Press Secretary Geoff Morrell also argued that "Where we exercise, when we exercise, with whom and how, using what assets and so forth, are determinations that are made by the United States Navy, . . . by the Department of Defense, by the United States government. . . . that is going to be the framework by which we make decisions such as joint exercises with the Republic of Korea forthcoming in the . . . Yellow Sea, or in the Sea of Japan."[44]

Despite such strong rhetoric, the ROK and the United States decided to hold the Invincible Spirit exercise in the East Sea (Sea of Japan) and keep the USS *George Washington* from entering the West Sea. A ROK Defense Ministry official admitted that Chinese objection was a factor in changing the original plan of having the exercise in the West Sea.[45] It should be noted that this decision was an important setback caused by China's unusually strong opposition. Throughout the six decades of bilateral alliance, Invincible Spirit is the first joint military exercise in which the Chinese government raised a strong objection in public and the ROK–U.S. alliance retreated. This event signals that a rising China is beginning to exercise its growing national power to influence the bilateral alliance in the name of protecting national security and regional stability.

One day, China may make an issue of the new U.S. base, which is under construction in Pyongtaek, a port city on the western coast of South Korea, about 100 km south of Seoul. U.S. Air Force bases in Osan and Kunsan are located nearby, which means that it will become a strategic hub combining U.S. air, naval, and army assets. Following the rationale of General Luo of the PLA Academy of Military Sciences, the Chinese could perceive the U.S. base in Pyongtaek as a threat to "the gateway to China's capital region and a vital passage to the heartland of Beijing and Tianjin." The move of the Invincible Spirit exercise to the East Sea opened the window for China's

---

[43] Asian Security Studies Center, 2010 Annual Meeting of Asian Security Initiative, July 8–9, 2010, Seoul, http://www.eai.or.kr/type_k/panelView.asp?bytag=n&catcode=&code=kor_event&idx=9124&page=1.

[44] DOD News Briefing with Geoff Morrell from the Pentagon, U.S. Department of Defense, Office of the Assistant Secretary of Defense (Public Affairs), July 14, 2010.

[45] "Compromise on drill by U.S., Korea," *JoongAng Daily*, July 16, 2010.

future claim that U.S. presence along the western coast of the Korean Peninsula should be constrained.

This may be a troublesome signal that the ROK–U.S. alliance will be influenced by a rising China, which raises concerns whether the alliance could effectively deal with future contingencies in North Korea. The Department of Defense recognizes possible Chinese intervention when such events occur. For example, a DOD report on China remarked that:[46]

> China's leaders hope to prevent regional instability from spilling across China's borders and thereby interfering with economic development or domestic stability. Changes in regional security dynamics—such as perceived threats to China's ability to access and transport foreign resources, or disruptions on the Korean Peninsula—could lead to shifts in China's military development and deployment patterns, likely with consequences for neighboring states.

Belatedly the United States expressed its intention to hold a joint exercise in the West Sea with the participation of the USS *George Washington*.[47] However, to curtail Chinese disruptive influence on the ROK–U.S. joint exercises and military alliance in the future, the two countries should maintain firm opposition to China's further interference. And they should conduct the annual *Cheonan* air and naval exercise in the West Sea for the memory of the ROK sailors lost in her sinking.

Lessons Learned from the North Korean Nuclear Crisis

There are two important lessons to be learned from the two-decade-long process of resolving North Korea's nuclear crisis. On the one hand, U.S. security commitment to South Korea has been diminished, at least in

---

[46] Military and Security Developments Involving the People's Republic of China 2010: A Report to Congress Pursuant to the National Defense Authorization Act for Fiscal Year 2010, Office of the Secretary of Defense, 2010, 16, http://www.defense.gov/pubs/pdfs/2010_CMPR_Final.pdf.

[47] Pentagon Press Secretary Geoff Morrell stated: "And we are also, obviously, planning other maritime and air exercises between our two militaries as part of the sequence we had talked about before. They will be taking place in both the East and West Sea, and both the Sea of Japan and the Yellow Sea. They will once again involve the USS *George Washington*. And the USS *George Washington* will exercise in the Yellow Sea, in the West Sea. But I don't have for you yet dates when that exercise involving that aircraft carrier will take place. But that will be ... part of the sequence of exercises that we conduct will be a return of the ... *George Washington*, including exercising in the Yellow Sea." U.S. Department of Defense, Office of the Assistant Secretary of Defense (Public Affairs), News Transcript, August 5, 2010, http://www.defense.gov/Transcripts/Transcript.aspx?TranscriptID=53001.

an indirect way, by its efforts to ally North Korea's security concerns during the course of various negotiations to resolve the crisis. On the other hand, American politicians' political interests effectively marginalized South Korea's security interests.

Repercussions of American Security Guarantee to North Korea

Since the outbreak of the North Korean nuclear crisis in the early 1990s, there have been constant worries that the U.S. security commitment, especially the nuclear umbrella, has weakened. The North Korean argument that it had to develop nuclear weapons due to the American nuclear threat has gained growing acceptance in the United States, thus this strategy can claim to have earned some measure of success.

For example, North Korea successfully used the nuclear issue as a lure to achieve the first U.S.–DPRK high-level talks after the Korean War in June 1993. In the joint statement, the United States formally pledged not to use or threaten to use armed force against North Korea, including nuclear weapons.[48] The United States made a similar promise in the Geneva Agreed Framework signed on October 21, 1994 in Article III.1: "The U.S. will provide formal assurances to the DPRK, against the threat or use of nuclear weapons by the U.S."[49] The September 19, 2005 Joint Declaration agreed upon at the fourth round of the Six-Party Talks also made a similar security guarantee to North Korea (Article 1): "The United States affirmed that it has no nuclear weapons on the Korean Peninsula and has no intention to attack or invade the DPRK with nuclear or conventional weapons."[50]

In short, in the early 1990s, North Korea used termination of its nuclear development programs as bait to extract repeated promises from the United States not to use military force especially nuclear weapons. And 20 years later, the DPRK is using abandonment of nuclear weapons as a pretext for insisting on the signing of a peace treaty and deactivating the armistice agreement which has formed the foundation of the ROK–U.S. joint

---

[48] Joint Statement of the Democratic People's Republic of Korea and the United States of America, New York, June 11, 1993.
[49] Agreed Framework between the United States of America and the Democratic People's Republic of Korea, Geneva, October 21, 1994.
[50] Joint Statement of the Fourth Round of the Six-Party Talks, Beijing, 19 September 2005.

deterrence against North Korea. This is the reality of the North Korean nuclear crisis today.

American Passion for Political Legacy Undermining South Korea's Security Interests

President William J. Clinton knew that the DPRK had operated a highly enriched uranium (HEU) program with the help of Pakistan in violation of the Geneva Agreed Framework. A report to the Speaker of House of Representatives in November 1999 stated that:[51]

> North Korea's WMD programs pose a major threat to the United States and its allies. This threat has advanced considerably over the past five years, particularly with the enhancement of North Korea's missile capabilities. There is significant evidence that undeclared nuclear weapons development activity continues, including efforts to acquire uranium enrichment technologies and recent nuclear-related high explosive tests. This means that the United States cannot discount the possibility that North Korea could produce additional nuclear weapons outside of the constraints imposed by the 1994 Agreed Framework.

President Clinton did not disclose this fact, however, concerned that his diplomatic legacy centered on the Agreed Framework might be damaged. Instead, he accelerated normalization talks with North Korea, exchanged high-ranking officials, and issued a joint communiqué as if the North loyally adhered to its non-nuclear promise. On October 12, 2000, the communiqué was agreed on the occasion that North Korea's special envoy, Vice Marshal Jo Myong-rok visited the United States and met with President Clinton. In return, Secretary of State Madeleine Albright visited Pyongyang and met Kim Jong-il. The joint communiqué stipulated various measures to improve the U.S.–DPRK relations, including that:[52]

> Building on the principles laid out in the June 11, 1993 U.S.–DPRK Joint Statement and reaffirmed in the October 21, 1994, Agreed Framework, the two sides agreed to work to remove

---

[51] North Korea Advisory Group, Report to the Speaker U.S. House of Representatives, November 1999, 2, http://www.house.gov/international_relations/nkag/report.htm.
[52] The U.S.–DPRK Joint Communiqué, October 12, 2000.

mistrust, build mutual confidence, and maintain an atmosphere in which they can deal constructively with issues of central concern. In this regard, the two sides reaffirmed that their relations should be based on the principles of respect for each other's sovereignty and non-interference in each other's internal affairs, and noted the value of regular diplomatic contacts, bilaterally and in broader fora.

In February 2000, President Clinton ignored a congressional request to certify that North Korea was not seeking to develop nuclear weapons. In response to the administration's request for funding the Korean Peninsula Energy Development Organization (KEDO), Congress asked the President to certify that:[53]

- North Korea is complying with all provisions of the Agreed Framework and progress is being made on the implementation of the Joint Denuclearization Agreement between North and South Korea;

- North Korea is cooperating fully in the canning and safe storage of all spent fuel from its 5 MWe reactor;

- North Korea has not significantly diverted assistance provided by the United States for purposes for which it was not intended, and

- The United States is fully engaged in efforts to impede North Korea's development and export of ballistic missiles.

On February 24, 2000, President Clinton spent 1.5 million dollars to fund KEDO by waiving the requirement to certify that North Korea has not diverted assistance provided by the United States for purposes for which it was not intended; and it was not seeking to develop or acquire the capability to enrich uranium, or any additional capability to reprocess spent nuclear fuel.[54]

The much-praised Perry Report which was produced in October 1999 by former Secretary of Defense William J. Perry, then U.S.–North Korea Policy Coordinator and Special Advisor to the President and the Secretary

---

[53] Special Report–KEDO Funding, October 30, 1998, NAPSNet@nautilus.org.
[54] "Presidential Memo on U.S. Contribution to KEDO," Presidential Determination No. 2000-15, Office of the Press Secretary, February 24, 2000, https://www.clintonfoundation.org/legacy/022400-presidential-memo-on-us-contribution-to-kedo.htm.

of State, set out last-ditch diplomatic efforts toward North Korea. However, the report articulated as its basic premise that "the policy review team has serious concerns about possible continuing nuclear weapons-related work in the DPRK."[55]

During the George W. Bush presidency, the U.S. State Department on October 11, 2008 removed North Korea from a list of state sponsors of terrorism, meeting Pyongyang's major demand in anticipation of its reciprocal good behavior in verifying North Korea denuclearization. Contrary to common expectations, this decision did not give the Kim Jong-il regime any substantial benefits. For the delisting to bear any meaningful fruit, North Korean society had to reform and open, and about 20 other sanctions remained without change. The U.S. decision, however, would have helped Kim Jong-il reinforce his political legitimacy and authorities that might have been weakened by his illness. Believing that their Dear Leader won a one-to-one match with President Bush, North Korean elites could have launched extensive propaganda campaign that Kim Jong-il brought Americans to their knees without forgoing a piece of nuclear weaponry. Internationally, the Bush administration's decision might encourage further reckless behaviors of other would-be proliferators.

A major motivation to rescind the designation of the DPRK as a state sponsor of terrorism is the Bush administration's aspiration for creating a legacy. Bogged down in the Iraq War, isolated on the world stage, and with no concrete domestic achievements, President Bush from his second term regarded the North Korean nuclear crisis as an opportunity to produce a political legacy. In the course of what former UN Ambassador John Bolton called "legacy frenzy,"[56] the Bush administration gave up key principles—such as not having direct bilateral contacts with North Korea and holding on to complete, verifiable, and irreversible dismantlement—set back from initial positions in the negotiations, and devoted itself to just producing an agreement. The outcome was disappointing with disablement much less thorough than originally promised in February 2007 with the declaration missing major parts of the DPRK nuclear programs such as the uranium enrichment and proliferation activities, it contained no assurance of when

---

[55] William Perry, Review of United States Policy Toward North Korea: Findings and Recommendations, October 12, 1999, http://www.state.gov/www.regions/eap/991012_northkorea_rpt.html.
[56] John Bolton, "Bush owes his successor a tough finish on foreign policy," *Wall Street Journal*, September 6, 2008, A11.

and how nuclear weapons be dismantled, and provided inadequate verification with many loopholes for the DPRK.

Under the motto of ABC (Anything But Clinton), Bush administration officials heavily criticized and vowed to overhaul Clinton's North Korea policy. The current nuclear crisis erupted in October 2002 when the Bush administration correctly revealed the DPRK's HEU program which had long been masked by the Clinton administration's legacy frenzy. Few would have believed that President Bush would have followed the exactly same path of his predecessor.

Critical observation of the American politicians' legacy drives is not an isolated view in South Korea. In his *Foreign Affairs* article, Yoichi Funabashi, the editor-in-chief of the *Asahi Shimbun*, cited veteran Japanese diplomats' views that Secretary of State Condoleezza Rice's drive to build her legacy by scoring a diplomatic success with North Korea in the later days of the Bush administration is similar to a disconcerting replay of Secretary Madeleine Albright's final days in the Clinton administration, when she feverishly tried to arrange a visit to Pyongyang for President Clinton.[57]

For the Future of the Alliance

The ROK–U.S. alliance has occasionally experienced difficult times in the six decades of the alliance history. The most turbulent period were the 10 years of progressive governments under South Korean Presidents Kim Dae-jung and Roh Moo-hyun. Gaping differences appeared over key issues, which adversely influenced the bilateral relations. The bilateral alliance cannot and should not remain a fixture of the Cold War era. The world as a whole and Northeast Asia in particular has experienced significant transformation and change since the war's end.

It should not be forgotten, however, that the Korean Peninsula is yet to escape the quagmire of the Cold War. Technically, North Korea and China on the one side and South Korea and the United States on the other side are still at war. The North Korean nuclear crisis is the most dangerous security threat South Korea has faced since the end of the Korean War. Furthermore, North Korean leader Kim Jong-il's illness and the ongoing

---

[57] Yoichi Funabashi, "Keeping up with Asia: America and the new balance of power," *Foreign Affairs*, September/October 2008, 110–25.

transfer of succession to his third son are creating unparalleled uncertainty and instability in the North–South Korean relations and the wider region. Thus, any change in the deterrent postures against the DPRK should be considered with maximum caution and sensitivity. The ROK–U.S. alliance should not be damaged by emotional distractions either. Seoul and Washington should not forget that it has been Pyongyang's strategic goal to drive a wedge between the two sides. In view of the worsened bilateral relationship during the Roh administration, several important remedial measures were presented for forging a better alliance relationship with a long-term vision and vigor.[58] Although the bilateral relationship has improved much after the change of governments on both sides, most of those measures are still valid today.

This paper adds three more policy measures for building a stronger and better alliance in the future: respecting and committing to each other's commitments, strengthening joint long-term vision and formulating common strategies, and protecting the armistice agreement and the United Nations Command (UNC). A fundamental principle driving these measures is that diplomatic engagement per se cannot be the right path in dealing with North Korea. To successfully change North Korea either through engagement or containment, what is needed is a clear understanding of the history and strategic meaning of the Korean division and an astute reading of North Korean strategies. In particular, engagement based on either sympathetic views of North Korea or wishful thinking is worse than no engagement, and much worse than principled engagement with clear-minded strategy and goals.[59]

Respecting and Committing to Each Other's Commitments

Every country has its own national interests, national objectives to meet those interests, and policy tools to achieve these objectives. That is, every

---

[58] Cheon Seongwhun, "North Korea and the ROK–U.S. security alliance," *Armed Forces & Society*, Vol. 34, No. 1, October 2007, 19–24.

[59] The following articles are examples of proposing engagement based on either wishful thinking or pro–North Korean regime views. Joel Wit, "Don't sink diplomacy," *New York Times*, May 18, 2010; Donald Gregg, "Testing North Korean waters," *New York Times*, August 31, 2010; Jimmy Carter, "North Korea wants to make a deal," *New York Times*, September 15, 2010.

country has its national commitments, and the ROK and the United States should respect and commit themselves to each other's major commitments. The commitments are varied depending on the issue area and the context (bilateral/regional/international).

Some national commitments are related to its alliance partner. For the ROK, for example, the commitments are peace and safety of the nation, peaceful North–South Korean relations and unification, economic, and cultural development and well-being of all Koreans, and active development and use of science and technology. For the United States, ROK-related national interests are, for instance, provision of effective deterrence, maintenance of peace and stability, denuclearization of the Korean Peninsula, nonproliferation of weapons of mass destruction, and more balanced trade with South Korea.

Sometimes, allies' national commitments conflict. Differences revealed during the bilateral consultations on the issue of the strategic stability concept is one such example. Another potential area where the two sides' national commitments might differ is the revision of the bilateral cooperation agreement for peaceful uses of nuclear energy. Seoul and Washington will start negotiation to update the agreement which will end in 2014. There exists concern that South Korea's commitment to peaceful uses of nuclear energy may be inconsistent with the United States' commitment to world-wide nonproliferation and the nuclear weapon–free world. In fact, Washington often has been hesitant regarding Seoul's research and development in the science and technology fields. For instance, the United States expressed doubts on some R&D projects in the peaceful uses of nuclear energy. And most South Koreans are curious about why Russia, instead of the United States, has become their primary partner for space development projects.

An obstacle to further strengthening the bilateral alliance is the American mind-set regarding South Korea. The current ROK is quite different from what it was in 1974 when the bilateral nuclear cooperation agreement was signed, not to mention the 1950s when the Korean War ended. But American politicians and military and civilian bureaucracies have a tendency to look at South Korea through the old lens. That was one of the causes of strong anti-American sentiments in South Korea during the candle-light demonstrations in December 2002. The United States mindset has failed to catch up with the rapid growth and changes in South Korean society. Such a mistake should not be repeated.

In regard to nuclear nonproliferation, despite North Korea's determined efforts for acquiring nuclear weapons, South Korea has firmly adhered to its non-nuclear weapon policy since its first announcement in 1990. Geostrategic circumstances on the Korean Peninsula, however, tend to provide a rationale for the international community to be suspicious of sincerity of South Korea's non-nuclear weapon policy. North Korea's nuclear weapon program has only added to the suspicions.

Contrary to this traditional thought, the nuclear crisis has actually increased the legitimacy of South Korea's non-nuclear weapon policy. Despite North Korea's two nuclear tests in 2006 and 2009, South Korean governments, both liberal and conservative, have shown no hint of changing current policy. Emotional voices in the country arguing for responding in kind by going nuclear are overwhelmed by sensible government policies and mature opinions of the majority of the public that call for following international nonproliferation norms and rules in a responsible manner. The Obama administration's reducing role of nuclear weapons will not disrupt the resolve of South Korea's current policy either.

To South Korea, its commitment to a non-nuclear weapon policy is on a par with its commitment to alliance with the United States in two ways. On the one hand, the United States' extended deterrence including its nuclear umbrella has filled the security vacuum incurred by the South's non-nuclear weapon policy. The history of the bilateral alliance proves that the U.S. nuclear umbrella is efficient and effective to deter North Korea. On the other hand, as a credible and responsible ally, South Korea is not careless enough to behave in a manner that displeases its strongest ally. Therefore, suspicion of South Korea's non-nuclear weapon policy is outdated and futile, and should not lay a shadow over the future partnership of the ROK–U.S. alliance.

The nuclear cooperation between Washington and Seoul should move beyond the force of habit of the old days when South Korea struggled to emerge from the rubble of the Korean War. With strong support and assistance from the United States, South Korea has developed to become the first donor-providing nation among the developing countries in the world. Nowadays, South Korean products, culture, technologies, humanitarian assistance, and diplomatic contributions reach out to many parts of the world. In the realm of nuclear nonproliferation, South Korea also is proud of becoming a role model to demonstrate that security can be attained without nuclear weapons, and credible and transparent nuclear energy policy brings prosperity and well-being to its people.

Strengthening Joint Long-term Vision and Formulating Common Strategies

Moving beyond the trite perception, stereotyped attitudes, and fixed mind-set, Seoul and Washington need a new vision with long-term perspectives and acute awareness of the rapidly changing security dynamics in East Asia, especially in the northeast. The two countries have just started this journey. At the summit in June 2009, President Lee Myung-bak and President Obama declared the joint vision for the alliance. It covers building the bilateral relationship onto three layers.[60]

First, in relation to the future of Korea, they agreed that

> Through our alliance we aim to build a better future for all people on the Korean Peninsula, establishing a durable peace on the peninsula and leading to peaceful reunification on the principles of free democracy and a market economy. We will work together to achieve the complete and verifiable elimination of North Korea's nuclear weapons and existing nuclear programs, as well as ballistic missile programs, and to promote respect for the fundamental human rights of the North Korean people.

Second, the joint vision enlarges the scope of cooperation to the Asia-Pacific region.

> In the Asia-Pacific region we will work jointly with regional institutions and partners to foster prosperity, keep the peace, and improve the daily lives of the people of the region. We believe that open societies and open economies create prosperity and support human dignity, and our nations and civic organizations will promote human rights, democracy, free markets, and trade and investment liberalization in the region. To enhance security in the

---

[60] Joint Vision For The Alliance Of The United States Of America And The Republic Of Korea, The White House, Office of the Press Secretary, Washington, DC, June 16, 2009.

> Asia-Pacific, our governments will advocate for, and take part in, effective cooperative regional efforts to promote mutual understanding, confidence and transparency regarding security issues among the nations of the region.

Third, the joint vision also proposes to work together on global security issues and transnational crimes.

> Our governments and our citizens will work closely to address the global challenges of terrorism, proliferation of weapons of mass destruction, piracy, organized crime and narcotics, climate change, poverty, infringement on human rights, energy security, and epidemic disease. The alliance will enhance coordination on peacekeeping, post-conflict stabilization and development assistance, as is being undertaken in Iraq and Afghanistan. We will also strengthen coordination in multilateral mechanisms aimed at global economic recovery such as the G20.

This new vision laid out by the two presidents should be strengthened and further developed in a number of ways. For example, on the future of the Korean Peninsula, Seoul and Washington should agree that peaceful unification must be led by South Korea based on democracy and a market economy, and that a prosperous unified Korea will enhance regional stability and world peace. In addition, the United States should confirm its extended deterrence, including the nuclear umbrella, for the future unified Korea.

At the same time, the two countries need to develop common strategies to put the joint vision into practice. Common strategies should be formulated on at least three different fronts with certain key components.

- Diplomatic—Close consultation and shared understanding are required to curtail any possible wedge in the bilateral relationship. For example, "who leads which issue" needs to be agreed upon in advance. For instance, South Korean concern about intimate ties between the United States and North Korea or being neglected in regional strategic matters and American worry of secret deal between the two Koreas should be eliminated.

- Defense—Deterrence should be reinforced against North Korea's asymmetric threat and joint military preparedness must be upgraded for possible contingencies in North Korea.

Washington also needs to address security concerns in Seoul which were triggered by its reducing the role of nuclear weapons and the nuclear umbrella.

- Economic—Bilateral economic cooperation must expand and increased economic ties will be an invaluable asset to support the bilateral partnership. Thus, failure of the pending bilateral free trade agreement is not an option for forging a better relationship between the two nations.

Protecting the Armistice Agreement and the UNC

The year 2010 marked the 60th anniversary of the Korean War. On July 7, 1950, the United Nations Command was formed to fight against North Korean forces that invaded South Korea on June 25 that year. Twenty-one nations joined the UNC, with 16 countries sending combat troops and five providing medical and material support. While the armistice system, signed on July 27, 1953, has been the backbone of providing security on the Korean Peninsula, the idea of replacing it with a new peace treaty is emerging as a possible solution to the North Korean nuclear crisis.

On January 11, 2010, North Korea's Foreign Ministry proposed to conclude a peace treaty with the United States before resolving the nuclear problem.[61] This is the latest version of Pyongyang's proposal since the Korean War, covering sequential linkage between nuclear and peace treaty issues. North Korea alleged that its denuclearization is impossible without mutual trust between the two countries, and that trust can only be built with a peace treaty formally ending the war—the source of hostility.

However, the Workers' Party of North Korea and its leadership have devoted two generations to realizing the policy of national revolution and unification by force on the peninsula. To North Koreans, the armistice agreement has symbolized failure of the policy and is an obstacle to the ultimate aim of unification on their terms. That is why replacing the armistice agreement has been a key strategic goal to North Korea. To achieve this, North Korea has launched a two-prong strategy from the early 1970s: "military provocation" and "peace offensive."

---

[61] Korean Central News Agency, January 11, 2010.

North Korea has specifically targeted the Northern Limit Line in the West Sea for military provocation, which was not included in the initial armistice agreement when the United Nations forces occupied the entire sea area surrounding the peninsula. Later, the UN defined the NLL in a manner to avoid unnecessary naval clashes. While adhering to this line until the early 1970s, North Korea began to question the authenticity of the NLL in an attempt to challenge the armistice agreement. Since 1999, there have been four naval clashes provoked by North Korea along the NLL in the West Sea, with the *Cheonan* sinking incident the latest deliberate attempt to stir regional debate over the armistice agreement.

In parallel, Pyongyang has proposed to sign a peace treaty with Washington, with the diverse involvement of relevant parties—China, the United Nations, and South Korea. Initially reluctant to Pyongyang's demand, Washington has gradually changed its position over the years. Especially, in conjunction with the dismantling of North Korea's nuclear programs, a growing number of American officials and academics are willing to accept the idea. While President George H. W. Bush scorned it in 1992 at the first high-level contact with North Korea, 14 years later in November 2006, the younger Bush expressed his willingness to sign a declaration ending the Korean War as a bid to denuclearize North Korea.[62]

It was President Clinton who erroneously accepted North Korea's proclaimed rhetoric that the pending threat of the United States and the armistice agreement are responsible for the North Korean nuclear problem. In the 1990s, he promised several times at the bilateral nuclear talks not to threaten or use nuclear weapons against North Korea and launched the four-party talks to build a permanent peace regime on the peninsula. It appears that officials in the Obama administration are taking similar stances. For example, Secretary Clinton remarked in February 2009 that the United States will be willing to "replace the peninsula's longstanding armistice agreements with a permanent peace treaty" if North Korea is genuinely prepared to

---

[62] In a meeting with President Roh Moo-hyun on November 18, 2006 in Hanoi, President George W. Bush said: "And as I've made clear in a speech as recently as two days ago in Singapore, that we want the North Korean leaders to hear that if it gives up its weapons—nuclear weapons ambitions, that we would be willing to enter into security arrangements with the North Koreans, as well as move forward new economic incentives for the North Korean people." President Bush Meets with President Roh of the Republic of Korea, The Sheraton Hanoi, Hanoi, Vietnam, Office of the Press Secretary, November 18, 2006, http://georgewbush-whitehouse.archives.gov/news/releases/2006/11/20061118-4.html.

dismantle its nuclear programs.[63] She made a similar remark at the ROK–U.S. Foreign and Defense Ministers' meeting held in Seoul on July 21, 2010.[64]

Traditionally, conservative governments in Seoul flatly rejected Pyongyang's demand. They regarded it as a cunning strategy with multiple purposes such as to exclude South Korea from the future peace building efforts on the Korean Peninsula, to uphold North Korea as the only legitimate entity to represent Koreans on the peninsula, to remove the USFK, and to achieve unification on its terms.

The previous progressive governments of Kim Dae-jung and Roh Moo-hyun took a quite different approach, however. With the political slogans of "dismantling the Cold War security framework" and "establishing a new peace structure" respectively, these pro-North Korea administrations attempted to change the existing armistice structure. It was carried out under a broader political campaign of denying and correcting the so-called "past of South Korea"—the establishment of conservative South Korean governments. In a chain of purging efforts under this campaign, the armistice agreement was a key element to overhaul the security area. When Secretary of State Rice proposed an idea of replacing the armistice agreement with a peace treaty, then ROK Minister of Foreign Affairs Ban Ki-moon welcomed her proposal with great enthusiasm.[65] The new conservative Lee Myung-bak administration understands the danger of rushing into a peace treaty, but seems willing to include it as a part of solution to the nuclear problem.

---

[63] She remarked that, "If North Korea is genuinely prepared to completely and verifiably eliminate their nuclear weapons program, the Obama administration will be willing to normalize bilateral relations, replace the peninsula's longstanding armistice agreements with a permanent peace treaty, and assist in meeting the energy and other economic needs of the North Korean people." Hillary Rodham Clinton, U.S.–Asia Relations: Indispensable to Our Future, Remarks at the Asia Society, New York, New York, February 13, 2009, http://www.state.gov/secretary/rm/2009a/02/117333.htm.

[64] She said: "North Korea can halt its provocative behavior, its threats and belligerence toward its neighbors, take irreversible steps to fulfill its denuclearization commitments, and comply with international law. And if North Korea chooses that path, sanctions will be lifted, energy and other economic assistance will be provided, its relations with the United States will be normalized, and the current armistice on the Peninsula will be replaced by a permanent peace agreement." Press Availability With Secretary Gates, Korean Foreign Minister Yu, and Korean Defense Minister Kim, Hillary Rodham Clinton, Secretary of State, Ministry of Foreign Affairs and Trade Seoul, South Korea, July 21, 2010, http://www.state.gov/secretary/rm/2010/07/145014.htm.

[65] Yoichi Funabashi, "The Peninsula Question" (*Joongangilbo News Magazine*, 2007), 571 (Korean translation).

Even though denuclearization of North Korea is important, trading off the armistice agreement is no more than a self-defeating policy for the United States and South Korea. And such a policy would be harmful to long-term stability in Northeast Asia. It will create the wrong impression that the armistice agreement and the UNC are responsible for North Korea's nuclear weapons development program—a long-held argument by North Korea. Also, a U.S.–North Korea peace treaty will lead to some critical strategic mistakes. It will:

- Support the long-lasting North Korean argument that the Korean War was a national liberation war against U.S. imperialism and that the USFK is a symbol of American aggression;

- Accept the parallel argument that Washington and Pyongyang are the sole parties of the war;

- Recognize Pyongyang as the only legitimate entity on the peninsula after independence in 1945 and endorse it as a winner of the decades-long constitutional struggle between parliamentarianism of the South versus communism of the North. (It should be noted that West Germany never recognized the legitimacy of the Eastern German regime.);

- Let Pyongyang win political, ideological, and psychological warfare vis-à-vis Seoul and Washington;

- Imply that North Korea deserves to play a key role in unification issues and marginalizing South Korean interests; and

- Strengthen pro–North Korea factions in South Korean society and intensifying ideological struggle within it.

Even if South Korea is invited to join a peace treaty, it is still premature and risky in the following reasons:

- The price of denuclearizing North Korea is too cheap to exchange for an armistice agreement. Hundreds of artillery guns and missiles along the DMZ can turn the Seoul metropolitan area into a sea of fire as North Korea has threatened. Pyongyang can deploy chemical weapons and has formidable special troops ready to infiltrate South Korea. A recent report by the U.S. State Department hints that North Korea has continued to develop biological weapons and may use them.[66] Unless these threats are taken away, permanent peace in Korea would be no more than an illusion.

- Peace building is a process, success of which will take time and effort. Although trust is important, the North Korean argument of building trust based solely on a mere peace treaty is absurd. Peace building should be a front-loading process. Without enduring efforts centered on initial confidence building and arms reduction, enough trust cannot be built to sign a peace treaty. As Alexander Vershbow, former U.S. ambassador to Seoul, remarked in October 2007, a peace treaty is "like the roof of a new house," to get to the point of which one needs to "complete work on the foundation—confidence building measures and increased openness on the part of North Korea—and the walls—full denuclearization."[67]

- Pyongyang is a chronic violator of agreements. History has shown North Korea with a notorious habit that agreement is one thing, and implementation is another. Unless the nature of the leadership undergoes fundamental changes, a peace treaty cannot guarantee genuine peace; it will only create a false sense of security. It will be misused by Pyongyang for a malicious campaign to unravel South Korean society as numerous other documents have done so in the past.

---

[66] The document reports: "Available information indicates that North Korea may still consider the use of biological weapons as a military option, and that it has continued its past effort to acquire specialized equipment, materials, and expertise, some of which could support biological weapon development. North Korea has yet to declare any of its biological research and development activities as part of the BWC confidence-building measures." Adherence to and Compliance with Arms Control, Nonproliferation, and Disarmament Agreements and Commitments, Washington, DC, Department of State, Bureau of Verification, Compliance, and Implementation, July 2010, 20–21.

[67] Alexander Vershbow, "A peace regime on the Korean peninsula: the way ahead," The IFANS Special Seminar on Peace Regime on the Korean Peninsula: Visions and Task, October 26, 2007, http://seoul.usembassy.gov/utils/eprintpage.html.

Despite occasional clashes, the Korean Peninsula has maintained a relatively stable peace since the Korea War, mainly because of the existing peace framework. This consists of the armistice agreement, the UNC, and the mutual defense treaty between the ROK and the United States. In particular, any discussion about a new peace framework in the peninsula must be based on positive appreciation of the armistice agreement and the UNC. As the former UNC Commander General Burwell B. Bell III remarked in March 2006, it is "the longest standing peace enforcement coalition in the history of the United Nations."[68] To exchange the valuable armistice system with North Korea's uncertain denuclearization commitment is nothing but yielding to its nuclear blackmail or being fooled by its peace offensive.

The Korean Peninsula remains home to the constitutional struggle between parliamentarianism and hybrid communism—the last frontier of the epochal struggle in the modern history. According to historian Philip Bobbitt, such a struggle ends only when the superior constitutional order dominates the weaker by bettering the welfare of the (Korean) nation and thus, resolving the underlying constitutional question.[69] A peace treaty must be a tool to hallmark ending the struggle, not a makeshift to avoid the fundamental strategic question.

---

[68] Statement of Gen B. B. Bell, Commander, United Nations Command; Commander, Republic of Korea–United States Combined Forces Command; and Commander, United States Forces Korea before the Senate Armed Services Committee, March 7, 2006, 21.

[69] Philip Bobbitt, *The Shield of Achilles: War, Peace and the Course of History* (New York: Anchor Books, 2002).

Chapter 4

The Lee Administration and Changes in ROK Strategic Culture

by Doug Joong Kim

The year 2010 marked the anniversary of major historical events in 1910, 1945, 1950, 1990, and 2000 that profoundly affected Korea's strategic culture. The manner in which the administration of President Lee Myung-bak has shaped the strategic culture of the Republic of Korea (ROK),[1] referred to as South Korea, since 2008 provides a remarkable contrast to that of his two predecessors, Presidents Kim Dae-jung (1998–2003) and Roh Moo-hyun (2003–8).

On August 22, 1910, Imperial Japan annexed Korea as a colony.[2] While the treaty was subsequently found to be illegal and nullified, Korean suffering was real and hard to reverse. The annexation lasted for 35 years, from August 29, 1910, to August 15, 1945.

That month, the millennia-old unified Korean nation entered a new phase of difficulty that still plagues modern Koreans while also threatening regional peace and global security. Colonized Korea was liberated when Imperial Japan unconditionally surrendered to the United States and Allied forces on August 15, ending World War II.[3] Liberation, however, brought new tragedy as the nation was promptly divided along the 38th parallel into two parts, which since the summer of 1948 have been governed by the ROK in the south and Democratic People's Republic of Korea (DPRK) in the

---

[1] This paper refers to South Korea as the Republic of Korea, ROK, Seoul, or simply "Korea."
[2] Tokyo announced the annexation on August 29, 1910. The author has been arguing for years to change the length of annexation from 36 to 35 years. Finally, the Korean Ministry of Foreign Affairs and Trade changed the number to 35 in its publication *Sixty Years of Diplomatic History of Korea, 1948-2008*, which was published in 2009. Still, most Koreans say 36. The historical record should be corrected.
[3] The two major catalysts to Tokyo's decision to surrender unconditionally were the atomic bombings of Hiroshima and Nagasaki and the Soviet Union's decision on August 8 to enter the war against Japan.

north.⁴ This national division produced the so-called "Korean question" of which government would govern the Korean Peninsula. To resolve this, the United Nations in 1947 called for UN-monitored free elections throughout the peninsula to establish a national government.⁵ The Soviet Union and North Korean authorities forbade such elections in the north. UN monitors observed the elections south of the 38th parallel, which led to the establishment of the freely elected ROK government on August 15, 1948. Four months later, the UN declared the ROK government to be the "only [lawful] Government" on the Korean ⁶. The struggle for a unified Korean government to govern all Koreans on the peninsula is the underlying reason for the ongoing Korean War.⁷

In 1950, to unify the Korean Peninsula under its control, North Korea invaded the ROK on June 25.⁸ The surprise amphibious landing at Inchon on September 15 by United Nations forces under General Douglas MacArthur changed the course of the war. U.S. and South Korean forces pushed the invaders deep into their own territory before "Chinese 'volunteers' intervened in October, ultimately enabling the DPRK to restore its authority in North Korea."⁹ By the time the cease-fire agreement was signed on July 27, 1953, both China and the Soviet Union had become

---

[4] On August 15, 1945, President Harry S. Truman proposed to Soviet Premier Josef Stalin that Korea be temporarily divided along the 38th parallel to facilitate the surrender of Japanese forces in Korea. Stalin agreed, evidently to avoid a confrontation with the United States by occupying the entire peninsula and perhaps to encourage a quid pro quo under which Washington would permit the Soviet Union to occupy the northern half of Hokkaido, which is the northernmost major Japanese island. The Soviet Union accepted the United States proposal to occupy the northern and southern parts separately. The United States was barely able to save the southern part of the Korean peninsula. On August 15, 1948, the ROK (South Korea) was proclaimed, prompting Kim Il-sung to announce the establishment of the communist Democratic People's Republic of Korea (DPRK, North Korea).

[5] UN General Assembly Resolution 112(III), November 14, 1947.

[6] UN General Assembly Resolution 195(III), December 12, 1948. The United Nations accepted the ROK and DPRK as members in 1991 (UNGA Resolution 702) but has not described the DPRK as a "lawful government."

[7] Major combatant commanders signed an Armistice Agreement on July 27, 1953 to halt major combat operations, transfer prisoners of war, and implement other measures. However, the Armistice Agreement did not end the war but will remain in effect until "the peaceful settlement of the Korean question" inter alia (Articles IV and V).

[8] UN Security Council Resolution 82 (S/1501) noted "with grave concern the armed attack on the Republic of Korea by forces from North Korea."

[9] "The Korean War 1950-53" in *South Korea: A Country Study, Federal Research Division* (Washington, DC: Library of Congress, 1990).

involved. While the 1953 Armistice Agreement did stop major combat operations, the signatories to the agreement understood that the Korean War would persist until the Korean question is resolved.[10]

In 1990, South Korea and the Soviet Union established diplomatic relations, raising South Korean hopes for a productive bilateral relationship. A major catalyst for Moscow's decision to establish diplomatic relations with Seoul seems to have been the Soviet economic crisis. This crisis prompted President of the Soviet Union Mikhail Gorbachev to seek better relations with all countries in the Asia-Pacific region regardless of sociopolitical system, as he explained in his July 1986 Vladivostok and August 1988 Krasnoyarsk speeches. Improved Seoul-Moscow relations appear to have been carefully and systematically planned to include sports, trade, and political relations. The Soviets were eager to participate in the 1988 Seoul Olympics, if only for the sake of the athletic competition. Moscow sent more than 6,000 athletes and fans to South Korea by ship through Pusan and Inchon and via Aeroflot aircraft destined for Kimpo Airport near Seoul. For its part, Seoul particularly honored Soviet athletes and guests, and the Soviet team did not go home with empty hands. Daewoo provided a range of souvenirs that included 36 South Korean television sets, seven minibuses, four large buses, and four cars.[11]

The year 2000 was an historic watershed in inter-Korea relations. In mid-June, ROK President Kim Dae-jung and DPRK Chairman Kim Jong-il conducted the first all-Korean summit meeting. This event and the resulting joint statement on June 15 raised hopes for improved relations. Stockholm's prestigious Nobel Foundation awarded its annual Peace Prize to President Kim for this apparent breakthrough. However, his achievement was tainted by revelations that his administration paid $500 million to Pyongyang just before the summit.[12] The Lee administration has declared that it will never offer such a "bribe."

Therefore, 2010 is the 100th anniversary of the annexation of Korea by Imperial Japan, the 65th anniversary of liberation, the 60th anniversary of

---

[10] Korean War Armistice Agreement—July 27, 1953, Articles IV and V. Article IV stipulates the importance of resolving the Korean question and Article V states, "this Armistice Agreement shall remain in effect until expressly superseded either by mutually acceptable amendments . . . or by provision in an appropriate agreement for a peaceful settlement."
[11] Ibid.
[12] Ibid.

the Korean War, the 20th anniversary of the establishment of diplomatic relations between Korea and the Soviet Union, and the 10th anniversary of the first South–North Korean summit meeting. Mindful of these major events, the Korean public began the year with hope that it could become one of reconciliation after sixty long years of tension and conflict.

Satisfying these hopes became more difficult, however, due to increased North Korean belligerence that prompted significant changes in South Korea's strategic culture from a time of unfulfilled idealism from 1998–2007 under Presidents Kim Dae-jung and Roh Moo-hyun to a more realistic culture since February 2008 under President Lee Myung-bak.

Pre-*Cheonan* ROK Strategic Culture

Ongoing threats from North Korea have been a constant factor in ROK security policy since Pyongyang launched the Korean War in 1950 to unify the Korean Peninsula under its control. The DPRK's emergence as a nuclear weapons state is an important case in point.

The administrations of Presidents Kim and Roh tried to manage these threats through historically generous engagement strategies from 1998–2007. Kim's "Sunshine" policy produced the first inter-Korea summit as noted and follow-on agreements that changed the way Seoul publicly described North Korea. Thus, the ROK Ministry of National Defense stopped referring to North Korea as the main security threat to South Korea in its biennial defense white papers. Moreover, Seoul seemed to look the other way as Pyongyang continued efforts to become a nuclear weapons state even after finally succeeding in October 2006.[13] One year later in October 2007 the Roh administration sought an apparent business-as-usual approach, which produced another generous set of initiatives in the second inter-Korea summit.[14]

Despite South Korean popular hopes for a more benign security environment based on the relatively progressive engagement policies and inter-Korea summit agreements achieved by Kim and Roh, the North Korean military threat had not diminished by late 2007. North Korea had

---

[13] David E. Sanger, "North Koreans Say They Tested Nuclear Device," *The New York Times*, October 9, 2006.

[14] Roh Moo-hyun and Kim Jong-il, "Declaration on the Advancement of South–North Korean Relations, Peace and Prosperity," ROK Ministry of Unification, October 5, 2007.

become a nuclear weapons state, and the possibility of denuclearizing the North was very low. The Six-Party Talks, which started during the Roh administration, were deadlocked due to Pyongyang's refusal to approve a credible verification process.

In 2007 presidential candidate Lee Myung-bak recognized that the Kim and Roh approaches had neither neutralized North Korea's threats nor substantively improved inter-Korea relations. Lee called for a new approach that included the need for mutual reciprocity. He was elected president with strong support from Korean conservatives and began to implement his new approach when he was inaugurated in February 2008.

The Lee administration's first defense white paper in 2008 discussed the North Korean threat more frankly than the previous two administrations. The 2008 Defense White Paper noted, "North Korea maintains its huge conventional military power as before, and continues to develop weapons of mass destruction (WMD). This creates a threat to the Korean Peninsula and to the general security of the region."[15] Moreover, Pyongyang's "proliferation of WMDs such as nuclear, biological, and chemical weapons, as well as the means to deliver them through ballistic missiles is considered one of the primary factors posing a major threat to global security today. It is particularly damaging to global security that some nations possess the technology to develop nuclear weapons and long-range missiles. In addition, they can easily acquire related parts and materials on the international black markets."[16]

Such changes in ROK public diplomacy puzzled the South Korean public, which had not realized the danger of the North Korean threat or the scope of change in Lee's North Korea policies. They did not appreciate the seriousness of the situation. Meanwhile, opposition parties continuously criticized the policy changes, warning that they might cause a deterioration of relations with the North. Seoul's new stance also puzzled North Korean leaders. Both groups needed to adjust to Lee's approach and sometimes they tried to turn the clock back.

Pyongyang took a more belligerent stance in 2009. On January 30, North Korea's Committee for the Peaceful Reunification of Korea issued a statement with the following key points that effectively nullified all inter-

---

[15] *Defense White Paper 2008* (Seoul: ROK Ministry of National Defense, 2008), 25.
[16] Ibid., 10–11.

Korea agreements:

> First, all the agreed points concerning the issue of putting an end to the political and military confrontation between the north and the south will be *nullified* [emphasis added].
>
> Second, the Agreement on Reconciliation, Non-aggression, Cooperation and Exchange between the North and the South and the points on the military boundary line in the West [Yellow] Sea stipulated in its appendix will be *nullified* [emphasis added].[17]

Pyongyang raised the stakes in the spring and summer. Ignoring several UN Security Council resolutions, North Korea conducted another long-range ballistic missile test on April 5.[18] On April 13, the president of the UNSC stated, "The Security Council this afternoon condemned the launch carried out on 5 April by the Democratic People's Republic of Korea, in contravention of Security Council resolution 1718 (2006), which barred the East Asian country from conducting missile-related activities."[19] The next day Pyongyang belligerently replied, "The DPRK will never participate in . . . Six-Party Talks nor will it be bound any longer to any agreement of the talks as they have been reduced to a platform for encroaching upon its sovereignty and forcing it to disarm itself and bringing down its system."[20]

On May 24, the DPRK conducted its second nuclear weapons test,[21] prompting the UN Security Council on June 12 to issue Resolution 1874 further condemning North Korea. In September, the Kim Jong-il regime sent a blunt letter to the UNSC, laying out a number of confrontational positions, including the following: "The DPRK totally rejects the UNSC 'Resolution 1874' which was unfairly orchestrated in June 13 in wanton

---

[17] "DPRK to Scrap All Points Agreed with S. Korea over Political and Military Issues," [North]Korea Central News Agency, January 30, 2009.

[18] Peter Foster, "North Korea launches missile in 'satellite test,'" *The Telegraph*, April 5, 2009, http://www.telegraph.co.uk/news/worldnews/asia/northkorea/5108535/North-Korea-launches-missile-in-satellite-test.html.

[19] UNSC 9634, "Security Council Condemns Launch by Democratic People's Republic of Korea: Agrees to Adjust Travel Ban, Assets Freeze, Arms Embargo Imposed in 2006," UN Security Council Department of Public Relations, April 13, 2009, http://www.un.org/News/Press/docs/2009/sc9634.doc.htm.

[20] "DPRK Foreign Ministry Vehemently Refutes UNSC's 'Presidential Statement,'" [North] *Korean News*, April 14, 2009, http://www.kcna.co.jp/index-e.htm.

[21] Choe Sang-hun, "North Korea Claims to Conduct 2nd Nuclear Test," *The New York Times*, May 24, 2009.

violation of the DPRK's sovereignty and dignity and that the DPRK will never be bound by this resolution."

Reprocessing of spent fuel rods is at its final phase and extracted plutonium is being weaponized. Experimental uranium enrichment has successfully been conducted to enter into completion phase.[22]

Despite these discouraging developments in 2009, the Korean public still envisioned 2010 as a potential landmark year for inter-Korea relations. They hoped that Seoul and Pyongyang could make efforts to heal the wounds of the Korean War, show cooperative gestures toward each other and other participating countries in the war, including the United States, China, and Russia. Over the course of 60 years since the Korean War, as its veterans get older and fewer in number, some Koreans thought it would be appropriate to invite those veterans—residing in Korea and abroad—to visit their old battlefields, and give them a chance to console their psychological and physical wounds and the memory of their fallen veterans, regardless of their nationalities. After these visits, the veterans would tell their children and friends about the importance of peace and security on the Korean Peninsula.[23]

These hopes were dashed on March 26, 2010, however, when North Korea sank the ROK Ship *Cheonan*, consigning it and 46 ROK sailors to become the most recent victims of the ongoing Korean War. This surprise attack reminded South Koreans that the North Korean threat could not be easily neutralized. Pyongyang and the South Korean public would see a significantly different response from the Lee administration compared to his predecessors.

Post-*Cheonan* ROK Strategic Culture

The news on March 26 was heartbreaking, especially for those whose loved ones were on the sinking 1,200-ton ROK Navy corvette. This incident produced a major turning point in South Korean strategic culture, inter-Korean relations, and the security environment in Northeast Asia.[24]

---

[22] "DPRK Permanent Representative Sends Letter to President of UNSC," [North] Korea Central News Agency, September 4, 2009.

[23] Does history repeat itself? Just before the 1988 Seoul Olympic Games, North Korea exploded a bomb on board a Korean jetliner in mid-air. One of the bombers is living in Korea, and recently made a trip to Japan.

[24] The term "*Cheonan* incident" is inappropriate because it does not indicate that the ship was attacked by the North and the North is responsible.

A multinational inspection team later concluded that a North Korean submarine sank the *Cheonan* with a single torpedo. Discussed below are the results of the multinational inspection team, the domestic and international responses, and initial ROK measures.

To determine what happened, Seoul invited 24 foreign experts to investigate the incident, which comprised four support teams from the United States, Australia, the United Kingdom, and Sweden. Their report was released on May 20, 2010, with the key finding that a North Korean submarine sank the *Cheonan* with a single, indigenous (CHT-02D) torpedo.

President Lee addressed the nation on May 24 to explain the results of the multinational investigation and their determination that North Korea was responsible.[25] He urged Koreans to be patient and tolerant, as many feared that the two Koreas were heading toward a resumption of large-scale combat operations on this the sixtieth anniversary of the Korean War. Fear of hot war in Korea was the main concern, and the responses between the government and the opposition parties were quite different.

The president outlined several countermeasures, which excluded a military role. He reminded the nation and foreign observers, "The overriding goal of the Republic of Korea is not military confrontation. Our goal has always been the attainment of real peace and stability on the Korean Peninsula. Our goal is to bring about prosperity for all Koreans. Our vision is to realize the peaceful reunification of the Korean Peninsula."

He demanded North Korea's apology, saying: "Apologize immediately to the Republic of Korea and the international community. Immediately punish those who are responsible for and those who were involved in the incident. These are basic measures that the North has to take before anything else. If the North continues to make excuses and wild assertions as it has always done in the past, they will not find any place to stand in the world." Lee also pointed out that the Korean military made mistakes, "We have to admit that our Armed Forces made mistakes as well. On the occasion of this incident, the Government will solidify the national security readiness. The discipline of the Armed Forces will be reestablished, military reform efforts will be expedited and combat capabilities will be reinforced drastically."[26]

---

[25] President Lee Myung-bak, "Special Address to the Nation," The Blue House, May 24, 2010.
[26] Ibid.

The Korean public received government statements and the report's findings with surprisingly mixed feelings that included a level of discontent.

The public became confused by conflicting news coverage and government statements at the time of the incident. The media reported the incident as if it was the Winter Olympic Games in which Yuna Kim was the star. The National Assembly was more interested in publicity, holding live hearings with responsible personnel from the Defense Ministry. The details of the rescue operations were broadcast like a video game. The government failed to quell important controversies over the issue. The performance of the administration in handling the *Cheonan* situation was, at the initial stage, embarrassing. President Lee called it "the mistakes."

Of more concern is the number of Koreans who challenge the report's findings, especially the many scholars and NGOs who favored the Kim and Roh engagement policies with the North. They even sent an e-mail to the United Nations to influence the UNSC process, which embarrassed the ROK government. Those groups still claim they acted properly. Meanwhile, those who support the government are cautious about dealing with the issue at academic conferences.

On balance, the Lee administration was wise to assemble a multinational team to investigate the *Cheonan* sinking. While the ensuing report is persuasive to most readers, certain aspects of this process were flawed.

Seoul should have invited experts from China, Russia, and Japan, as they are members of the Six-Party Talks. Including Chinese and Russian experts could have helped build stronger consensus to support Seoul's requests for relatively strong UN action.

The official documents and presidential statements regarding the incident were not well circulated among the Korean public. The news media did not handle the issue as well as it did in the previous two administrations. The government did not persuade the public to accept the investigation team's findings or successfully mobilize public awareness of the severity of the problem and Pyongyang's responsibility for another act of aggression against South Korea.

Reaction to the *Cheonan* attack and the results of the international investigation team varied among the key actors: North Korea, the United Nations Security Council, and the surrounding powers—China, Russia, and the United States.

North Korea predictably denied any involvement in the *Cheonan* incident. On May 23, for example, the [North] Korea Central News Agency (KCNA) reported a "signed commentary" in the *Rodong Sinmun* that stated,

> The "investigation into the case" was nothing but a red herring as it was aimed to zealously spread a rumor about the "north's involvement in the case" and thus fan up atmosphere for extreme animosity toward fellow countrymen and confrontation with them among south Koreans of different circles and, at the same time, openly unleash a war of aggression against the DPRK in collusion with foreign forces under the pretext of what it called "security crisis."[27]

On May 25, one day after President Lee Myung-bak informed the public of the findings by the international investigation team, KCNA reported, "the 'story about the north's torpedo attack' is a whopping lie."[28] Pyongyang has steadfastly denied any involvement in the incident, despite the incontrovertible evidence examined by the multinational team.

The UN Security Council issued a presidential statement on July 9, 2010, with two key sentences. One, "the Security Council condemns the attack, which led to the sinking of the Republic of Korea Ship *Cheonan*." Two, "In view of the findings [of the South Korean-led multinational investigation] which concluded that [North Korea] was responsible for sinking the *Cheonan*, the Security Council expresses its deep concern."[29] The statement mentions North Korea three times, including Pyongyang's claim that "it had nothing to do with the incident."[30] But it did not blame Pyongyang for this act of aggression.

This result was not fully satisfactory for the Lee administration. The administration had focused its diplomatic efforts on persuading the United Nations to levy strong sanctions against the North. The UNSC

---

[27] "S. Korean Puppets' Moves for Confrontation and War Flailed," [North] Korea Central News Agency, May 23, 2010.

[28] "Military Commentator on Truth behind 'Story of Attack by North,'" [North] Korea Central News Agency, May 25, 2010.

[29] "Security Council Condemns Attack on Republic of Korea Ship *Cheonan*," United Nations Security Council (SC/9975), July 9, 2010, http://www.un.org/News/Press/docs/2010/sc9975.doc.htm.

[30] Ibid.

fundamentally discounted the ROK's basic position that "the North's sinking of the South Korean ship was an outright military provocation that goes against all international treaties including the armistice [agreement] and UN Charter and needs to be dealt in a firm manner."[31] The UNSC stance basically constitutes a South Korean defeat. On the other hand, the UNSC statement represents a North Korean victory because it did not hold Pyongyang accountable for sinking the warship.

Internationally, the Lee administration's efforts to punish or sanction the North were not so successful. Only the United States came to the ROK's aid with the first "Two-plus-Two" meetings of both countries' defense and foreign affairs ministers, and several military exercises. China and Russia were not fully cooperative and there is criticism of Korea-China and Korea-Russia relations, saying the strategic partnerships were not working in this case.

Since mid-June, Seoul's decisions to improve certain aspects of its defense posture and public outreach through the president's Liberation Day address reveal more changes in Korea's strategic culture. On the 65th anniversary of national liberation, August 15, 2010, Lee warned the North through several messages in his annual address to the nation:

- This [attack on the *Cheonan*] should never have happened. The North must never venture to carry out another provocation nor will South Korea tolerate it if they do so again.

- It is about time Pyongyang looked straight at reality, made a courageous change and came up with a drastic decision.

- [T]he two Koreas first need to form a peace community that assures security and peace on the peninsula. What is most important in this connection is the denuclearization of the peninsula.

- The next step is to carry out comprehensive inter-Korean exchanges and cooperation with a view to developing the North's economy dramatically. The result will be an economic community in which the two will work for economic integration.

---

[31] "Korea, U.S. agree to delay OPCON transfer to 2015," www.president.go.kr, June 28, 2010.

- Building on such a foundation, the two Koreas will eventually be able to remove the wall of different systems and establish a community of the Korean nation that will ensure dignity, freedom and basic rights of all individuals. Through this process, Koreans can ultimately bring about the peaceful unification of Korea.

- Reunification will happen. It is therefore our duty to start thinking about real and substantive ways to prepare for reunification such as the adoption of a unification tax.[32]

The unification tax proposal came under instant criticism. One newspaper said, "[Lee's] remarks came in the midst of high tension on the Korean Peninsula since the deadly *Cheonan* sinking."[33] A newspaper editorial pointed out,

> President Lee Myung-bak's proposal to introduce a unification tax is creating quite a stir.... The opposition camp is strongly opposed to Lee's idea, saying that it is an absurd move, considering the administration is using a meager three percent of the fund created to promote exchange and cooperation between South and North Korea.[34]

The controversies over the unification tax and President Lee's vision of unification might be perceived as an exit strategy from the *Cheonan* incident and the following tensions on the Korean peninsula. Alternatively, the proposal could represent the beginning of a national debate on a subject of profound importance: shall Koreans become proactive on peaceful unification or continue to be passive on reunification, leaving future generations to cope with it?

The *Cheonan* sinking produced several major changes in South Korea's defense posture, including military leadership and organization. In addition, others made by President Roh Moo-hyun are to be reversed or modified.

On June 26, one day after the 60th anniversary of the Korean War invasion by the North, Presidents Lee Myung-bak and Barack Obama

---

[32] "Address by President Lee Myung-bak on the 65th anniversary of National Liberation," August 15, 2010, www.president.go.kr.

[33] *JoongAng Daily*, August 16, 2010.

[34] "Division on Unification," *JoongAng Daily* editorial, August 19, 2010.

announced that the transfer of wartime operational control (OpCon) from the ROK–U.S. Combined Forces Command will be delayed three years to 2015. This is a major departure from the Roh administration initiative in 2007 to assume wartime OpCon by April 17, 2012, which many Koreans believed provided the country with insufficient time to acquire new capabilities.

North Korea's second nuclear test in May 2009 persuaded many Koreans that the OpCon transfer in 2012 would be premature. Defense Minister Kim Tae-young pointed out that transferring OpCon then could be "the worst-case scenario for the military," because North Korea will celebrate founder Kim Il-sung's 100th birthday in April 2012 and probably would have bolstered its nuclear capabilities for the event.[35] Deferring the transfer to 2015 would provide Seoul with more time to secure its own intelligence gathering ability, strategic command and communication system, and precision bombing skills.

After the June 16 summit meeting with President Obama, Lee said, "In due consideration of the changed circumstances in the region, the two presidents—in line with the prior request of the South Korean government—reviewed the appropriateness of the timeline for conversion and decided to delay the date by three years to December 2015." By then, the North will also have made it official that Kim Jong-il's son will be designated the next leader of North Korea. The Lee administration made it clear that the delay was requested by South Korea. Surprisingly, the opposition parties did not object.

Security Focus

Foreign Minister Yu Myung-hwan, Defense Minister Kim Tae-young, and Unification Minister Hyun In-taek were not affected by the August 8 cabinet reshuffle. Keeping them in position reinforced their reputations as "the top executors of the Lee Myung-bak administration's uncompromising policies against North Korea." The media interpreted it in the following way:

> The survival of the three security-related ministers in Lee's shake-up of his cabinet on August 8th reflects Seoul's intention to continue pressing Pyongyang over the sinking of the *Cheonan* warship, according to political insiders. . . . The official said the

---

[35] www.mnd.go.kr

important task of preparing for the G-20 Summit in November and of preventing additional provocation from North Korea leading up to the summit were considerations in keeping the three ministers.... Analysts said the government took into consideration the possibility that replacing the three ministers could send a wrong signal to the North.

In addition, they are well aware of the measures to be taken to correct the weak point of the Korean government in terms of national defense, foreign, and unification policy, which were revealed by the *Cheonan* incident. "They should fix the cowshed after they lost the cow."[36]

Military Service Review

The duration of military service is to be reviewed. South Korea expects its active-duty troops to shrink from 690,000 to 517,000 under a national project called Defense Reform 2020. In 2007, the Roh government decided to shorten the mandatory service term to 18 months by 2014. However, after the *Cheonan*, this decision was questioned.

Lee Sang-woo, head of the Presidential Commission for National Security Review that was established after the sinking, said that the duration of military service should be at least 24 months to maintain professional armed forces at full operational capacity. Shortening the duration of military service would force South Korea to eventually reduce the number of its troops to about 500,000 by 2020, from the current 655,000.[37]

This change will draw criticism from candidate recruits who can be expected to question why the service period was shortened from 24 to 18 months in the first place. The threat from North Korea had not changed. Therefore, the background and intention of the Roh decision needs to be re-examined.

North Korea's attack on the *Cheonan* prompted significant changes in South Korea's strategic culture with respect to national security planning and unification, although some Koreans seem more inclined to accept North Korean propaganda blaming the Lee administration for weakening inter-Korea relations than they are to hold Pyongyang accountable for its aggression.

---

[36] *JoongAng Daily*, August 10, 2010.
[37] *JoongAng Daily*, August 14, 2010.

For most Koreans and the administration, however, the incident prompted new, more realistic perceptions regarding their security environment and unification. These include awareness that engagement with North Korea had not reduced its hostility toward the ROK and South Korea's military capabilities neither deterred the North Korean attack nor enabled an effective response. North Korea's denials and the refusal of China, Russia, and the United Nations to hold Pyongyang accountable for the attack profoundly disappointed Koreans who had hoped for a more responsible stance from these key actors.

The attack and its aftermath shocked most Koreans into considering several key points: North Korea will remain a serious threat until the peaceful unification of a democratic Korea; engagement is desirable but must be mutually beneficial and productive; the surrounding powers pursue their own interests at ROK's expense, although Washington's firm support and willingness to accept Seoul's request to defer OpCon transfer to 2015 were a welcome exception; and ROK military capabilities require enhancement.

Consequently, Koreans have tended to accept the Lee administration's initiatives to postpone the assumption of wartime OpCon transfer until 2015 and review the duration of military service. Developing a consensus on the efficacy of inter-Korea engagement and unification planning are clear challenges for the public and administration.

The Lee administration took some important new steps on these subjects as of the date of this paper. What else can it do in the future?

Beyond 2010

Mobilizing public support is essential for achieving ROK objectives to deter North Korean aggression and ultimately achieve the peaceful unification of a democratic Korea that would enhance regional peace and prosperity. To supplement the previously discussed initiatives launched by the Lee administration, four additional measures are suggested: improve ROK relations with China, contain the North Korean threat, strengthen ROK public awareness, and establish a new Korean National Guard.

Korea should pay more attention to enlisting China's support for Korean national interests, or at least neutralizing its opposition. China is a member of the Six-Party Talks as well as a permanent member of the United Nations Security Council. No progress can be made in either forum without China's support.

At the same time, the Lee administration needs to address an apparent yearning among Korean intellectuals for China to become the "G-2" (with the United States) and stand against U.S. dominance in Northeast Asia. For them, the rise of China is great news. They welcome such news items as the *New York Times'* "China Passes Japan as Second-Largest Economy." This story notes that China's economy now ranks second to the United States and opines that "the rest of the world will have to reckon with a new economic superpower."[38] Why these Korean intellectuals want China to become the region's dominant power is an important question with significant implications for Korea's security planning.

To get China's support, Korea should expand its official—state-to-state—and public diplomacy toward China.

The Lee administration failed to persuade China of North Korea's culpability for sinking the *Cheonan* and should have invited China to participate in the investigation from the start. It is not too late to strengthen state-to-state diplomacy to gain Beijing's support for the future.

Stronger public diplomacy is needed to reach the Chinese public. Key audiences should be public officials, members of the armed forces, news media members and other opinion leaders, scholars, and Internet users, whose numbers are rapidly increasing every year. The number of Chinese using the Internet soared from about 2 percent of the population (23 million users) in 2000 to about 31 percent (420 million users) in 2010.[39] Similar growth in the years to come is expected.

Important messages should describe the Korean perspective on a range of controversial themes. One might remind the audiences of North Korea's continuing aggression. Another might address China's support for the North Korean system that produces so much suffering among its people. A third could be the benefits of a peacefully unified democratic Korea for China, affirming that a unified democratic Korea would be a much better neighbor than North Korea.

---

[38] David Barboza, "China Passes Japan as Second-Largest Economy," *The New York Times*, August 15, 2010.

Another part of public diplomacy should be to invite Korean War veterans from China, who fought against South Korea and the United States during the Korean War, to visit South Korea. Those who suffered from the war understand the tragedy of war better than anybody else. The goal would be to empower and encourage these aging Chinese veterans to become strong supporters of peace on the Korean Peninsula and to tell their fellow citizens about the danger of war. The number of Chinese tourists to Korea is growing fast, and the numbers will continue to increase as long as it is a safe travel destination. Interestingly, the more Chinese visitors that come to Korea, the safer it will become.

North Korea remains belligerent and unchanging. President Lee reminded Koreans in his Liberation Day address on August 15th: "The entire world is changing. Changes are taking place faster than ever. But, what is the situation in North Korea? Nothing has changed over the last sixty years.... It is now time for the North Korean regime to change.... It is time for the North Korean regime to start thinking about what is truly good for the regime itself and its people."[40]

Of course, Lee understands that change is the last thing the North Korean regime wants, but this rhetoric is necessary for the sake of domestic politics. When Lee explained the lessons of the *Cheonan* incident, he said, "We had been forgetting the reality that the nation faces the most belligerent regime in the world."[41]

It is the reality that "options are limited for retaliation against the North."[42] "Even if we decided to take military action, we'd be limited by the Combined Forces commander's right to hold back action under the Combined Delegated Authority," said Grand National Party legislator Kim Jang-soo, a former defense minister. Then what can Koreans do about it?

Bruce Bechtol Jr. believes Korea needs need both containment and cooperation: "While many hope for an eventual peaceful end state for the Korean Peninsula, as long as North Korea continues to develop, deploy, and

---

[39] "China Internet Usage Stats and Population Report," Internet World Stats, February 2010, http://www.internetworldstats.com/asia/cn.htm.
[40] "Address by President Lee Myung-bak on the 65th anniversary of National Liberation," August 15, 2010.
[41] Ibid.
[42] *JoongAng Daily*, April 19, 2010.

proliferate its robust WMD programs, only containment and cooperation among allies will maintain security and stability in the region."[43] Containing the North will be highly controversial but important to consider.

If Korea and the international community cannot make North Korea change, the second best option is to keep the North from making further provocations against the South. There are at least two approaches to be considered: review the "special relationship" with the North, and build foreign support through international fora.

The view of the relationship between the South and the North needs to be reexamined. In 1991 both Koreas agreed to a "special relationship" in the Agreement on Reconciliation, Nonaggression, and Exchanges and Cooperation between South and North Korea, the so-called Basic Agreement.[44] That special relationship put the South at a disadvantage. There should be no aggression or killings such as occurred in the attack on the *Cheonan* among participants of relationships established in a nonaggression agreement. This relationship also embodies the rationale of the wealthy elder brother who has a moral obligation to help his poor younger brother because it is the wise course of action. There is a story about these rich and the poor brothers. If the two fight each other, the poor one claims that he has nothing to lose, while the rich one is afraid he might lose everything. The "special relationship" needs to be reevaluated the in light of North Korea nullifying the Basic Agreement in 2009.[45]

Koreans should accept that the Korean War is ongoing until resolution of the longstanding "Korean question." The only way to resolve the question is to achieve the peaceful unification of a democratic Korea. In the meantime, Korea needs to improve its deterrence capabilities through diplomacy and developing better military skills.

Korea has hosted a number of major international conferences that provide opportunities to inform visitors about key topics of national security. The November 2010 G20 meeting is one example, and another is the next

---

[43] Bruce E. Bechtol Jr., "The North Korean WMD Threat: Nuclear Programs, Missiles, and Proliferation," Korea Institute for Maritime Strategy, *Strategy 21*, Volume 13, Number 1 (Summer 2010), 250.

[44] Chung Won-shik (South Korea's chief delegate) and Yon Hyong-muk (North Korea's chief delegate), *Agreement on Reconciliation, Nonaggression, and Exchanges and Cooperation between South and North Korea*, signed on December 13, 1991 and entered into force on February 19, 1992.

[45] "DPRK to Scrap All Points Agreed with S. Korea over Political and Military Issues,' [North] Korea Central News Agency, January 30, 2009.

Nuclear Security Summit in 2012. If it attracts the same participation as the first such summit in Washington, DC, in 2010, it will be the largest summit Korea will have ever hosted. The Washington summit was the largest gathering of world leaders hosted by the United States in recent history.[46]

The Lee administration recognizes this will provide another opportunity to "help rally the international community to make a stronger commitment to resolving the North Korean nuclear problem."[47] Of course, Seoul needs a sophisticated approach to inform the knowledgeable participants in these high-level conferences. Blatant propaganda will be counterproductive.

On August 13, 2010, the Asan Institute for Policy Studies held a symposium on "Post-*Cheonan* Regional Security" at which the author asked the question, "Will North Korea do the following in the near future—conduct a nuclear test, launch a long-range missile, and engage in military provocation?" The answer was "yes, yes, and yes." One of the presenters asked the author, "How will South Korea respond?"

In answering this question, the author reminded the audience of President Lee's address on May 24: "Public awareness of the importance of national security will be strengthened as well. We must never waver in the face of threats, provocations, and divisive schemes by the North. We must become one when it comes to national security."

The author noted that achieving President Lee's envisioned consensus will be a tough task. The Lee administration's perceptions and policies regarding North Korea are significantly different from those of the Kim and Roh governments, because their engagement was not truly productive. The Korean people are more interested in sports, the Olympic Games, soccer, sports stars playing overseas, movies, video games, and so on. The general public is not interested in national security. Debates on security issues are very rare and seminars on such issues are very few. There have been no congressional hearings since the findings in the *Cheonan* incident. When China did not support the South Korean position at the UN Security Council, the views of security experts and China experts were scarcely reported in the news media. That resulted in disbelief, mistrust, suspicion,

---

[46] "Korea Designated as Host of the 2012 Nuclear Security Summit," The Blue House, April 14, 2010.
[47] Ibid.

and a lack of confidence in the military because the general public tends to agree with those who appear on the media and the Internet.

The *Cheonan* should not be forgotten by the Korean people. One way to preserve its name in memoriam is to establish an on-site memorial to the ship and its 46 sailors who went down with her. The U.S. memorial to the USS *Arizona* (BB 39) in Pearl Harbor is a good model.[48]

Strengthening the military reserve with a national guard would greatly bolster Korea's defense capabilities. In 1961, Korea adopted America's ROTC system, and it turned out to be a great success. A Korean National Guard, patterned on the U.S. model, would be cost-effective and provide a higher-caliber back-up to active duty forces than the current reserve force.

Most Korean army soldiers are draftees, but the military is gradually recruiting volunteers to be professional soldiers, starting with the Marine Corps, Air Force, and some areas of the Army. However, a volunteer military costs a huge amount of money, due to the need to compete for talent with private industry. What is urgent at this point is to invest more money in advanced weapon systems, not on manpower.

The reserve forces currently comprise individuals who have finished their mandatory military service. But insufficient training, poor equipment, and low morale reduce their ability to perform combat missions as reservists. Many Korean men and women wish to serve their country. If they were well trained and equipped with updated weapons, they could serve much longer than their mandatory service terms. They would constitute an army of volunteers and should be promoted according to their capability and achievements, thus enhancing professionalism. Moreover, the budget requirements would be minimal, as they will be paid only when called to active duty. For most reservists, this would amount to one weekend a month and two weeks annually for training, i.e. a total period of 38 days.

To further enhance Korea's defense capabilities, the Lee administration should establish a Korean National Guard based on the U.S. model.

Since the cease-fire in July 1953, South Korea has never used its military to retaliate against North Korea's provocations. It is agreed that "Military action means dialogue has broken down and the situation can only be

---

[48] No navy ship in the future is to bear the name *Cheonan*, for it should be reserved for the ship sunk on March 26, 2010.

changed through the use of force. It should always be the last resort; never the first."⁴⁹ The loss of human lives because of military clashes is not acceptable, for human life is more important than anything else. To deter future North Korean provocations, the Lee administration should build support among neighboring countries to constrain Pyongyang. The ROK–U.S. security alliance is the most important guarantee for the security of Korea, and Korea-Japan cooperation is also essential. Improving relations with China and Russia is also necessary. In reaching out to the surrounding powers, Seoul can work with them to make the Korean Peninsula a safer place and may carve out an important role as a mediator in Northeast Asia.

The year 2010 was not the landmark year that many Koreans had hoped it would be because of the advent of a significantly more dangerous strategic environment. Consequently, South Korea's strategic culture had become less idealistic and more pragmatic under the Lee Myung-bak administration.

Thus, the Lee administration's North Korea policy is different from that of the Kim or Roh administrations. It still causes some confusion among the Korean people and continues to draw criticism from the opposition parties, which favor a relatively generous engagement policy with the North. The inability of the former "sunshine" type policies to produce a substantive improvement in inter-Korea relations and a reduction in North Korea's military capabilities should undercut the credibility of those advocating a return to those policies. Moreover, the *Cheonan* incident in March 2010 clarified that serious nature of the North Korean threat.

To ensure peace and security on the Korean Peninsula, the following measures are recommended.

First, Korea should secure the support of the surrounding powers or at least neutralize their opposition. Korea will then be secure. While each of the powers is important for the security and the eventual unification of Korea, China is especially so. Its role as a significant benefactor to Pyongyang provides Beijing with inherent influence to dissuade the North from threatening the South. Therefore, the Korean government should expand its official and public diplomacy to build support among Chinese government officials and its public. The Internet provides one good method for reaching these audiences.

---

[49] Chris Ryan, *Fight to Win* (London: Arrow Books, 2009), 275.

Second, containing North Korea's threat is important, while maintaining military preparedness and deterrence. This is the minimum defense. Resolution of the nuclear issue should remain a precondition for the Lee administration to improve relations with the North.

Third, to maximize the combat readiness of Korean reserve forces, a Korean National Guard should be established. It would be an army of volunteers similar to the U.S. National Guard.

Fourth, the government should increase efforts to mobilize public support of its policies to neutralize the North Korean threat and prepare for peaceful unification.

Fifth, the 46 sailors lost in the *Cheonan* sinking should be the last casualties of confrontation between the Koreas. Establishing a memorial for the corvette and its lost crew members would be appropriate.

Finally, Koreans need to acknowledge the importance of developing a patient plan to achieve peaceful unification in coordination with our only ally. Peaceful unification of a democratic Korea ultimately is the only way to end the Korean War and create a peaceful, prosperous region.

Chapter 5

The North Korean Military Threat[1]

by Joseph S. Bermudez Jr.

The Korean people have many scores to settle with the U.S.
—Kim Myong-ch'ol, unofficial spokesperson for Kim Jong-il and the DPRK, 2006[2]

Overview[3]

Anyone with an interest in either the security and political affairs in East Asia or the international proliferation of weapons of mass destruction (WMD) and ballistic missiles understands that for at least the past thirty years the Democratic People's Republic of Korea (DPRK, more commonly known as North Korea) has presented the international community with a wide array of threats to regional security and global stability. Included among the more salient components of this threat are: the world's fourth largest military, one of the world's largest special operations forces, an active nuclear weapons development program and the proliferation of related technologies, active ballistic missile development programs and the proliferation of ballistic missiles and related technologies, the largest ballistic missile force in the developing world, significant inventory of deployed chemical weapons and the proliferation of related technologies, an active biological warfare research program, continued provocative military and intelligence operations against the Republic of Korea (ROK) and Japan, the

---

[1] This paper draws heavily upon interview data collected by Joseph S. Bermudez Jr. and his publications including: *Defense White Paper, 1990 thru 2008* (Seoul: Ministry of National Defense, Republic of Korea, 1990-2008), *Shield of the Great Leader: The Armed Forces of North Korea* (Sydney: Allen & Unwin, 2001), *Armed Forces of North Korea*, 2d ed. (draft manuscript), "North Korea" in *Jane's Sentinel Country Risk Assessments: China and Northeast Asia*, Issue Twenty-Seven–2010 (London: IHS Jane's, 2010), and *North Korea: The Foundations for Military Strength–Update 1995*, PC-1510-101-96 (Washington, DC: Defense Intelligence Agency, March 1996), hereafter *Foundations Update*.

[2] Kim Myong-ch'ol, "Why Pyongyang is going Nuclear," *Asia Times*, August 31, 2006, http://www.atimes.com/atimes/Korea/HH31Dg01.html.

[3] *Defense White Paper, 2008* (Seoul: Ministry of National Defense, Republic of Korea, 2008), 25–40, 316.

intermittent provision of military training and assistance to terrorist and revolutionary organizations, systematic engagement in illicit narcotics production and distribution, counterfeiting and money-laundering activities, and a failed economy.[4]

Influencing and compounding the volatility of these characteristics are two underlying factors—the national policy known as Military First (*son'gun chongch'i*) and the ongoing transition of power from Kim Jong-il to his son Kim Jong-un.

The Military First policy instituted by Kim Jong-il places the Korean People's Army (KPA) and its leadership at the center of power and resource allocation within the DPRK. A clear indicator of the success of the policy is that the pinnacle of power within the DPRK is the National Defense Commission (NDC), which consists of 13 members. Of these, eight are general grade officers. The power of the KPA and the influence of the Military First policy are more clearly understood by the fact that the army is the DPRK's single largest employer, consumer, and industry.[5] Although the question of a transition of power from Kim Jong-il to a successor has likely been an important factor in maneuvering among the DPRK's power-holding elite for the past 10 years, it has risen to become one of the primary concerns since Kim's reported stroke in 2008. All available information indicates that his 27-year-old son Kim Jong-un (reportedly given the titles of "Brilliant Comrade" or "Morning Star General") is the designated heir.[6] The maneuverings surrounding this

---

[4] Several of the more readily accessible analyses of the threat poised by the DPRK include: Bruce E. Bechtol Jr., *Defiant Failed State: The North Korean Threat to International Security* (Dulles: Potomac Books Inc., 2010); Paul Rexton Kan, Bruce E. Bechtol Jr., and Robert M. Collins, *Criminal Sovereignty: Understanding North Korea's Illicit International Activities* (Carlisle Barracks: Strategic Studies Institute, 2010); Gen Walter Sharp, 2010 testimony before the Senate Armed Services Committee, http://www.usfk.mil/usfk/Uploads/110/HACMILCON_March 2010.pdf; Bechtol, *Red Rogue: The Persistent Challenge of North Korea* (Dulles: Potomac Books Inc., 2007); Gen B. B. Bell, 2006 testimony before the Senate Armed Services Committee, http://armed-services.senate.gov/statemnt/2006/March/Bell%2003-07-06.pdf; Bermudez, *Shield of the Great Leader*; U.S. Marine Corps, *North Korea Country Handbook*, Marine Corps Intelligence Activity, MCIA-2630-NK-016-97, Washington, DC, May 1997; *North Korea: The Foundations for Military Strength* (Washington, DC: Defense Intelligence Agency, October 1991); *Foundations Update*; and Ministry of National Defense, Republic of Korea, *Defense White Paper*, Seoul, 1991–2009.

[5] This statement includes the Munitions Industry Department, which is responsible for the weapons research, development, production, and sales infrastructure.

transition have witnessed substantial changes among the power-holding elite during the past several years. Because of these and numerous other personnel adjustments to ensure fealty to the Kim family and replace aging leaders, the majority of the current power-holding elite, while being consummate domestic political survivors, possess neither significant combat, nor broad international diplomatic experience.[7] This is a dangerous situation, fraught with genuine possibilities for miscalculation for a nation that is heavily engaged in ongoing aggressive diplomatic and military brinkmanship.[8]

The KPA is a unified armed force that is the fourth largest in the world (behind China, the United States, and India). Out of a population of 24 million, approximately 1.19 million (ground forces 1.02 million, navy .06 million, and air force .11 million) serve as active-duty personnel.[9] A reserve force numbering approximately 7.7 million augments this active-duty component.[10] These forces are equipped with approximately 1,500 aircraft and helicopters, 770 naval vessels and submarines, 3,900 tanks, 2,100 armored fighting vehicles, 8,500 artillery systems, 5,100 multiple rocket

---

[6] The website North Korea Leadership Watch, http://nkleadershipwatch.wordpress.com/, provides an up-to-date source for information concerning the DPRK's succession process, as well as its leadership dynamics.; "Rare N. Korean Party Meeting 'to Anoint Kim Jong-il's Successor'," *Chosun Ilbo*, June 28, 2010, http://english.chosun.com/site/data/html_dir/2010/06/28/2010062801266.html; and Martin Fackler, "North Korea Appears to Tap Leader's Son as Enigmatic Heir," *New York Times*, April 24, 2010.

[7] "N. Korea's Succession Campaign Stirs Up More Discontent," *Chosun Ilbo*, April 18, 2010, http://english.chosun.com/site/data/html_dir/2010/05/18/2010051801337.html.

[8] Some of the best studies concerning the Military First policy, dynamics of the DPRK leadership, and the current transition of leadership can be found in: Ken E. Gause, *North Korean Civil-Military Trends: Military-First Politics to a Point* (Carlisle Barracks: Strategic Studies Institute, 2006), www.strategicstudiesinstitute.army.mil/pdffiles/pub728.pdf; Ken E. Gause, "The North Korean Leadership: Systems Dynamics and Fault Lines," in Kongdan Oh Hassig, (ed.), *North Korean Policy Elites* (Washington, DC: Institute for Defense Analyses, 2004) http://www.brookings.edu/views/papers/fellows/oh20040601intro.pdf; and Michael Madden's North Korean Leadership blog, www.nkleadershipwatch.wordpress.com/. See also: Sang-hun Choe, "Succession May Be Behind N. Korea's New Belligerence," *New York Times*, May 27, 2010, http://www.nytimes.com/2010/05/28/world/asia/28north.html; "Bigwigs in North vie for Power over Investments," *JoongAng Daily*, July 5, 2010, http://joongangdaily.joins.com/article/ view.asp?aid=2922711; "N. Korean Regime Tries to Regain Grip on Power," *Chosun Ilbo*, June 8, 2010, http://english.chosun.com/site/data/html_dir/2010/06/08/2010060801330.html; and David E. Sanger and Thom Shanker, "U.S. Sees North Korea as Rattling Sabers for Heir" *New York Times*, August 13, 2010.

[9] *Defense White Paper, 2008*, 316. An estimated 4 percent of active-duty and 8 percent of reserve KPA personnel are female.

[10] Ibid., 36–37, 316.

launchers, and 800 to 900 ballistic missiles. An estimated 70 percent of the ground forces and 50 percent of air and naval forces are deployed within 100 kilometers of the Demilitarized Zone (DMZ) south of a line running west to east through Pyongyang and Wonsan. These forward deployed forces are protected by a network of more than 4,000 underground facilities that allows them to launch an invasion with minimal preparation or conduct a defense in depth of the nation's southern border.[11]

As impressive as this might appear, it belies the fact that the overall conventional military capabilities of the armed forces of the DPRK have slowly declined over the past 15 years and will continue to do so for the foreseeable future. There are many reasons for this, but the primary underlying factors are more than a decade of famine and economic collapse. Officers and enlisted personnel are generally undernourished and at the extreme low end of being fit for service by ROK standards, despite the armed forces being a high priority in the national budget. The economic collapse has also severely restricted training, maintenance, and the acquisition of modern weapons.

Despite being faced with such challenges the KPA remains a potent, relatively well-trained, highly disciplined, conventional military threat to the ROK force, which is undergoing continual, albeit slow, modernization. Understanding that it could not match the growing sophistication and technologically advanced war fighting capabilities of combined ROK and U.S. forces, the KPA, since the 1960s, has pursued force expansion and doctrinal developments emphasizing the use of asymmetric forces (e.g., information warfare, ballistic missiles, long-range artillery, special operations forces, and weapons of mass destruction) in any future war on the Korean Peninsula. These asymmetric capabilities are formidable and are continuing to develop. That they present a significant threat to the ROK and all of East Asia is evidenced by the dramatic expansion of its special operations forces, the April 2009 ballistic missile test campaign, the May 2009 nuclear weapons test, and July 2010 sinking of the ROK Navy corvette *Cheonan*. Aside from the sheer size of the KPA, these asymmetric capabilities represent its most distinguishing and lethal feature.[12]

Barring an unforeseen event, or series of events, of remarkable

---

[11] There are an estimated total of 8,000–10,000 underground facilities located throughout the nation.
[12] "New Threat from N. Korea's 'Asymmetrical' Warfare," *Chosun Ilbo*, April 29, 2010, http://english.chosun.com/site/data/html_dir/2010/04/29/2010042901362.html; and "North Adopts New War Invasion Strategy," *JoongAng Daily*, April 27, 2010, http://joongangdaily.joins.com/article/view.asp?aid=2919725.

proportions, the above characteristics will ensure that the DPRK will continue to present a wide array of threats to regional security and global stability for the foreseeable future. Significantly, the DPRK represents the country most likely to involve the United States in a large-scale war. Any such war will undoubtedly be sudden, violent, and extremely expensive in terms of human and economic costs. It will likely experience the widespread use of chemical weapons and ballistic missiles, and has the very real potential of witnessing the first post-World War II use of nuclear weapons—by the DPRK.

Command and Control[13]

All power within the DPRK originates with Kim Jong-il, who is simultaneously Chairman of the National Defense Commission, General Secretary of the Korean Workers' Party (KWP), and Supreme Commander of the KPA. Under the 1997 Constitution, the National Defense Commission is the highest decision-making body.[14] It is, in reality, the pinnacle of power within the DPRK. The primary path for command and control of the KPA extends from the National Defense Commission to the General Staff Department (GSD). From here, command and control flows to the Korean People's Navy Command, Korean People's Air and Air Defense Command, various bureaus and operational units. The Ministry of People's Armed Forces represents the military externally and exercises administrative authority over the KPA. Two secondary paths exist to ensure political control of the KPA. The first extends through the KWP Central Committee to the Central Military Committee and onto the KPA General Political Bureau subordinate to the National Defense Commission. From the KPA General Political Bureau it extends down via a separate chain of command to the lowest levels of the KPA. The second extends from the National Defense Commission to the Security Command, which also maintains representatives to the lowest levels of the KPA. As a unified armed force the Chief of the General Staff not only directly commands the ground forces but also the naval and air forces.

During late 2008 Kim Jong-il suffered what has been widely reported

---

[13] *Defense White Paper, 2008*, 31; Bermudez, *Shield of the Great Leader*, 20–55; Bermudez, *Armed Forces of North Korea*, 2d ed. (draft manuscript); Bermudez, *Jane's Sentinel Country Risk Assessments*, 466–7; and *Foundations Update*, 1–4.

[14] While it had no practical effects, the DPRK Constitution was amended in April 2009 to state that the Chairman of the Nation Defense Commission is the nation's "Supreme Commander."

to be a stroke from which he has slowly recovered. By early 2009 he had resumed much of his former responsibilities. During his incapacitation, however, de facto control of the DPRK passed to the National Defense Commission and a small group of power-holding elites. While there were undoubtedly some minor power struggles, the process of assuming power and then returning it appears to have proceeded relatively smoothly. Some adjustments were made within the leadership as a result of these experiences and a number of personnel appointments were announced following the first session of the Twelfth Supreme People's Assembly on April 9, 2009. A number of these were for natural reasons (for example, age, illness, retirement, and so on), while the remaining were for political reasons.

During 2009-10 the DPRK initiated a number of personnel and organizational changes within the National Defense Commission and intelligence and internal security community that would bring about the most dramatic reorganization in years. Most significantly, the commission was expanded to 13 members. Of these, five now control the entire intelligence and internal security community. While the Ministry of People's Security was transferred from the Cabinet to the commission, press reports also indicate that numerous organizational changes occurred within those intelligence organizations tasked with activities against the ROK and foreign intelligence operations. Most significant was the reorganization of the Ministry of People's Armed Forces' (MPAF) Reconnaissance Bureau into the Reconnaissance General Bureau (RGB). This organization, while it remains institutionally subordinate to the MPAF, apparently reports directly to the commission Vice Chairman General O Kuk-ryol.[15] The RGB is under the directorship of Lieutenant General Kim Yong-ch'ol and is tasked with the coordination and control of all operations against the ROK and foreign intelligence operations.

At the Third Plenum of the Twelfth Supreme People's Assembly held on June 7, 2010, Jang Song-taek, the director of the KWP Administration Department, was appointed to vice chairman of the National Defense Commission.[16] In his position as director, both the State Security

---

[15] O Kuk Ryol is considered an expert on intelligence operations having been the director of the KWP's Operations Department since 1989 and having overseen numerous anti-ROK operations as well as the development of a number of classes of infiltration vessels, semi-submersible infiltration landing craft, and mini-submarines. With his promotion to National Defense Commission vice chairman it is unclear if he will continue as director of the Operations Department, now under the new Reconnaissance General Bureau.

Department and Ministry of People's Security report directly to him. Jang's appointment means that all foreign intelligence (including anti-ROK operations) and internal security organizations are under the control of two of the four vice chairmen of the commission—General O Kuk-ryol and Jang Song-taek respectively. The consolidation of these powerful agencies one level immediately below Kim Jong-il more clearly delineates the areas of responsibilities for each agency and reduces operating inefficiencies within the various agencies. Significantly, it also solidifies the powerbase for the upcoming succession of Kim Jong-il by his son Kim Jong-un.

This consolidation of capabilities under General O Kuk-ryol suggests that the DPRK is adopting a policy calling for more provocative infiltrations and operations against the ROK in the future. The early 2010 attempted assassination of former KWP Party Secretary Hwang Jang-yop, who defected to the ROK, by two Reconnaissance General Bureau operatives and the March 2010 sinking of the ROKN corvette *Cheonan* by what is believed to be a Reconnaissance General Bureau Yeono-class midget submarine may be indications of this.[17]

A noteworthy characteristic of the National Defense Commission specifically, and the power-holding elite in general, is that a number of members occupy multiple leadership positions within the KPA, KWP, and intelligence and internal security services. This cross-pollination and concentration of power within the hands of a few individuals enables Kim Jong-il, through the National Defense Commission, to easily maintain firm control over all aspects of DPRK society and the flow of information. It also means that the typical decision-making process and poles of political power apparent in most nations are not present within the DPRK.

Ground Forces[18]

With approximately 1.02 million active-duty troops—augmented by a reserve force of approximately 7.7 million—the ground forces are the largest

---

[16] Jang Song-taek is married to Kim Jong-il's sister Kim Kyong-hui and has been the director of the KWP's Administration Department since 2007.

[17] These recent operations are strongly reminiscent of the aggressive insurgency operations undertaken by the Reconnaissance Bureau during the mid to late 1960s.

[18] *Defense White Paper*, 2008, 32-33; Bermudez, *Shield of the Great Leader*, 56–91; Bermudez, *Armed Forces of North Korea*, 2d ed. (draft manuscript); Bermudez, *Jane's Sentinel Country Risk Assessments*, 469–75; and *Foundations Update*, 13-15.

and most formidable component of the KPA. The reserves include, among others, the paramilitary forces of the Guard Command, Ministry of People's Security, Speed Battle Youth Shock Troops, and General Bureau of Logistics Mobilization.[19] The size, organization, and combat capabilities of the ground forces provide the DPRK with substantial defensive and offensive capabilities. One of the KPA's most salient aspects is its formidable special operations force, totaling approximately 180,000 personnel. The primary mission of the ground forces component is the defense of the DPRK and the protection of the Kim Jong-il regime. Secondary missions include the reunification of the Korean Peninsula, conducting special operations, internal security, and responding to natural disasters.

With the majority of the KPA's active-duty ground forces deployed within 100 kilometers of the DMZ, while dictated by terrain, allows for the rapid commitment of second and third echelon forces and facilitates an attack upon the ROK with minimal redeployment and warning. It is estimated that should the DPRK decide to initiate hostilities, under ideal conditions the ROK and United States would have 24 to 72 hours warning at most—or as little as 12 to 24 hours if the KPA was already at an alerted status.

The GSD-level mechanized infantry and tank divisions are deployed along the primary avenues of approach to the ROK to provide effective support. They are also ideally positioned for exploiting breakthroughs and to cover strategic rear areas from invasion. The KPA's sole remaining artillery division and GSD-level artillery brigades are forward deployed and well protected in underground facilities. Without moving, these long-range artillery units are capable of barraging Seoul and providing deep fire support to attacking KPA ground troops. The Pyongyang Defense Command is deployed in and around the capital city to provide protection in the case of invasion and to serve as a counter-coup force if required.

Beginning in approximately 2000, the KPA initiated a comprehensive program involving the reorganization, re-equipping, and redeployment of ground force units as well as the restructuring and upgrading of reserve forces and the rear-area command structure. Notable improvements include the production and deployment of new tanks and long-range self-propelled artillery systems (primarily 240mm multiple-rocket launchers and 170mm

---

[19] With the exception of the Reserve Military Training Units the majority of the reserves will likely be employed as reinforcements or replacements for regular KPA units or utilized as rear area security units.

self-propelled guns); the restructuring of two mechanized corps, one tank corps, and one artillery corps into divisions; the expansion of existing light infantry battalions into regiments; and the establishment of a number of mechanized light infantry divisions.

This has been accomplished during a period of economic crisis, which has limited access to foreign equipment and precipitated fuel shortages, restricting training and operations. Complicating this has been a series of floods and famines that have affected every aspect of life within the DPRK. Despite preferential treatment, the effects of these domestic crises on the KPA ground component have been significant, especially upon units deployed within the rear areas. Morale and discipline problems have reportedly increased, training has fluctuated and some second and third echelon units have had difficulty in maintaining operational readiness.

The Ministry of People's Armed Forces has also been forced to lower the minimum entry requirements for service in the armed forces several times to address the slow decline in the health of the general population. This itself has resulted in a slow but steady erosion of the physical stature and well-being of the average KPA soldier. The trend is toward shorter troops with extremely little body fat and less muscle mass.[20] Additionally, the past seven years have reportedly witnessed a slow increase in the number of females within the KPA. Whether this is a result of changing demographics within the DPRK, or a means of addressing the declining number of males fit for military service, is unclear.

The factors leading to declining operational readiness within the KPA appear to be most noticeable among the reserve units, moderately apparent in units deployed along the DMZ, and least obvious within elite special operations and ballistic missile units. Despite these problems the KPA ground force component is currently judged to be capable of defending the territory of the DPRK, conducting special operations against the ROK and Japan, and maintaining internal security. It currently maintains the capability to initiate a war of reunification against the ROK with little warning; however, it has a declining capability to prosecute such a war for an extended period of time.[21]

---

[20] "Healthier children through free lunch," *JoongAng Daily*, March 24, 2010, http://joongangdaily.joins.com/article/view.asp?aid=2918237.

[21] *Defense White Paper, 2008*, 40. The best available estimates are that the KPA maintains war readiness reserves of two to three months worth of oil and ammunition.

Reconnaissance General Bureau[22]

The Reconnaissance General Bureau is the primary organization tasked with collecting foreign tactical and strategic intelligence and coordinating or conducting all external special operations. It also exercises operational control over agents engaged in military intelligence activities and oversees the training, maintenance, and deployment of guerrilla teams available for operation in the ROK. The bureau director is Lieutenant General Kim Yong-ch'ol.

While information concerning organizational changes within the DPRK's intelligence community is limited, that which is available suggests that the Reconnaissance General Bureau was established by combining the KWP's Operations Bureau and Office No. 35 with the MPAF's Reconnaissance Bureau. The Unification Front Department and External Liaison Department were reduced to bureau-level organizations and remain subordinate to the KWP's Secretariat.

At this early stage there have been only a few significant organizational changes within the various agencies subordinated to the Reconnaissance General Bureau. Major changes will undoubtedly occur as the bureau develops and redundancies are eliminated. For example, both the former Operations Department and the Reconnaissance Bureau maintain large sea escort or naval components. It would seem likely that these would be combined in some fashion in the future. It is probable that coordination and competition between the various agencies, frequently problem areas in the past, will improve under the unified leadership thereby having the potential to make the intelligence community more efficient.

The RGB is headquartered in Pyongyang and organized into a headquarters and six bureaus: First Bureau—Operations, Second—Reconnaissance, Third—Foreign Intelligence, Fifth—Inter-Korean

---

[22] Interview data acquired by Joseph S. Bermudez Jr.; "N. Korea's Command Center of Clandestine Operations," *Chosun Ilbo*, April 21, 2010, http://english.chosun.com/site/data/html_dir/2010/04/21/2010042101137.html; Bermudez, "A New Emphasis on Operations Against South Korea?," 38 North, posted 11 June 2010, http://38north.org/2010/06/a-new-emphasis-on-operations-against-south-korea/; "Reconnaissance General Bureau is Heart of N.K. Terrorism," *Korea Herald*, May 26, 2010; Yu Yong-won and An Yong-hyon. "Dangerous Man' O Kuk Ryol," *Chosun Ilbo*, June 8, 2009; and Ch'oe Son-yong and Chang Yong-hun. "North Korea Integrates Maneuvering Organs Targeting the South and Overseas Into Reconnaissance General Bureau," *Yonhap*, May 10, 2009, http://english.yonhapnews.co.kr.

Dialogue, Sixth—Technical, and Seventh—Rear Services.[23]

Special Operations Forces[24]

According to ROK intelligence sources the KPA deploys one of the largest special operations forces in the world. This force is organized into approximately seven light infantry divisions, 25 special operations forces brigades (12 light infantry/mechanized light infantry, three reconnaissance, three airborne, two air force sniper, two navy sniper, and three sniper brigades) and five to seven reconnaissance battalions. Additionally, infantry divisions possess an organic light infantry battalion or regiment.[25]

The primary missions of these special forces are: reconnaissance; establishing a "Second Front" within the ROK/U.S. strategic rear; decapitation and disruption of the ROK/U.S. command, control, communications, computers, intelligence, surveillance, and reconnaissance (C4ISR) structure; neutralization of ROK and U.S. air bases; and neutralization of ROK and U.S. missiles and weapons of mass destruction.

The Light Infantry Training Guidance Bureau is the primary organization within the KPA tasked with the training and conduction of unconventional and special warfare operations. During peacetime it is believed to exercise administrative control over all special operations units, including those of the Korean People's Air Force (KPAF), Korean People's Navy (KPN), and possibly the Reconnaissance General Bureau. During wartime it will function as the primary headquarters coordinating all special operations.

Beginning in 2000 but more significantly from 2003 to the present, the KPA has undertaken a number of important organizational changes within its ground forces units. Among the more significant changes was the expan-

---

[23] Some sources identify the bureaus as being numbered 1 thru 7. There is no Fourth Bureau as a result of Korean cultural traditions.

[24] *Defense White Paper, 2008*, 33; Joseph S. Bermudez Jr., *North Korean Special Forces*, 2d ed. (Annapolis: Naval Institute Press, 1997); Bermudez, *Jane's Sentinel Country Risk Assessments*, 472–73; *Foundations Update*, 21–23; "N. Korea Moves 50,000 Special Forces to Frontline," *Chosun Ilbo*, April 6, 2010, http://english.chosun.com/site/data/html_dir/2010/05/06/2010050600371.html; and "N. Korea 'Has 180,000 Special Forces Ready to Cross into South'," *Chosun Ilbo*, June 16, 2010, http://english.chosun.com/site/data/html_dir/2010/06/16/2010061601318.html.

[25] U.S. sources, however, credit the KPA with a significantly lower number. The discrepancy arises from the fact that ROK estimates include light infantry units organic to divisions and corps, as well as infantry units converted to light infantry.

sion of existing division-level light infantry battalions within the DMZ corps to regiments and the reorganization of seven infantry or mechanized infantry divisions (approximately 50,000 troops) into light infantry divisions. These later organizational developments were apparently achieved by stripping the divisions of the majority of their combat and combat support units (for example artillery, armor, air defense, and so on). Accompanying these organizational developments was the expansion of urban, nighttime, and mountaineering training for all special operations units.[26]

It is believed that the KPA undertook these changes following a strategic review of a future conflict on the Korean Peninsula, combined with lessons learned from the recent conflicts in the Balkans, Iraq, and Afghanistan, which convinced the KPA of the need for a greater number of "light" units. This is possibly one of the most significant developments in KPA conventional forces in the past 20 years.

The KPA takes great pride in its special operations forces, which it frequently identifies as the "invincibles" (in the air force), "bombs" (in the army), and "human torpedoes" (in the navy).[27]

Korean People's Navy[28]

The KPN is the smallest of the three services with a personnel strength of approximately 60,000. It is headquartered in Pyongyang and is organized into a Naval Command headquarters, Naval Staff, two fleet headquarters

---

[26] "'Human Torpedoes' Are the North's Secret Naval Weapon," *Chosun Ilbo*, April 22, 2010, http://english.chosun.com/site/data/html_dir/2010/04/22/2010042201171.html, and Baek Seung-joo. "How to Deal with the Threat of N. Korea's Special Forces?," *Chosun Ilbo*, May 12, 2010, http://english.chosun.com/site/data/html_dir/2010/05/12/2010051201255.html.

[27] "N Korea 'Runs Naval Suicide Squads'," *Chosun Ilbo*, March 30, 2010, http://english.chosun.com/site/data/html_dir/2010/03/30/2010033000884.html.

[28] *Defense White Paper, 2008*, 33–35; "Secret Report on Shwe Mann's Visit Says Burma To Copy DPRK, PRC Military Models," Dr Lun Swe (blog), July 2, 2009, Open Source Center, SEP20090709043001001; Bermudez, *Shield of the Great Leader*, 92–122; Bermudez, *Armed Forces of North Korea*, 2d ed. (draft manuscript); Bermudez, *Jane's Sentinel Country Risk Assessments*, 492–7; *Foundations Update*, 16; "N. Korean Subs 'Hard to Track All the Time'," *Chosun Ilbo*, June 9, 2010, http://english.chosun.com/site/data/html_dir/2010/04/09/2010040900289.html; "N. Korean Subs Ply East Sea with Impunity," *Chosun Ilbo*, May 27, 2007, http://english.chosun.com/site/data/html_dir/2010/05/27/2010052701296.html; "4 N. Korean Subs Disappear from Radar," *Chosun Ilbo*, May 26, 2010; http://english.chosun.com/site/data/html_dir/2010/05/26/2010052601246.html; and "Kim Jong-il Called for Stronger Navy After Defeat in Skirmish," *Chosun Ilbo*, May 6, 2010, http://english.chosun.com/site/data/html_dir/2010/05/06/2010050601362.html

(the East and West Sea Fleets), 13 to 16 squadrons, two navy sniper brigades, a reconnaissance unit, two coastal defense missile regiments, an unknown number of surveillance radar companies, and a naval support/antisubmarine warfare air battalion/regiment. Approximately 40 to 60 percent of the navy's combat vessels are deployed south of the Pyongyang-Wonsan line. The navy controls a number of ocean-going merchant vessels and coordinates with the Ministry of Land and Marine Transportation the operations of the DPRK's merchant marine fleet; provides support to the Reconnaissance General Bureau's Maritime and Operations Departments, which operate a number of Sang-O–class coastal submarines, and Yeono- and Yugo-class midget submarines in the infiltration role; coordinates coastal defense with the KPA's coastal defense artillery batteries; and coordinates coastal surveillance and security with the Coastal Security Bureau and paramilitary organizations.

The navy's primary mission is to provide an afloat defense for the approaches to the DPRK's main ports and defend the territorial waters and national coastlines. Secondary missions include the insertion of special operations forces, coastal surveillance, and the protection and control of coastal shipping and fishing operations. In the event of hostilities the KPN would be tasked with amphibious lift and fire-support operations, support to army ground force units, naval mine warfare, interdiction of enemy shipping in waters adjacent to the Korean peninsula, and rear area security. KPN submarines may extend this by conducting short-range offensive patrols off both Japanese coasts; long-range offensive patrols in the East China Sea, Philippine Sea, and approaches to Japan; and the insertion of special operation forces throughout the region.

The KPN has the appearance of being a modestly capable littoral force with a relatively constant combat ship strength of approximately 770 vessels (420 combat vessels, 130 air-cushioned vehicles, 90 infantry/mechanized landing craft, 30 mine warfare, 30 support vessels, and 70 submarines), which ranks it as one of the world's largest navies. The reality is, however, significantly different. The prolonged economic crises engulfing the country limited access to equipment from abroad, and chronic fuel shortages have impacted training and operations. Approximately 10 to 15 percent of the KPN's surface fleet is laid up for engine or hull repair in dry dock or at graving docks. Additionally, another 10 to 15 percent of the surface fleet is stored on land, both in the open and in tunnels. These vessels require maintenance to be restored to full service. Thus the overall number of surface vessels is significantly lower than the figure of 700. Submarine forces (including those assigned to the Reconnaissance General Bureau), however, appear to be in a higher state of readiness.

Additional factors negatively impacting operational readiness and capabilities include: limited training, obsolescing equipment, the poor material condition of a number of principal combatant ships, lack of sophisticated electronic warfare (EW) equipment, shortage of modern weapons, an inefficient and inadequate logistic system, cumbersome administrative procedures, completely inadequate C4ISR, and moderate morale. The fact that the navy is also divided into two fleets, one on each side of the Korean Peninsula, virtually precludes the service from bringing its full potential to bear in either sea or the possibility of reinforcing either fleet.

The combined KPN and Reconnaissance General Bureau's submarine force consists of approximately 70 boats—20 Romeo-class diesel-attack, 40 Sang-O–class coastal diesel-attack, approximately 5 Yeono-class midget diesel-attack/reconnaissance, and 5 Yugo-class midget diesel-attack/reconnaissance submarines. Although a significant portion of this force is obsolete by Western naval standards, it poses a significant threat. The presence of even a single KPN or Reconnaissance General Bureau submarine during wartime is a threat that cannot be ignored as seen by the sinking of the ROKN corvette *Cheonan* (PCC-772).

At approximately 2122 (local time) on March 26, 2010, the *Cheonan* exploded and sank while on patrol near Baengnyeong Island in the West (Yellow) Sea near the Northern Limit Line. Forty-six ROK Navy crewmembers were killed. While the immediate cause was unknown, subsequent investigation concluded that it was attacked by a DPRK submarine launching a CHT-20D torpedo. It is likely that the submarine was a Yeono-class midget from the Reconnaissance General Bureau.[29]

Aside from its submarines the Reconnaissance General Bureau operates approximately 20 "mother ships" and numerous different classes of high-speed semisubmersible infiltration landing craft.

---

[29] The single most comprehensive source concerning this incident is *Joint Investigation Report: On the Attack Against the ROK Ship* Cheonan (Seoul: Republic of Korea Ministry of Defense, 2010).

The navy sniper brigades are primarily tasked with the seizure, disruption, or destruction of key installations within coastal areas; assisting the advance of KPA ground force units by enveloping coastal flanks; assault landings to seize and control a beachhead to allow the landing of standard ground force units; assisting standard ground force units during river crossing/bridging operations within coastal areas; establishment of a new front within the ROK's strategic rear; and reconnaissance and special operations.

The KPN is primarily a coastal defense force and ill-equipped and ill-trained for "blue water" operations. It is judged to have a limited capability to guard DPRK's territorial waters (out to 12 nm) and insert special operations forces into the Republic of Korea during peacetime. It is unable, however, to enforce the claimed two hundred nm exclusive economic zone. In the event of hostilities, the KPN possesses the capability to conduct limited short-term offensive and defensive wartime operations. It can deploy attack forces—surface and submarine—into both the Yellow and East (Sea of Japan) Seas capable of interdicting commercial shipping to and from the ROK and Japan, as well as temporarily serving as a serious obstacle to hostile naval operations. The KPN's experiences with operating an inventory of both coastal and midget submarines provides it with a limited wartime ability to interdict Japan's eastern ports and conduct special operations landings in the region. It also possesses the ability to conduct two battalion-brigade and several company-battalion–sized amphibious lift operations against the South. These wartime capabilities are likely to be limited to the initial stages (the first 30 days) of a renewed war.

The KPN's limited abilities and weaknesses portend that in a future war the advanced weaponry and combined operations capabilities of the U.S. Navy and Republic of Korea Navy, combined with air supremacy, would quickly neutralize the vast majority of the KPN's surface combatants, but not before it had conducted a number of amphibious landings, laid numerous sea mines, and began the interdiction of coastal shipping. KPN midget and coastal submarine operations would undoubtedly prove more problematic for the U.S. and ROK navies and would likely survive longer than the surface fleet.

Korean People's Air Force[30]

With a personnel strength of approximately 110,000 (27,000 officers and 83,000 enlisted) and 1,600–1,700 aircraft, the KPAF surpasses the Republic of Korea Air Force (ROKAF) and U.S. air components deployed in the ROK in terms of personnel and number of aircraft in inventory. This ascendancy, however, is purely numerical since the KPAF is qualitatively inferior in all aspects of combat capability and measures of effectiveness.

The primary mission of the KPAF is the air defense of the DPRK mainland and territorial waters. Secondary missions include reconnaissance, transportation and logistic support, insertion of special operations forces, strategic bombing, and provision of tactical air support to elements of the KPA and KPN.

KPAF Supreme Headquarters and Air Defense Command Headquarters, as well as the Western Air Defense Direction Headquarters, are located in Pyongyang adjacent to the Miram Air Base. The Eastern Air Defense Direction Headquarters is at Songdong-ni Air Base.

The KPAF is organized into a command element, air staff, air defense headquarters, six air divisions, several independent air battalions, two air force sniper brigades, a reconnaissance unit, unmanned aerial vehicle unit, hot-air balloon units, sailplane units, approximately 19 surface-to-air missile (SAM) brigades [organized into three air defense sectors], a SAM maintenance depot, an unknown number of antiaircraft artillery (AAA) regiments, unknown number of radar regiments, one to four searchlight battalions, a communications regiment, an air traffic control regiment, and several aircraft production and repair facilities. The national air carrier, Air Koryo, is directly subordinate to the KPAF.

Aviation assets are primarily of Russian and Chinese origin, including approximately 200 Y-5 (An-2) biplanes and about 300 helicopters. A significant, but unknown, percentage of the KPAF's older aircraft inventory is non-flyable and has been relegated to use as decoys, training aids for special operations forces, cannibalized for spare parts, or simply left

---

[30] *Defense White Paper, 2008*, 35–36; "Secret Report on Shwe Mann's Visit Says Burma To Copy DPRK, PRC Military Models," Dr Lun Swe (blog), July 2, 2009, Open Source Center, SEP20090709043001001, hereafter "Secret Report"; Bermudez, *Shield of the Great Leader*, 123–60; Bermudez, *Armed Forces of North Korea*, 2d ed. (draft manuscript); Bermudez, *Jane's Sentinel Country Risk Assessments*, 480–7; and *Foundations Update*, 16–21.

abandoned on KPAF airfields. The combat readiness rate of the operational aircraft is estimated to be 65 to 75 percent for MiG-29, MiG-23, MiG-21, and Su-25 types; 70 to 80 percent for F-5, F-6, and H-5; 75 to 85 percent for Y-5; and 65 to 76 percent for helicopters. During his May 2010 visit to China, Kim Jong-il is reported to have requested that China provide the KPAF with the J-10 (F-10) next-generation fighter.[31] It appears, however, that the Chinese have declined to supply the aircraft at this time.

The DPRK's air defense network is arguably one of the densest in the world. It is, however, based on obsolete weapons, missiles, and radars; and is most effective at lower altitudes where masses of AAA fire can be brought to bear on an intruder. Its high altitude SA-2/3/5 surface-to-air missiles are, however, ineffective in a modern electronic-warfare (EW) environment. The DPRK has made modest progress since the mid-1990s in introducing modernized radars and EW equipment to service. Among the items that have been brought into use are global positioning satellite and airborne warning and control system radar jammers.[32]

The KPAF's sniper brigades are primarily tasked with the neutralization of ROK/U.S. air bases and C4ISR assets. Due to the importance assigned to this wartime mission they receive priority tasking for the use of An-2 transports and helicopters.

There are approximately 106 known airfields and heliports of various types and levels of usability within North Korea. Of these, 12 are abandoned, not usable, or their status is unknown but believed unusable. The remaining 94 can be broken down as follows: 21 air bases (includes Sunan International Airport); 28 airfields; 17 highway strips; two helicopter bases; four VIP heliports, and more than 21 miscellaneous heliports/helipads. All primary air bases are hardened to some extent, with many featuring underground maintenance facilities, aircraft shelters, and dispersal areas. Even secondary airfields have elements of hardening, often having roads leading from the runway to fortified dispersal tunnels bored into hillsides; in some cases, these may be one to two kilometers distant from the airfield itself. The KPAF possesses at least two "underground" air bases, Onch'on-up on the west coast and Kangja-ri on the east. These are distinguished from

---

[31] "Kim Jong-il Demands Fighter Jets from China," *Chosun Ilbo*, June 17, 2010, http://english.chosun.com/site/data/html_dir/2010/06/17/2010061700535.html.
[32] *Defense White Paper, 2008*, 36; and "Secret Report."

other hardened air bases in having runways and hardstands that extend out from underneath mountains, thus allowing aircraft the possibility of taking-off from under the mountain and landing directly into it.

With an inflexible and unsophisticated command and control system, large numbers of obsolete aircraft, limited access to spare parts for its few modern aircraft, and continual fuel shortages, significant deficiencies in pilot training (some sources report that KPAF pilots average only 15 to 25 flying hours per year), the KPAF is judged to possess only limited offensive and defensive wartime capabilities and to be capable of conducting a surge of offensive operations only during the initial phase of any hostilities. It is also considered to have only a limited capability of guarding DPRK airspace during peacetime.

Information Warfare[33]

One of the increasingly important and expanding components of the Korean People's Army offensive strategy is electronic warfare. This is understood by the KPA—which believes it will play a major role in all future conflicts—to consist of operations using the electromagnetic spectrum to attack the enemy. During the 1990s the KPA identified "electronic intelligence warfare" (EIW, *chonja chinungjon*) as a new type of warfare, the essence of which is the disruption or destruction of the opponent's computer networks thus paralyzing the enemy's military command and control system.[34] Although this appears to be analogous to information warfare (IW), the Ministry of People's Armed Forces' understanding may also include elements of reconnaissance, cryptanalysis, intelligence collection, and disinformation operations, as well as the use of the Internet to cause disruption within the enemy's social and economic homeland. During a future conflict the KPA will likely employ IW capabilities to both protect the DPRK's C4ISR structure and to attack those of the ROK, United States, and Japan.

---

[33] Joseph S. Bermudez Jr., "SIGINT, EW and EIW in the Korean People's Army: An Overview of Development and Organization" in *Bytes and Bullets: Information Technology Revolution and National Security on the Korean Peninsula*, ed. Alexandre Y. Mansourov (Honolulu: Asia Pacific Center for Security Studies, 2005), 234–75, http://www.apcss.org/Publications/Edited%20Volumes/BytesAndBullets/TOC.pdf; and Bermudez, *Jane's Sentinel Country Risk Assessments*, 464–65, 473–74.

[34] "Future electronic warfare Discussed," *Nodong Sinmun*, December 5, 1999, 6, Open Source Center.

Kim Jong-il stated in 2000 that the DPRK should "not prepare for electronic warfare just because that is what others are doing. In modern warfare, modern and conventional weapons must be massed and combined."[35] Also in 2000, Kim Jong-il proclaimed that information technology (IT) was a national priority. Defectors state that Kim's oldest son, Kim Jong-nam, was placed in charge of developing the IT sector. This has led to the computerization of the KPA. By 2005 most battalions were equipped with a small number of computers. At this stage, these are only typically used for exchanging documents between headquarters and disseminating KWP publications and orders.

During 2003, in an effort to both support the fledgling information technology sector and boost the KPA's EIW capabilities, the DPRK initiated a five-year campaign to expand and enhance the nation's computer technology. The importance of this was re-emphasized by the KWP in 2006.

The Internet is perceived by the DPRK leadership as both a propaganda and information warfare tool of considerable importance. This is attested to by a January 2007 complaint that the ROK government's blocking of access to more than thirty websites considered pro-North was "a fascist action against democracy and human rights" that "infringes upon the South Koreans' freedom of speech."

In November 2007 the ROK and DPRK announced a joint project to develop a Korean version of the Linux operating system to be known as Hana Linux.[36]

Throughout the decade from 2000 to 2010, the DPRK has continued to expand its IW capabilities and is believed to have engaged in numerous electronic attacks against ROK, U.S., and Japanese defense and government computer networks and systems. The vast majority of these attacks have originated from within China or Japan using compromised computer systems. DPRK IW troops are frequently asserted as being very capable. In December 2008 the ROK Ministry of Defense stated that the KPA was continuing to strengthen its IW capabilities.

---

[35] Yong-hun Yi, "KPA Must Change in 21st Century," *Pukhan*, January 2000, 86–93, Open Source Center, FTS20000126000399.

[36] Tim Alper, "Can Linux Finally Unite Korea?," *Guardian*, January 17, 2008, http://www.guardian.co.uk/technology/2008/jan/17/linux.korea; and "North and South Korea unite over Linux," *ZDnet*, November 30, 2007, http://news.zdnet.co.uk/software/0,1000000121,39291201,00.htm.

Preliminary information suggests that EW and signals intelligence (SIGINT) operations are conducted at all levels of the KPA and intelligence community. EIW operations are conducted at the national level by the General Staff Department, Reconnaissance General Bureau, and Ministry of State Security, among others. Within the KPA, EIW elements are located at General Staff Department, corps, division, brigade, and regiment levels. Directly subordinate to the General Staff Department are the Electronic Warfare Bureau—which holds the primary mission for EIW—the 121st Surveillance Bureau (a.k.a., Unit 121), 204th Enemy Attack Bureau (Enemy Attack Bureau No. 204) and No. 110 Research Center, although the subordination of the last two units is unclear. Additionally, there are EIW elements within the navy and air force. The KPA believes that EW and EIW are complimentary and must be integrated with conventional forces and operations to be effective on the modern battlefield.[37]

The 121st Surveillance Bureau, which reportedly consists of 300 personnel, is subordinate to the General Staff Department's Reconnaissance General Bureau. Until 1997 is was primarily concerned with military communications intelligence (COMINT), including cryptographic technology and the decryption of ROK, U.S., and Japanese military cryptographic systems. Since then it has expanded its responsibilities to include operating system technology and network traffic analysis. The unit reportedly conducts hacking activities and offensive military IW operations.[38]

The 204th Enemy Attack Bureau, reportedly established in 2002 and consisting of 100 personnel, is also believed to be subordinate to the Reconnaissance General Bureau. It is responsible for conducting cyber-psychological warfare operations against the ROK armed forces personnel and disseminating false information to the South's general public.[39]

The No. 110 Research Center is subordinate to the Reconnaissance General Bureau. It reportedly has 500 to 600 personnel, maintains overseas detachments, and conducts a wide range of offensive IW operations, although these are believed to concentrate upon military and intelligence targets.[40]

---

[37] Interview data acquired by Joseph S. Bermudez Jr.; Ko So'ng-p'yo, "There is a 'CIA-Class' Hacker Group in North Korea's Ministry of People's Armed Forces," *JoongAng Ilbo*, April 20, 2009, http://joongangdaily.joins.com; and "North Korea Poised for Cyber Salvo," *Defensetech*, April 20, 2009, http://defensetech.org/2009/04/20/north-korea-poised-for-cyber-salvo/.
[38] Ibid.
[39] Ibid.
[40] Ibid.

Within the KWP are at least two IW organizations, the Basic Materials Investigation Office and Operations Office.[41] The first is subordinate to KWP Office 35 (a.k.a. Room 35), the intelligence unit in charge of collecting political, economic, and social information on the ROK, Japan, China, Southeast Asia, and Europe. The basic materials office reportedly consists of 50 personnel and is responsible for hacking activities and offensive IW operations against political and economic targets and social organizations. The Operations Office is subordinate to the KWP's United Front Department, and reportedly consists of 50 personnel who conduct cyber-psychological warfare against the ROK public. It disseminates false information and antiwar messages to manipulate public opinion by positively influencing citizens toward the DPRK and create a sense of mistrust and dissatisfaction with the ROK government.

In addition to the above organizations, the Ministry of State Security reportedly maintains a sizeable IW organization.

Ballistic Missiles[42]

"...the heroic people's army that is equipped with the spirit of human bombs and outer space striking means and can defeat any formidable enemy in the world..."

—KCNA December 4, 1998[43]

---

[41] Ibid.

[42] Joseph S. Bermudez Jr., "Scud SRBM," *KPA Journal*, Vol. 1, No. 3, March 2010, 5–9, http://nkleadershipwatch.files.wordpress.com/2010/03/kpa-journal-vol-1-no-3.pdf; and Bermudez, "KN-02," *KPA Journal*, Vol. 1, No. 2, February 2010, 7–12, http://nkleadershipwatch.files.wordpress.com/2010/02/kpa-journal-vol-1-no-2.pdf; "Secret Report"; Steven A. Hildreth, *North Korean Ballistic Missile Threat to the United States* (Washington, DC: Congressional Research Service, January 2009); Bermudez, *Jane's Sentinel Country Risk Assessments*, 517–27; *Defense White Paper, 2008*, 38–39; Bermudez, *Shield of the Great Leader*, 236–91; Bermudez, *Armed Forces of North Korea*, 2d ed. (draft manuscript); Joseph S. Bermudez Jr., *A History of Ballistic Missile Development in the DPRK*, Center for Nonproliferation Studies, Monterrey Institute for International Studies, Occasional Paper No. 2, 1999, http://cns.miis.edu/opapers/op2/op2.pdf, hereafter *History of Ballistic Missile Development*; Daniel A. Pinkston, *The North Korean Ballistic Missile Program* (Carlisle Barracks: U.S. Army Strategic Studies Institute, 2008), http://www.strategicstudiesinstitute.army.mil/pdffiles/pub842.pdf; and *Foundations Update*, 21.

[43] "Nodong Sinmun Essay Urges 'Mercilessly' Fighting US," KCNA, December 4, 1998, Open Source Center, FBIS-EAS-98-338.

North Korea has pursued a robust and expanding ballistic missile development program since the late 1970s that has been assigned a national priority at least equal to the nation's nuclear program. Due to this emphasis, the missile program has steadily progressed in spite of national economic failure and cyclical famines since the late 1980s. All current indications suggest that the missile development program is likely to continue as long as the regime survives.

The DPRK possesses the largest ballistic missile force in the developing world and is on the threshold of deploying space launch vehicles (SLVs) and intercontinental ballistic missiles (ICBMs) that could eventually threaten the continental United States.[44] This is an ominous development since there is little doubt that the DPRK perceives the ballistic missile to be the delivery system of choice for nuclear weapons. Considerably more disconcerting are the reports that during the 1990s the A. Q. Khan nuclear-proliferation network provided the DPRK with the design for an implosion-type nuclear warhead that could be carried by a ballistic missile.

Operational ballistic missiles within the KPA are under the administrative and operational control of the Ballistic Missile Training and Guidance Bureau, but wartime control of the missile units would likely be ceded to the General Staff Department, or more likely, directly to the National Defense Commission. The KPA's ballistic missile units are deployed in two belts—forward and strategic rear. The forward belt is located 50–100 kilometers from the DMZ, while the strategic rear belt is located 130–230 kilometers from the zone.

Among the ballistic missiles and space launch vehicles that are in KPA inventory or under active development are:

- Short Range Ballistic Missiles (KN-02, Scud B, Scud C, Scud D/Scud ER)

- Medium Range Ballistic Missiles (Nodong, Taepodong-1)

- Intermediate Range Ballistic Missiles (Taepodong-1, Musudan [BM-25])

---

[44] Short-Range Ballistic Missile (SRBM): Range < 1,000 km; Medium-Range Ballistic Missile (MRBM): Range 1,000–3,000 km; Intermediate-Range Ballistic Missile (IRBM): Range 3,000–5,500 km; Intercontinental Ballistic Missile (ICBM): Range > 5,500 km; and Space Launch Vehicle (SLV): Any rocket designed to place a payload into space.

- Intercontinental Ballistic Missiles (Taepodong-2)

- Space Launch Vehicle (Paektusan-1 [Taepodong-1 SLV], U'nha 1 [Taepodong-2 SLV])

It is estimated that since the start of ballistic missile production within the DPRK a total of 1,150–1,350 systems have been produced. Of these 325–400 have been sold to other nations, and another 20 to 30 have been used for initial operations, test, and evaluation, thus leaving a current inventory of 800 to 900 missiles (some estimates go as high as 1,000). Of these, U.S. sources estimate that approximately 600+ are Scud B/C/D/ER, 200 Nodong, and fewer than 50 other medium, intermediate, and intercontinental missiles. ROK government sources present a somewhat different inventory of 400 Scud and 450 Nodong missiles, with the capability to build approximately 15 Taepodong systems.

Among analysts there is a growing discussion as to the viability of a DPRK ballistic missile inventory of 800–900 systems. This discussion centers on the DPRK's production capabilities, quality control, maintenance competence, and C4ISR capabilities, all of which are below the standards of all the states in East Asia. The net result is that while the DPRK may physically possess this inventory, there is a high probability that only 85 to 95 percent are actually serviceable. Of these only 85 to 90 percent could be effectively employed due to C4ISR limitations and a generally low level of realistic training among KPA missile troops. Nevertheless, the operational realities within the region are such that even an inventory of 575 to 750 ballistic missiles presents a significant strategic threat. Even at the lower inventory level, the KPA is capable of sustaining a rate-of-fire of 50 to 75 ballistic missiles an hour for the first few hours of a renewed conflict and 10 to 20 per day thereafter until the inventory is depleted. Notably, it is a threat for which no state in the region currently possesses an effective defense.

The DPRK is reported to possess a variety of warheads for its various ballistic missile systems. These include unitary high-explosive, high-explosive fragmentation, cluster/bomblet, and chemical, biological, radiological dispersion, and nuclear. It is probable that at least some research has been conducted into the development of fuel-air explosive, electromagnetic pulse, and penetrating warheads.

While a rudimentary chemical and biological warhead for ballistic missiles is relatively simple to design and construct, that of an effective and reliable one faces a number of technological challenges, such as high re-entry velocity, severely high temperatures, and effectiveness of dispersal mechanisms. These requirements are just within the scientific and military capabilities of the DPRK, although it is likely that they received some foreign assistance during their initial efforts.

The requirements for the design and development of a reliable nuclear warhead are an order-of-magnitude more demanding than those for chemical and biological warheads. They are at the outer limit of the scientific and military capabilities of the DPRK, and it is probable this development program has also received some foreign assistance.[45]

The question of whether the DPRK possesses a workable nuclear warhead design for ballistic missiles is a contentious one. In early 2007 senior DPRK diplomat Kim Kye-kwan strongly suggested to David Albright, the president of the Institute for Science and International Security, that his nation did in fact possess such a capability.[46] However, Japanese, ROK, and U.S. sources generally believe that it has not yet achieved this. For example, in October 2009 the ROK Ministry of National Defense stated that the DPRK might not have achieved the technological advancements required to develop nuclear warheads for use on ballistic missiles. Two months later, the Korea Institute of Defense Analyses, in its annual report, supported this opinion. Three months later, in January 2010, the U.S. Department of Defense stated that, "we must assume that sooner or later [the DPRK] will have a successful test of its TD-2 and, if there are no major changes in its national security strategy in the next decade, it will be able to mate a nuclear warhead to a proven delivery system."[47]

These assessments stand in contrast to information released in December 2009 citing a previously unpublicized account by A. Q. Khan. In this account, Khan states that during a visit to the DPRK in 1999, he was shown boxes containing components of three completed ballistic missile nuclear warheads. He was informed that these could be assembled for use within an hour. He further stated that "While they explained the construction [design of their

---

[45] "Report Casts Doubt on N. Korea's Ability to Deploy Nukes," *Chosun Ilbo*, July 30, 2020, http://english.chosun.com/site/data/html_dir/2010/07/30/2010073000795.html.

[46] David Albright, *North Korea's Alleged Large-Scale Enrichment Plant: Yet Another Questionable Extrapolation Based on Aluminum Tubes* (Washington, DC: Institute for Science and International Security, February 23, 2007), http://www.isis-online.org/publications/dprk/DPRKenrichment 22Feb.pdf.

[47] *Ballistic Missiles Defense Review Report* (Washington, DC: Department of Defense, February 2010), 4.

bombs], they quietly showed me the six boxes" containing split cores for the warheads, as well as "sixty-four igniters/detonators per bomb packed in six separate boxes."[48]

For the foreseeable future it is unlikely that the DPRK nuclear weapons program could develop a workable nuclear warhead design in the 100–400 kg range without foreign assistance. It is likely that current generation nuclear warhead designs—of unknown reliability—are in the 650–750 kg weight range.

Since the late 1980s North Korea has sold abroad approximately 325 to 400 Scud B/C/D/ER, Nodong, and Scud-ER ballistic missiles, as well as components or the technology to produce these systems (and possibly the Taepodong family of ballistic missiles). States to which the DPRK has sold or attempted to sell ballistic missiles, components or technology include Egypt, Iran, Iraq, Libya, Myanmar (Burma), Pakistan, Nigeria, Syria, UAE, Vietnam, and Yemen.

As U.S. and international counter-proliferation efforts (for example, the Proliferation Security Initiative) have come into force, the nature of the DPRK's ballistic missile efforts have changed from the provision of complete systems to specific sub-systems and technology transfers. This in turn has led the North and its proliferation partners (for example, Syria and Iran) to make more extensive use of air routes rather than sea transportation as a means to transfer ballistic missile components and technologies. As of 2008, the United States, in cooperation with its allies and other interested states, were working to limit the DPRK's use of these air routes.

As a means to develop ballistic missile technology and to earn international prestige the DPRK has pursued the development and testing of space launch vehicles including three attempted satellite launches—August 31, 1998; July 5–6, 2006; and April 5, 2009. All three failed.[49]

---

[48] Arun Kumar, "Pakistan Helped North Korea Build Nuke?," *Washington Post*, December 29, 2009; and David Albright and Corey Hinderstein, "The A. Q. Khan Illicit Nuclear Trade Network and Implications for Nonproliferation Efforts," *Strategic Insights*, Volume V, Issue 6, July 2006, http://www.nps.edu/Academics/centers/ccc/publications/OnlineJournal/2006/Jul/albrightJul06.html.

[49] Joseph S. Bermudez Jr. in: "Launch Failure Frustrates North Korea's Missile Aspirations," *Jane's Defence Weekly*, April 7, 2009, jdw.janes.com; "Fully Assembled Unha SLV Sits on North Korean Launch Pad," *Jane's Defence Weekly*, March 30, 2009, jdw.janes.com; "North Korea Set to Launch Taepo Dong 2," *Jane's Defence Weekly*, July 5, 2006, jdw.janes.com; "Musudan-ni Launch Facility Keeps its Secrets," *Jane's Defence Weekly*, July 5, 2006, jdw.janes.com; Taepo-dong Launch Brings DPRK Missiles Back Into the Spotlight," *Jane's Intelligence Review*, Volume 10, Number 10, October 1998, 30–32; and "North Koreans Test Two-stage IRBM Over Japan," *Jane's Defence Weekly*, Volume 30, Number 10, 9 September, 1998, 28.

For the foreseeable future the DPRK will continue the development and production of a range of new and existing ballistic missile systems, and will continue its attempts to place a satellite into low-earth orbit. These later efforts will provide a significant contribution to its IRBM and ICBM development and production efforts.

Nuclear Weapons[50]

The world does not deserve to exist without the DPRK... [and should the DPRK implode] ... we will take the rest of the world with us.

—Kim Jong-il[51]

The more desperately the U.S. imperialists brandish their nukes and the more zealously their lackeys follow them, the more rapidly the [DPRK's] nuclear deterrence will be bolstered up along the orbit of self-defense and the more remote the prospect for the denuclearization of the Korean peninsula will be become.

—National Defense Commission statement, July 2010[52]

Over the past 40 years the DPRK has pursued an expanding nuclear program to the point where it now possesses all the requisite technologies, personnel, and infrastructure to produce nuclear weapons that are, at a minimum, comparable to first-generation U.S. nuclear weapons. It is capable of employing such weapons throughout the Korean Peninsula and to a lesser degree against Japan. To date, North Korea has conducted two tests of what appear to be first generation Pu-239 implosion weapons. The country has publicly stated that it has the right to conduct future tests when and where it wants. During late summer 2009, unconfirmed reports suggested that the DPRK was preparing for a third nuclear test. As of July 2011, no such test has occurred.

---

[50] Larry A. Niksch, *North Korea's Nuclear Weapons Developments and Diplomacy* (Washington, DC: Congressional Research Service, January 2010); Mary Beth Nikitin, *North Korea's Nuclear Weapons* (Washington, DC: Congressional Research Service, May 2009); Joseph S. Bermudez Jr., "North Korea's Nuclear Site" in "Nuclear Fallout—North Korea Returns to Proliferation Programme," *Jane's Intelligence Review*, June 19, 2009, jir.janes.com; *Defense White Paper, 2008*, 37–38; Bermudez, *Shield of the Great Leader*, 212–22; Bermudez, *Armed Forces of North Korea*, 2d ed. (draft manuscript); Bermudez, *Jane's Sentinel Country Risk Assessments*, 528–32; and *Foundations Update*, 11.

[51] "Hwang Jang-yop Speaks: Preparations for War in North Korea," http://www.nis.go.kr:7000/democratic/index.html, accessed July 11, 2000.

[52] "Quotations Of The Day," Associated Press, July 24, 2010.

Plutonium

Estimates of the DPRK nuclear weapons inventory are based upon the level of weapons design technology and quantity of Pu-239 it possesses. At present the best estimates available are that between 1989–2008 the DPRK discharged spent fuel rods with a content of 46 to 64 kg of Pu-239 from all its reactors combined. Of this total approximately 28 to 50 kg of Pu-239 was separated and available for weapons production as of early 2008. If this is reduced by the estimated 5 to 10 kg used in the October 2006 and May 2009 nuclear weapons tests, the total inventory of Pu-239 is 18 to 40 kg. Assuming that the state of nuclear weapons design technology achieved by the DPRK allows them to produce a weapon with approximately 5 kg of Pu-239, the total amount available would provide for four to eight weapons.[53]

These figures compare favorably with the February 2008 statement by Michael McConnell, the director of U.S. National Intelligence, that "if Pyongyang has sophisticated technologies, it can make 12 nuclear bombs with the 50 kilograms of plutonium thought to have been extracted. And if not, the number can be lowered to six, which is more likely to be true."[54]

During April 2009 the DPRK expelled American and International Atomic Energy Agency (IAEA) inspectors from Yongbyon and resumed reprocessing activities at the Radio-Chemistry Laboratory. Given that it would take three to six months to process the remaining fuel rods, and assuming that no major obstacles were encountered, the reprocessing should have been completed by the end of September 2009. On June 13, 2009 the DPRK declared that "More than one third of the spent fuel rods has been reprocessed to date."[55] Then on September 4, 2009 it announced that "We are also finalizing the reprocessing of the spent fuel rods and the plutonium

---

[53] "Report Casts Doubt" *Chosun Ilbo*; David Albright, Paul Brannan, and Jacqueline Shire, *North Korea's Plutonium Declaration: A Starting Point for an Initial Verification Process* (Washington, DC:ISIS, January 10, 2008), http://isis-online.org/uploads/isis-reports/documents/NorthKoreaDeclaration10Jan2008.pdf; Niksch, *North Korea's Nuclear Weapons*; Nikitin, *North Korea's Nuclear Weapons*; and "Purported Ex-General Says DPRK Posses 'Tens of Nuclear Weapons,'" AFP, May 14, 2003.

[54] "ROK Daily US DIA Director: DPRK Continuing To Develop Long-Range Ballistic Missile," *Dong-A Ilbo*, February 28, 2008, Open Source Center.

[55] Sam Kim, "N. Korea to Push Ahead With Uranium Enrichment Over U.N. Sanctions," *Yonhap*, June 12, 2009, http://english.yonhapnews.co.kr.

extracted are being weaponized."⁵⁶ Precisely how much this will add to Pu-239 inventory is currently uncertain.

These and other estimates of the DPRK's possible nuclear weapons inventory are currently based solely upon the amount of Pu-239 extracted from its reactors at Yongbyon. Should, however, the DPRK have obtained highly-enriched uranium (HEU) from foreign sources or a covert indigenous uranium enrichment program, the stockpile of nuclear weapons could be larger.

Uranium⁵⁷

While the current estimates of the DPRK's nuclear inventory are based on Pu-239 weapons, revelations during 2002–4 that the DPRK had been pursuing a HEU program with the assistance of Pakistan's A. Q. Khan Laboratories raised numerous additional concerns. Political developments during 2004–10 have only contributed to the uncertainty surrounding the program.

During October 2002, in a meeting with U.S. Assistant Secretary of State James Kelly, DPRK First Vice Foreign Minister Kang Sok-ju admitted that his country was pursuing a HEU program. The clear implication of the admission was that this program was to produce fissile material for nuclear weapons. That the DPRK had, until this time, denied all suggestions concerning a HEU program came as no surprise. It denied its Pu-239 program during the late 1980s and early 1990s until it was presented with incontrovertible proof by the IAEA, and it was only after Kelly presented equally undeniable proof of a covert HEU effort that minister Kang made his admission. The revelations center on the transfer of technology, equipment, and the exchange of personnel, primarily between the DPRK and Pakistan, although Russia and China are reported to have played a secondary role.

It is unclear when the current highly-enriched uranium program was initiated, however, most analysts date it to the early 1990s and an expansion of DPRK-Pakistan relations, which date to the early 1970s. The nuclear

---

[56] "DPRK Permanent Representative Sends Letter to President of UNSC," KCNA, September 4, 2009, http://www.kcna.co.jp/index-e.htm.

[57] Kumar, "Pakistan Helped North Korea;" Pervez Musharraf, *In the Line of Fire: A Memoir* (New York: Free Press, 2008); and Albright and Hinderstein, "The A.Q. Khan Illicit Nuclear Trade Network."

relationship only began in late 1993 or early 1994, following Benazir Bhutto's re-election as Pakistan's prime minister.

In December 1993 Bhutto initiated negotiations for the purchase of a small number of the DPRK-produced Nodong ballistic missiles as well as production technology. Within Pakistan the Nodong program, known locally as the Ghauri, was centered at the Khan (Kahuta) Research Laboratories.[58] At this point A. Q. Khan, the director of the laboratories, undertook a number of business transactions within the DPRK to provide it with HEU technologies, centrifuges, drawings, and technical advice. According to Khan, one Pakistani P-1 centrifuge was provided to the DPRK during the 1990s and approximately 12 in 2000. Subsequent reports in the Pakistani press speculated that the DPRK could have been enriching uranium on a small scale by 2002. In a 2003 letter allegedly written by A. Q. Khan to his wife and daughter he stated "(A retired general) brought three million dollars from North Korea and asked me to provide a design plan and machines." Khan's assistance to the North's highly-enriched uranium program lasted for at least six years. He is reported to have stated that in return for Pakistan's aid it received both the technology to produce krytrons (high-speed switches used in nuclear trigger mechanisms) and assistance in mating a nuclear warhead to the Ghauri ballistic missile. President Pervez Musharraf of Pakistan wrote in a 2006 memoir that he became aware of Pakistani involvement in 1999 when he received reports that DPRK nuclear experts, under the guise of ballistic missile engineers, were being given secret nuclear briefings. The extent of official Pakistani government involvement in these exchanges is unclear.[59]

The nuclear relationship is reported to have continued until late 2001 or early 2002 when it is believed to have been terminated (although some sources suggest it continued longer). The DPRK is currently judged to be in the early stages of developing a gas-centrifuge HEU capability.

In February 2005 the ROK National Intelligence Service judgment was that the North had "not yet built or possessed HEU nuclear bombs as it has

---

[58] Joseph S. Bermudez Jr., "Pakistan Achieves Ghauri Launch Success," *Jane's Defence Weekly*, February 13, 2008, jdw.janes.com; and Bermudez, *History of Ballistic Missile Development*.

[59] "N. Korea 'Had Enriched Uranium in 2002,'" *Chosun Ilbo*, http://english.chosun.com/site/data/html_dir/2009/12/29/2009122900357.html; and Myung-hwan Yu, "N. Korea 'Started Enriching Uranium in Late '90s,'" *Chosun Ilbo*, http://english.chosun.com/site/data/html_dir/2010/01/07/2010010700540.html.

not yet reached the stage of building the HEU factory."[60] The primary reason for this was that the flow of key equipment from Khan Laboratories in Pakistan had been halted. Given the previous lack of international controls upon the DPRK, some U.S. officials believe that a rudimentary research-scale HEU program—based on Pakistani technology—could have been operational by early 2005. Although estimates vary considerably, such a program could produce enough HEU for one additional nuclear weapon each year.

In February 2008, U.S. National Intelligence Director Michael McConnell stated that, "although North Korea denies it has HEU programs and its proliferation activities, we think it is involved with both."[61] Concerns over an HEU program continued to grow and on April 29, 2009 the DPRK Foreign Ministry declared, "the DPRK will make a decision to build a light-water reactor power plant and start the technological development for ensuring self-production of nuclear fuel [that is uranium enrichment] as its first process without delay."[62] Two months later, on June 13, 2009, the North declared, "Pursuant to the decision to build its own light-water reactor, enough success has been made in developing uranium enrichment technology to provide nuclear fuel to allow the experimental procedure."[63] Responding to this two days later, ROK Unification Minister Hyun In-taek stated, "As the U.S. raised the accusation in 2002, I believe [the HEU program] had started before that. I believe it has been there for at least seven to eight years." Most recently on September 4, 2009 the DPRK Foreign Ministry announced, "We've successfully done the experiment for enrichment of uranium and it has entered the final stage".

Any uranium enrichment facilities would most likely be located in P'yongan-bukto or P'yongan-namdo Provinces. The area bounded by Kusong-Subch'on-Pukchin would appear to be most suited based upon the power distribution and rail grids.

---

[60] "N. Korea Has Yet to Build HEU-Based Nuke Bombs," *Yonhap*, February 25, 2005, http://english.yonhapnews.co.kr.
[61] Ed Johnson, "North Korea Maintains Uranium Enrichment Program, U.S. Says," Bloomberg, February 5, 2008, http://www.bloomberg.com/.
[62] "North Korea Threatens Nuclear Test," Reuters, April 29, 2009.
[63] "DPRK FM Statement Announces 'Strong Counter-Measures' Against UNSC's 'Resolution 1874,'" KCNA, June 13, 2009, http://www.kcna.co.jp/index-e.htm.

Possible Early EMIS Program[64]

One of the questions concerning the production of highly-enriched uranium within the DPRK is whether it ever pursued an electromagnetic isotope separation (EMIS) effort. Calutrons—mass spectrometers used in the uranium isotope separation process—use a great amount of electricity, are expensive, and require constant maintenance. They are, however, relatively simple to produce and the technology was declassified decades ago. In reviewing a timeline of nuclear developments within the DPRK a conspicuous gap exists in the construction of nuclear-related facilities and the establishment of nuclear-related organizations during the 1970s and early 1980s. This same period coincides with a high point in DPRK economic and industrial capability to pursue an indigenous EMIS program. Both the political climate on the Korean Peninsula and the status of the ROK nuclear program at the time would suggest that it would be an opportune time for the DPRK to initiate such a program. A possible early EMIS program has not figured into any of the Six-Party Talks and the assessment of various intelligence agencies is that if it did exist, it did not contribute significantly to the DPRK's current inventory of fissile material.

Biological Weapons[65]

Despite public statements to the contrary, the DPRK possesses the indigenous capability to produce large quantities and varieties of biological weapons. It also possesses the ability to employ such weapons both on the Korean Peninsula and, to a lesser degree, worldwide using unconventional methods of delivery. It is believed by most sources that while the DPRK has an active biological warfare research effort, it has not weaponized biological agents.

In general, the potential offensive use of biological weapons by the KPA has not received the attention as that of chemical weapons. This is probably due to the DPRK's limitations in biotechnology and the realization that, once employed, there is almost no control over such weapons. Additionally, the KPA must calculate that biological warfare (BW) is potentially a greater

---

[64] Interview data acquired by Joseph S. Bermudez Jr.
[65] *Defense White Paper, 2008,* 39–40; Bermudez, *Shield of the Great Leader,* 222–31; Bermudez, *Armed Forces of North Korea,* 2d ed. (draft manuscript); Bermudez, *Jane's Sentinel Country Risk Assessments,* 523–33; and *Foundations Update,* 12

threat to the KPA than to the ROK or United States because of its limited medical and bio-medical capabilities and poor public health system. This last point was emphasized during the first half of 2007 by outbreaks of foot-and-mouth disease and measles, both of which required significant international assistance. For this reason, however, defensive biological warfare has received significant attention.

While the former Soviet Union and China have provided the DPRK with chemical agents, they are not believed to have provided any direct assistance in the development of biological weapons. Such capabilities are believed to have been developed indigenously. Biological warfare research is thought to have begun sometime during the early 1960s and to have focused primarily on ten to thirteen different strains of bacteria. At present, it is believed that the DPRK has not employed genetic engineering or advanced biotechnology to develop these bacteria.

Biological agents currently reported to be in the KPA inventory, although uncertain, include anthrax (Bacillus anthracis), botulism (Clostridium botulinum), cholera (Vibrio cholerae 01), hemorrhagic fever (probably the Korean strain), various strains of the influenza, plague (Yersinia pestis), smallpox (Variola), typhoid (Salmonella typhi), and yellow fever. In October 2009 the ROK Ministry of Defense cited the above agents and added dysentery.

Despite several reports of DPRK biological weapons proliferation activities with Iran, this remains unconfirmed. It is known that MPAF personnel, during the early 1990s, signed a military cooperation agreement with Cuba and visited a "genetic-bioengineering institute." Whether this is an indicator of biological weapons cooperation between the two nations, or not, is unclear.

Chemical Weapons[66]

The DPRK currently produces and possesses the capability to effectively employ throughout the Korean Peninsula significant quantities and varieties of chemical weapons. It also has, to a lesser extent, the ability to employ

---

[66] *Defense White Paper, 2008*, 39–40; Bermudez, *Shield of the Great Leader*, 231–35; Bermudez, *Armed Forces of North Korea*, 2d ed. (draft manuscript); Bermudez, *Jane's Sentinel Country Risk Assessments*, 534–35; and *Foundations Update*, 12.

these weapons worldwide using unconventional methods of delivery.

The KPA believes that chemical weapons will be a normal component of any renewed conflict on the Korean Peninsula. Release authority for their employment is believed to have been given to corps commanders should they lose contact with Pyongyang. Additionally, the ROK Ministry of Defense has identified six special corps munitions depots located at Sanumni (two sites—III Corps or Pyongyang Defense Command), Hwangch'on (III Corps), Samsan-dong (II Corps or the Artillery Corps), Sariwon (IV Corps), and Wangjaebong (V Corps). KPA defectors generally agree with this deployment, indicating that such depots exist only with the corps deployed along the DMZ (I, II, IV, and V) and not the rear area corps (III, VI, VIII, and XI).[67]

Chemical weapons research, development, and production is the responsibility of organizations subordinate to the KWP's Munitions Industry Department, specifically the Second Academy of Natural Sciences and the Second Economic Committee's Fifth Machine Industry Bureau. Both organizations receive the cooperation and assistance from the Academy of Sciences. The Fifth Machine Industry Bureau, with the assistance of the KPA's Nuclear Chemical Defense Bureau, control all facilities, or subfacilities, that manufacture chemical weapons. Additional assistance is believed to be provided by the Third Machine Industry (artillery shells), Fourth Machine Industry (missile warheads) and Seventh Machine Industry (air delivered weapons) Bureaus.[68]

The bureaus of the Second Economic Committee maintain regional offices throughout the country, which not only manage its own production facilities but also control certain production lines in various factories that are operated by the ministries and departments subordinate to the cabinet. In general, cabinet plants give higher priority to implementing the Second Economic Committee's production orders than other production orders.

The DPRK is almost certainly self-sufficient in the production of all necessary precursor chemicals for first generation chemical agents, including nerve agents. The best estimates available credit the North with an annual production potential of 4,500 tons of chemical agents in peacetime and

---

[67] *Defense White Paper, 1990* (Seoul: Ministry of National Defense, Republic of Korea, 1990), 74.
[68] Interview data acquired by Joseph S. Bermudez Jr.; "Status of North Korea's Science and Technology Development and Exchange, Part II," *Pukhan*, March 1996, 121–30, Open Source Center.

12,000 tons in wartime. Estimates of chemical weapons inventory have varied considerably over the past ten years. In 1989, the inventory was estimated to be "180 to 250 tons of chemical weapons of several kinds."[69] During October 2008 ROK Minister of Defense Kim Tae-young stated that the DPRK possessed 5,000 tonnes of chemical agents.[70] Current estimates suggest an inventory of 2,500–5,000 metric tons of agents, the majority of which is believed to be in the form of mustard, phosgene, sarin, and V-agents.[71] It is further believed that this inventory includes as many as 150 ballistic missile warheads. The KPA may also possess limited numbers of binary (GB, GF, or VX) chemical munitions.

It is difficult to differentiate between locations associated with just the production of feed stocks or precursors and those that actually produce chemical agents. This difficulty arises from several factors, most significantly, facilities that produce dual-use chemicals are sometimes described as being chemical agent factories. A possible example of this is the Hyesan Chemical Factory in Yanggang-do that is sometimes identified as producing chemical agents. Yet it is known to produce only intermediate products such as benzene, phenol, hydrochloric acid, and sulfuric acid. It is also important to note that the DPRK's larger chemical complexes are sizable facilities consisting of several smaller factories with different process units. Some of these complexes (for example, February 8th Vinalon Complex) apparently produce feed stocks, precursors and agents, but in different units within the complex. In reality, however, only a small portion of any one complex is involved in chemical agent production and these are probably purpose-built units.

When required, stored chemical agents are shipped in bulk form to either the Kanggye Chemical Weapons Factory in Kanggye, Chagang-do, or the Sakchu Chemical Weapons Factory in Sakchu, P'yongan-bukto. Here the chemical agents are brought together with the munitions or warheads to be filled.

Chemical agents currently reported to be in the KPA inventory include, but are not necessarily limited to adamsite (DM), chloroacetophenone

---

[69] "Daily Says North Stockpiling Biochemical Weapons," *Yonhap*, June 23, 1990, http://english.yonhapnews.co.kr; and "Daily Says North Stockpiling Biochemical Weapons" and "N. Korea is Mass Producing Chemical Weapons: U.S. Report," *FPI International*, 8 June 1986, 4.

[70] Byun Duk-kun: "N. Korea Unlikely to Possess Nuclear Weapons: Military Chief," *Yonhap*, October 8, 2008, http://www.yonhapnews.net/.

[71] *Defense White Paper, 2008*, 39–40.

(CN), chlorobenzylidene malononitrile (CS), chlorine (CL), cyanogen chloride (CK), hydrogen cyanide (AC), mustard-family (H, HD or HL), phosgene (CG and CX), sarin (GB), soman (GD), tabun (GA), and V-agents (VM and VX). It is important to note that according to KPA defectors the DPRK produces a total of twenty different chemical agents for use in weapons. For a variety of reasons, not the least of which is the DPRK's capability to produce or acquire certain precursors, it is believed that the KPA has concentrated upon mustard, chlorine, phosgene, sarin, and the V-agents. While not as toxic as cyanide, mustard, or nerve agents—and thus need to be employed in significantly larger quantities—chlorine and phosgene are industrial chemicals that are easily manufactured. As an example of production challenges the DPRK faces the production of soman requires the use of pinacolyl alcohol, which is currently produced by only a few companies in the world and in extremely small amounts, has no commercial uses, and is on the Australia Group's list of restricted products.[72]

To date, there have been no public indications that the DPRK produces binary chemical agents. However, given the benefits of such weapons (such as safety and a longer shelf-life), it is likely that some binary chemical agents are in production. Additionally, the KPA has conducted extensive studies of the Iran-Iraq War and Operation Desert Storm. Those studies have probably led them to follow the Iraqi model with regard to binary chemical weapons. For example, the Iraqis made the decision to produce binary sarin, however because the DF precursor produced by Iraq was very impure—which would result in an extremely short shelf life of sarin—they filled their munitions with isopropyl and cyclohexyl alcohols and stored the DF separately. Immediately prior to using the munitions the DF was added by hand.

Throughout the past 20 years there have been repeated reports that the DPRK has provided chemical weapons, agents, or technology to Egypt, Iran, Libya, and Syria. Most of these reports center on the sales of or assistance in developing chemical warheads for Scud-class ballistic missiles. Reports originating in the Middle East indicate that there was an acceleration of chemical weapons–related activity between Syria and North Korea during early 2007. These reports identify the city of Aleppo as the centre of this activity. It was near Aleppo that a chemical related accident

---

[72] The Australia Group is an informal association of 41 countries, which attempts to "ensure that exports do not contribute to the development of chemical or biological weapons," http://www.australiagroup.net/en/index.html.

allegedly occurred in July 2007 in which both Syrian and DPRK personnel were killed when a missile with a chemical warhead exploded prematurely. These reports, while numerous, remain to be confirmed.

Chapter 6

Irregular Warfare on the Korean Peninsula
by Colonel David S. Maxwell, U.S. Army

There are only two ways to approach planning for the collapse of North Korea: to be ill-prepared or to be really ill-prepared.

— Kurt Campbell, DASD, May 1, 1998[1]

What is going to happen on the Korean Peninsula? This is the question that plagues policy makers, strategists, and military planners in the Republic of Korea (ROK), the United States, and in Northeast Asia (NEA). If this question can be answered, the next question is: How will the ROK, United States, and the international community deal with what happens on the peninsula?

While optimistic planners and policy makers hope for a so-called "soft landing" with a peaceful reunification of the peninsula, prudence calls for planning for the worst-case scenarios. This contradicts the current focus of the United States on having to "win the wars it is currently fighting" as stated in the *2010 Quadrennial Defense Review*. The worst cases are, however, in the author's opinion at once both the most dangerous and the most likely threats in Northeast Asia and they should be considered. Therefore soft landing and peaceful reunification scenarios will not be addressed. While intentionally provocative, the ideas presented focus only on one of the many complexities of the Korean Peninsula and Northeast Asia: irregular warfare (IW).

Eliot Cohen and John Gooch in their seminal work on military failures determined that militaries are generally unsuccessful for three reasons: the failure to learn, adapt, and anticipate.[2] With those in mind, the ROK-U.S.

---

[1] Kurt Campbell, Deputy Assistant Secretary of Defense for International Security Affairs—Asia Pacific (DASD-ISA-APAC), remarks to USFK planners during a briefing at the Pentagon, 1 May 1998.
[2] Eliot A. Cohen and John Gooch, *Military Misfortunes: The Anatomy of Failure in War* (New York: Free Press, 1990).

alliance should learn from operations in Afghanistan and Iraq, adapt irregular warfare concepts to the security challenges on the Korean Peninsula, and anticipate the collapse of the Kim family regime and the complex, irregular threats that collapse will bring.

The conventional wisdom would postulate that the worst-case situation would be an attack by the North Korean military because surely the devastation and widespread humanitarian suffering as well as global economic impact would be on a scale that would far exceed any crisis that has occurred since the end of World War II. While that could very well be the case, there is little doubt about the military outcome of an attack by the North on the South and its allies and that would be the destruction of the [North] Korean People's Army and the Kim family regime. Victory will surely be in the South's favor; however, the real worst-case scenario comes from dealing with the aftermath, either post-regime collapse or post-conflict.

Assumptions

The fundamental assumption is that the threats that may emerge following collapse or conflict on the peninsula will be characterized by being irregular and these irregular threats will pose a dangerous and complex situation that if not properly planned and prepared for could destabilize the Korean Peninsula and the Northeast Asian region for years to come. These threats will be a source of human suffering in the region, as well as cause significant security threats and economic turmoil, perhaps on a global scale. It is imperative that these potential irregular threats be identified and understood and that countermeasures be developed.

The second fundamental assumption is that the North Korean people will not welcome the Republic of Korea and its allies with open arms. They may be welcomed by some, perhaps many, but certainly not by all and therein is a significant threat. It should be recalled that an assumption regarding the liberation of Iraq was made in 2003 that postulated the Iraqi people would welcome the United States as liberators. This incorrect assumption led to years of insurgency that was only countered after belated recognition of the conditions that fostered the resistance and then undertaking a significant shift in strategy.

The third assumption is that while irregular warfare is the current 21st-century term for the conflicts that the United States is likely to face, planners and policy makers do not appear to view the Irregular Warfare Joint Operating Concept (IW JOC)[3] as applying to the problems that can be expected to be posed by a post-Kim family regime—North Korea. While the IW JOC appears to be predisposed to countering the violent extremism of non-state actors as well as asymmetric threats from state actors, a post-Kim North Korea will at once have many characteristics of violent extremism (although based on a different belief: the religious-like *Juche* ideology) and at the same time use many of the already existing asymmetric capabilities developed by the North Korean state. Additionally, and perhaps most important, the assumption is made that remnants of the North Korean military, Communist Party, and population will oppose the introduction of non-North Korean forces and conduct a uniquely North Korean insurgency to accomplish the classic insurgent goal of ridding a land of an occupying power. It should be noted that the term "irregular warfare" in Korean is the same as "unconventional warfare" and this breeds confusion within the alliance.

The fourth assumption is that despite wishful thinking otherwise, China is going to intervene during a crisis in the North in order to protect four major interests. It must prevent the spillover of any conflict into China. Second, it must prevent the flow of refugees into an area where there are already some two million ethnic Koreans. Third, it will want to prevent not only the loss of control of nuclear weapons, but also prevent nuclear weapons from falling into ROK hands and simultaneously securing any information and evidence that might demonstrate Chinese complicity in the North Korean nuclear development program. Finally, China will want to ensure access to the natural resources that it has already secured through multi-year leases (in some cases one hundred years) with the North Korean government. These interests will drive Chinese actions in the event of crisis, either conflict or collapse.

The fifth and final assumption is that while some planning has taken place to deal with North Korean instability and the effects of a Kim regime collapse, there has been insufficient preparation. Furthermore, in addition to planning, actions can and should be taken prior to collapse to mitigate the conditions and deal with the collapse effects. Unfortunately, despite some

---

[3] Department of Defense, "Irregular Warfare: Countering Irregular Threats Joint Operating Concept, Version 2.0," 17 May 2010.

planning efforts to counter specific irregular threats, the ROK and the United States in particular, have been distracted by the very real and dangerous threat of North Korean nuclear weapons, delivery capabilities, and proliferation while at the same time ensuring deterrence of an attack by the North. Deterrence is paramount and the nuclear problem is a critical international problem; however, successful deterrence over time will likely result in the eventual collapse of the regime and the associated security and humanitarian crises that it will bring.

Irregular Warfare and an End State for the Korean Peninsula

If you concentrate exclusively on victory, while no thought for the after effect, you may be too exhausted to profit by peace, while it is almost certain that the peace will be a bad one, containing the germs of another war.

—B. H. Liddel-Hart[4]

To view the above assumptions from the perspective of the IW JOC with the purpose of looking at the Korean Peninsula in light of irregular warfare, it is necessary to begin with the concept's definitions of both IW and counterinsurgency:

> Irregular warfare. A violent struggle among state and non-state actors for legitimacy and influence over the relevant populations. Irregular warfare favors indirect and asymmetric approaches, though it may employ the full range of military and other capabilities, in order to erode an adversary's power, influence, and will. (JP 1-02)

> Counterinsurgency. Comprehensive civilian and military efforts taken to defeat an insurgency and to address any core grievances. (JP 3-24)[5]

The post-Kim regime North Korea is very likely to be a violent struggle between state actors on the one hand—the ROK, United States, and international community; and non-state actors on the other—the remnants of the North Korean People's Army (NKPA) and the Communist Party,

---

[4] B. H. Liddel-Hart quoted in Maj Susan E. Strednansky, USAF, "Balancing the Trinity: The Fine Art of Conflict Termination" (Maxwell AFB, AL: Air University Press, February 1996), 1.
[5] Department of Defense, "Irregular Warfare."

and members of a thoroughly indoctrinated population. Responses will require indirect and asymmetric approaches. However, it not only may, but also most likely will, require the full range of military and other capabilities to erode—and in this case defeat—North Korean military remnants and the legacy of the Kim family regime's power, influence, and will over the former North Korean population. Furthermore, it will most likely be necessary for the ROK to conduct a counterinsurgency campaign in the North to defeat an insurgency being executed by remnants of the North Korean military and elite with the support of the coerced population.

Before the future problems can be addressed, however, a proposed answer to the "Korea Question"—the division of the peninsula—should be established. The 1953 Armistice Agreement recommended that the political leaders of all parties meet and determine a solution.[6] Since no answer to this question has been forthcoming in some 60 years and it is apparent that there will be no capitulation by either the North or South, particularly as long as the Kim family remains in power, it is necessary to define a possible answer.

During a meeting between President Lee Myung-bak and President Barack Obama in June 2009, they reaffirmed the ROK-U.S. alliance and set forth a vision:

> Through our Alliance we aim to build a better future for all people on the Korean Peninsula, establishing a durable peace on the peninsula and leading to peaceful reunification on the principles of free democracy and a market economy. We will work together to achieve the complete and verifiable elimination of North Korea's nuclear weapons and existing nuclear programs, as well as ballistic missile programs, and to promote respect for the fundamental human rights of the North Korean people.[7]

---

[6] The phrase "Korea question" is derived from the 1953 Armistice Agreement, Section IV, paragraph 60, which states: "In order to insure the peaceful settlement of the *Korean question* [emphasis added], the military Commanders of both sides hereby recommend to the governments of the countries concerned on both sides that, within three (3) months after the Armistice Agreement is signed and becomes effective, a political conference of a higher level of both sides be held by representatives appointed respectively to settle through negotiation the questions of the withdrawal of all foreign forces from Korea, the peaceful settlement of the Korean question, etc."

[7] White House Press Release, "Joint Vision for the Alliance of the United States of American and the Republic of Korea," 16 June 2009, Washington, DC, http://www.whitehouse.gov/the_press_office/Joint-vision-for-the-alliance-of-the-United-States-of-America-and-the-Republic-of-Korea/.

This vision can and should be the basis for policy and strategy development. The foundation for any effective strategy is to have clearly defined end state and following the collapse of the regime it will be necessary to have an end state that will focus policy makers and military and civilian planners. A working proposed end state that would answer the so-called "Korea question" could be this:

A stable, secure, peaceful, economically vibrant, non-nuclear peninsula, reunified under a liberal constitutional form of government determined by the Korean people.[8]

This is an end state that the ROK and international community should strive to achieve and one that the ROK and U.S. alliance should agree upon and base future planning. This can ensure legitimacy of a reunified Korea in the struggle for influence over the Korean people. Irregular warfare and counterinsurgency are complex undertakings as evidenced by the past 10 years of war in Afghanistan and Iraq where there is no clear understandable and attainable end state. There is an opportunity now to establish an end state for the Korean Peninsula that will allow for planning and preparation and when crisis occurs, policy makers and planners will have a clear understanding of what must be achieved.

Nature of the Kim Family Regime and its Influence over the North Korean People

War embraces much more than politics: it is always an expression of culture, often a determinant of cultural forms, in some societies the culture itself.

—John Keegan in *A History of Warfare*[9]

Much has been written about the nature of the Kim family regime and its affect on the Korean people and their psyche. However, the most succinct, useful, and brilliant description can be found in the work of Adrian Buzo as he describes the beginnings of the "guerrilla dynasty" built around the

---

[8] This end state was proposed in the author's 2004 thesis. David S. Maxwell, "Beyond the Nuclear Crisis: A Strategy for the Korean Peninsula," National War College, National Defense University, April 2004, 14.
[9] John Keegan, *A History of Warfare*, (New York: Alfred A. Knopf, 1993), 12.

cult-like worship of Kim Il-sung. The following provides the foundation for understanding how the North Korean elite as well as much of the population is likely to act:

> In the course of this struggle against factional opponents, for the first time Kim began to emphasize nationalism as a means of rallying the population to the enormous sacrifices needed for postwar recovery. This was a nationalism that first took shape in the environment of the anti-Japanese guerrilla movement and developed into a creed through the destruction of both the non-Communist nationalist forces and much of the leftist intellectual tradition of the domestic Communists. Kim's nationalism did not draw inspiration from Korean history, nor did it dwell on past cultural achievements, for the serious study of history and traditional culture soon effectively ceased in the DPRK [Democratic People's Republic of Korea]. Rather, DPRK nationalism drew inspiration from the Spartan outlook of the former Manchurian guerrillas. It was a harsh nationalism that dwelt on past wrongs and promises of retribution for "national traitors" and their foreign backers. DPRK nationalism stressed the "purity" of all things Korean against the "contamination" of foreign ideas, and inculcated in the population a sense of fear and animosity toward the outside world. *Above all, DPRK nationalism stressed that the guerrilla ethos was not only the supreme, but also the only legitimate basis on which to reconstitute a reunified Korea.*[10]

A close reading of the above paragraph reveals a number of insights that can foretell the actions of the remnants of the regime and the military and a vast amount of the population. Sixty years of political indoctrination emphasizing the myth of anti-Japanese partisan warfare and the guerrilla exploits of Kim Il-sung as well as the total hostility to any foreign influence has laid the foundation for a popular resistance to any intervention from outside of North Korea, to include Koreans from the South. An analysis of Buzo's observations will show that a defeated NKPA and North Korean people may fight to the death or live to fight another day. In either case the result will be irregular threats against whatever outside force intervenes to attempt to stabilize the chaos that will follow wartime defeat or regime collapse.

---

[10] Adrian Buzo, *The Guerrilla Dynasty: Politics and Leadership in North Korea*, (Boulder, CO: Westview Press, 1999), 27. Emphasis added.

Although the North Korea people are suffering horrifically from living under the harsh conditions of the past 60 years and, since the mid-1990s, after the fall of the Soviet Union and the loss of economic aid it provided, because of the indoctrination and mindset of the people, it does not necessarily translate that they will welcome the collapse of the regime and reunification of the peninsula. For the past six decades the people have been so thoroughly indoctrinated that they have tremendous fear of anything outside of North Korea. Combined with the guerrilla mindset, it should be assumed in the worst case that the people will resist reunification that is not brought about by the Kim family. The guerrilla mindset will likely be the root cause of the irregular threats that occur in and emanate from North Korea.

Asymmetric Threats in North Korea

Although the current focus is on North Korea's nuclear program, it should be remembered that the North has developed a range of asymmetric threats to support its campaign plans to reunify the peninsula under its control. First and foremost it has the largest special operations force in the world. The North Korean regime has invested heavily in its SOF and they have proven very adept over the years as illustrated by the numerous infiltration operations. Much has been written about North Korean SOF, but suffice it to say given the large numbers that have been trained over the years, combined with the guerrilla mindset indoctrination of the population, prudent planners will recognize that this is a recipe for a significant threat during conflict and both post-conflict operations and a post-collapse situation.

In addition to the nuclear program, other weapons of mass destruction have been under development for years including large stockpiles of chemical weapons as well as probably some limited biological capabilities. Nuclear, chemical, and biological weapons and associated material pose not only direct threats to military and civilian personnel on the peninsula and in the region, they potentially can be sold on the global arms market, which could very well include terrorist organizations. The regime has a track record of proliferation of military hardware and any remnants of the regime will likely exploit overseas contacts as a source of funding and leverage.

In addition to weapons of mass destruction, North Korea has worked hard to develop missile delivery capabilities that it has sold to clients particularly in the Middle East. The presence of these systems in the North could provide an insurgency with capabilities never before seen and would push the description of the insurgency toward the hybrid warfare model that the Israelis faced in dealing with Hezbollah and has been well described by Frank Hoffman, among others.

In addition to SOF and weapons capabilities, North Korea has developed an extensive global network to support the regime through a myriad of illicit activities which range from counterfeiting U.S. currency to drug manufacturing and distribution to the counterfeiting of a range of goods from cigarettes to Viagra. This provides the capability to raise funds to support an insurgency as well as a means to sell military technology as an additional source of income. Of course that military technology could include WMD.

Analysis of the existing asymmetric threats shows that these capabilities will be well suited to insurgent operations by remnants of the toppled regime and its military. These, if exploited, will be far more complex and dangerous than any that were present in Afghanistan and Iraq.

Dealing with the Worst Case: The Kim Family Regime's Legacy of Irregular Threats

If in taking a native den one thinks chiefly of the market that he will establish there on the morrow, one does not take it in the ordinary way.

—Louis H. G. Lyautey: "The Colonial Role of the Army," *Revue Des Deux Mondes*, February 15, 1900[11]

While planning has taken place at various times over the years to allow the alliance to react to such threats as terrorism, use of WMD, humanitarian disaster and internally displaced persons/refugee flow, and internal civil war two questions should be asked:

- Has the alliance prepared for the worst case—an insurgency that opposes reunification—following collapse of the Kim family regime?

- What can and should be done prior to collapse to assist in mitigating the threats and shaping the outcome on the peninsula?

---

[11] Robert Debs Heinl Jr., ed., *Dictionary of Military and Naval Quotations* (Annapolis, MD: Naval Institute Press, 1966), 69.

Although the "to-do list" is long, there are five key fundamental tasks that the ROK-U.S. alliance and the international community must do to prepare for the collapse of the Kim family regime. While not exhaustive, focusing on these five tasks will provide the foundation needed to mitigate the effects of irregular threats and improve the conditions for successful alliance and international efforts to deal with the effects of regime collapse.

First, a decision must be made as to the end state envisioned for the Korean Peninsula. As noted earlier, the ROK-U.S. alliance requires an end state that could be along these lines: A stable, secure, peaceful, economically vibrant, non-nuclear peninsula, reunified under a liberal constitutional form of government determined by the Korean people.[12]

The imperative of an end state will provide focus for planners and policy makers and also yield the foundation for an influence campaign that is critical to shaping the environment after the regime's collapse.

Along with the establishment of the end state, a decision must be made regarding alliance transformation and leadership of operations in North Korea. It is imperative that South Korea leads the effort in reunification and operations in the North because this will help to undermine the 60-plus years of propaganda in which the South has been portrayed as a U.S. puppet. However, as evidenced by the so-called "OPCON transfer" that was originally scheduled for 2012 and was recently pushed back until 2015, the ROK military does not yet have the resources to conduct independent operations. In addition, the reality of the OPCON transfer issue is not solely about command and control of ROK military forces. This action is actually the dissolution of the ROK/U.S. Combined Forces Command (CFC) which has been one of the most effective combined commands in the world since 1978. It is commanded by an American four-star general with a ROK four-star deputy. Rather than dissolve the command, perhaps it should remain intact and its leadership shift to a ROK general in command with a U.S. deputy. In this way the ROK would be in charge of operations in the North and would still be able to exploit the expertise and full capabilities of the combined command.[13]

---

[12] Maxwell, "Beyond the Nuclear Crisis," 14.
[13] Bruce Bechtol, *Defiant Failed State: The North Korea Threat to International Security* (Washington, DC: Potomac Books, 2010), 165–74.

Irregular Warfare on the Korean Peninsula

The second most important action is to execute an influence campaign focusing on the second-tier leaders to maintain control of their organizations to prevent attack and a future insurgency. This tier consists of those corps, maneuver, and special operations commanders who control not only forces but also WMD capabilities. These leaders are key to maintaining control of the NKPA. In addition, an active influence campaign is necessary to prepare the North Korean population for a post-regime end state that results in a reunified peninsula. This is the most difficult, complex, and time consuming effort, but one that is critical to beginning to undo the years of political and social indoctrination that has used the *Juche* ideology as a de facto religion for social control. Additionally, this indoctrination has developed such high levels of distrust and fear of outsiders that any stability operations will be extremely difficult. It also has made the population ripe to support an insurgency especially if that continues to perpetuate the regime myths of the legitimacy of North Korea being based on anti-Japanese partisan warfare. Following regime collapse "anti-Japanese" will be substituted with "anti-foreigner."

Furthermore, a decision must be made to avoid the mistakes of the Iraq war. The North Korean military must be kept intact. It is one of the North's very few functioning institutions and can be a critical component for maintaining internal stability as well as executing support and stabilization operations. Most important, an intact military is one of the best methods to prevent a future insurgency. However, keeping the military intact requires a successful influence campaign to target those commanders who can and should maintain control of their forces and work with the ROK military and civilian leadership.

Eight years after Operation Enduring Freedom began in Afghanistan, the "Afghanistan-Pakistan Hands" program was developed. This recognized the importance of having planners, both military and civilian, with sufficient cultural expertise to understand the problems in the region and allow for effective plans and policies to be developed that incorporate cultural awareness and understanding. The same mistake should not be made in terms of North Korea. ROK and U.S. military and civilian North Korean experts should be brought together and dedicated to planning for a North Korean collapse. An investment should be made in developing younger "North Korea Hands" to be ready to deal with the aftermath of the Kim family regime. A competent staff and organization of experts cannot be created rapidly after the crisis occurs. This group needs to span the professional spectrum and assist in the development of policy and strategy as well as the campaign plan to deal with collapse. They will also be able to assist in the training and readiness of the military forces and civilian agencies that will execute the operations to achieve the end state of a reunified Korea.

Last, an international coalition must be established to support reunification of the peninsula. Most important, the ROK and the United States must engage with China. Chinese actions will play a critical role in the outcome of crisis on the peninsula in either post-conflict or post-collapse. The ROK-U.S. alliance and China must find common ground in interests and, through engagement and transparency, develop plans and methods for minimizing the potential for conflict between the two.

These efforts must, again, be undertaken prior to the crisis of regime collapse. Reunification, while the responsibility of the ROK, will require enormous resources not only in terms of manpower and material but also funding. Numerous studies attest to the huge costs of reunification. Those in Korea are likely to make German reunification pale in comparison because of the vast differences in infrastructure and standards of living between North and South. Failure to support reunification efforts and quell an insurgency in the North will, however, as already stated, likely bring instability in terms of security to Northeast Asia and also have global economic impact. It is in the interest of the regional as well as the global economic powers to support reunification. But the effort to build this coalition must occur now, even if done behind closed doors, to prevent political conflict prior to the collapse of the Kim regime.

The irregular threats that will be present on the Korean Peninsula when the regime collapses will be extremely complex and dangerous. While the wars in Iraq and Afghanistan have been difficult, the worst-case scenarios on the peninsula will be far more difficult. The threats must be understood and planners and policy makers must take an objective and realistic look at the problems that will have to be faced. While everyone may hope for a "soft landing" and peaceful reunification, the alliance and international community needs to prepare for the most likely and dangerous outcomes. This requires active preparatory actions by the ROK-U.S. alliance across the instruments of national power.

Planning is good, but preparation is better. While the regime has demonstrated enormous resiliency muddling through severe internal crises since the death of Kim Il-sung in 1994, a course of action cannot be to hope that it will continue to survive. The pressures on North Korea are likely to someday cause attack or collapse, either of which will be catastrophic for the ROK, the region, and international community.

Chapter 7

Understanding North Korea's Human Rights Abuses

by Chuck Downs

It is possible that this title for my presentation was assigned simply to allow wide latitude for covering the topic of human rights in general. But sometimes titles have a way of focusing a question, and this one caused me to wonder what most needs to be understood about North Korea's human rights abuses.

The fundamental aspects of this dire situation, after all, are well known. Basic freedoms, even those guaranteed by international agreements the North Korean regime has signed, are routinely denied to North Korea's citizens. The regime's food distribution policy and its political caste system predetermine that large segments of the North Korean population receive none of the food provided by international relief agencies and other countries. North Korea's political prison camps operate with an unmatched level of brutality. Its human rights crisis has serious regional and international consequences; it has caused a flow of refugees who often end up as victims of exploitation, violence, or crime when they cross into neighboring countries, and China's approach to this humanitarian crisis is to send the refugees back to the North where they face certain persecution. These and the other human rights concerns are merely the tip of the iceberg. The regime is so oppressive we cannot be certain we know the full dimensions of its human rights abuses.

Bruce Bechtol reminded me recently that we originally met some ten years ago in a small meeting called to discuss North Korean proliferation. During that session's broad discussion of the nature of the regime, I made an example of collective punishment as a characteristic of the regime's method of coercion and control. A well-known specialist in China responded that there was nothing new or unique about North Korea's use of collective punishment; it had been used throughout Asia, and had historical roots in Korea's kingdoms. I recognize the accuracy of his assertion, and understand that collective punishment was used not only in Asia, but in medieval Europe, and ancient Rome and Greece as well. It is by no means a purely Asian means of punishment. Its use today, however, is a matter of considerable contemporary concern. It violates not only codified declarations of human rights but also internationally accepted standards of appropriate governmental behavior. Its use by the modern North Korean regime cannot be dismissed as culturally Korean or justified on the basis of longstanding practice. Because Kim Il-sung decreed that three generations of a traitor's family must be wiped out, innocent people who often have no idea what the offense of their accused relative did or said are also incarcerated in North Korea's political prisons.

At about the same time, a colleague published a book on the North's negotiating style that took a decidedly different view from mine on what motivates the Kim regime's negotiating behavior. He wrote that Kim Il-sung's emphasis on the importance of centralized political power emerged from the rigorous demands of life in guerrilla camps.[1] If that is meant as an explanation for Kim's advocacy and adherence to absolute rule by one man—himself—it is completely misleading. Kim Il-sung and his son have been guided by the same greed and megalomania that has motivated tyrants since the dawn of history.

We Americans benefit from a long cultural tradition of fighting to defend human rights, one that has roots thousands of years before the founding of our republic. Our nation's birth was accompanied by a declaration of rights. Our cultural tradition of fighting for freedom, however, did not start in 1776. The notions that guided the founding fathers, among whom lived close to our session today in Quantico—Washington, Jefferson, Madison, and Mason—were in their minds because their classical education taught them that tyranny must be challenged and subdued.

Such an understanding of history, gained through an analysis of the tortuous and difficult history of the Western tradition—from the wars of the ancient democracies in Greece and Rome through the development of concepts of sovereignty and political legitimacy in Europe—has a global relevance, even to cultures as distant as Korea and even to histories as

---

[1] See, for example, "Factors Shaping North Korean Worldviews," chap. 1 in Scott Snyder, *Negotiating on the Edge* (Washington, DC: U.S. Institute of Peace Press, 1999), 17–28.

troubled as China's. We should not discard our historical traditions when we discuss the human rights abuses of a place like North Korea.

Thucydides' histories are replete with examples of the rise and fall of the fortunes of various governments of ancient Greece. His verdict on one-man rule, however, applies equally well to modern North Korea. He describes "their habit of providing simply for themselves, of looking solely to their personal comfort and family aggrandizement."[2] Aristotle echoed that conclusion. A tyrannical government he said, governed "with a view to its own advantage, not to that of its subjects."[3]

These were matters that weighed heavily on the minds of the American founding fathers. Washington wrote letters to Jefferson in which he mentioned the excesses of Roman Emperor Nero as though his corrupt tyrannical rule were the stuff of contemporary news. We may not be so attentive to classical precedents, but the reign of Nero gives plenty of grounds for comparison with the reign of Kim Jong-il. On May 22, 2009, we were able to pick up a copy of the *Wall Street Journal* to read the front page article about how Curtis Melvin and Joshua Stanton, two expert analysts of publicly available satellite images, had located the waterslide and wave pool at one of Kim Jong-il's many villas.[4] The prison camp survivor Kang Chul-hwan has also done an excellent job of finding evidence of the Kim family's lavish lifestyle. Excessive luxury is the norm for a profligate regime that rules an impoverished, starving citizenry.

Lincoln compared such misappropriation of public resources to slavery. He described it as the same logic that says, "You work and toil and earn bread, and I'll eat it." He said, "No matter in what shape it comes, whether from the mouth of a king who seeks to bestride the people of his own nation and live by the fruit of their labor, or from one race of men as an apology for enslaving another race, it is the same tyrannical principle."[5]

---

[2] Thucydides, 1.17 *Hellas*, in Robert B. Strassler, ed., *The Landmark Thucydides*, (New York: The Free Press, 1996), 13.
[3] Aristotle, *Politics*, Book IV, chap. X, in Ernest Barker, *The Politics of Aristotle* (New York: Oxford University Press, 1971), 179.
[4] Evan Ramstad, "Gulags, Nukes, and a Water Slide: Citizen Spies Lift North Korea's Veil," *Wall Street Journal*, May 22, 2009, 1.
[5] Abraham Lincoln quoted in John George Nicolay and John Hay, *Abraham Lincoln: A History*, vol. 2, part 3 of 8, http://www.fullbooks.com/Abraham-Lincoln-A-History-Volume-23.html.

The Regime's Starvation Policy and Human Rights

Aristotle saw public impoverishment as an objective of tyranny: "so that the common citizens will be occupied with earning their livelihood and will have neither leisure nor opportunity to engage in conspiratorial acts." We have seen this phenomenon in contemporary North Korea. Haggard and Noland, in their study "Hunger and Human Rights," observed that between 1995 and 1998, as famine approached, the North Korean regime failed to request international assistance. They explained that in the ensuing years, North Koreans suffered through a catastrophe that resulted in as many as one million deaths from starvation and hunger-related diseases; this represented between three to five percent of the population. The regime ignored internationally accepted norms for aid distribution, which are designed to ensure that the aid reaches those who need it most. Instead, it rewarded those whom it deemed loyal to the regime, and withholding food from those it deemed disloyal.[6]

As the crisis deepened and information about the ongoing catastrophe leaked out, Japan and South Korea began providing food and humanitarian supplies in June 1995. Later, the United States and European Union nations also contributed massive amounts of assistance, as well as private aid from NGOs such as the Red Cross, and through the UN World Food Program. As aid began arriving, the North Korean government demonstrated its venal duplicity by reducing the amount the regime had been spending on purchasing food from external sources. Put simply, the government did not use the world's aid to supplement the available food supply; it reduced the domestic food supply.[7]

When it received aid, the regime pursued several policies designed to control aid distribution, hinder effective monitoring, and create opportunities for controlling and diverting aid for the government's purposes. Due to the lack of transparency and effective monitoring, there

---

[6] The information on human rights abuses in North Korea presented here is taken directly from publications of the Committee for Human Rights in North Korea (HRNK). The majority of the information presented was originally published in: Stephan Haggard and Marcus Noland, "Hunger and Human Rights," (Washington, DC: HRNK, 2005) and DLA Piper et al., *Failure to Protect: A Call for the UN Security Council to Act in North Korea*, (Washington, DC: DLA Piper and HRNK, 2006). The specific references to statistics on hunger in North Korea are found in Haggard and Noland, 14–15, 23–29, and DLA Piper, 12–13.

[7] See Haggard and Noland, 14–15.

were widespread reports that significant amounts of foreign aid were not reaching the most deserving recipients. Aid was diverted to the same privileged persons the party favored under the public distribution system, including the military, party officials, and party loyalists.[8]

Aristotle also pointed out that "it is part of these tyrannical measures to impoverish the nation so as to bolster the funds available for military defense." Pyongyang took advantage of the foreign aid to divert government revenue away from food assistance and use the savings to fund the government's other priorities, such as military weapons programs.[9] North Korea's *songun*—military first—policy fits well with Thucydides' observation that tyrants "make safety the great aim of their accomplishments."[10] As it was cutting its purchases of food imports in 1999, the North Korean government bought 40 MiG-21 fighters and eight military helicopters from Kazakhstan. Further, the government continued to pursue its expensive nuclear programs during the famine, spending currency that should have been used to feed its people. Even at the height of the famine, the government demonstrated that it prioritizes its military over the basic survival needs of its population.[11]

Kim Jong-il's Ill-gotten Wealth

Aristotle defined tyranny as "that arbitrary power of an individual which is responsible to no one."[12] We should not be surprised that a regime like North Korea engages in illicit activities within and outside its borders. In order to finance its military programs, security services, and loyal elite, the North Korean regime has systematically engaged in weapons proliferation,

---

[8] Haggard and Noland have questioned whether outright direct diversion to privileged persons, including the military, occurred on a large scale. They argue that the military and other privileged persons had the means to purchase and acquire food on their own, and presumably they were given the first portions of the aid from China and South Korea, which was given with no monitoring or commitment that the aid be distributed on the basis of need rather than class. Instead, Haggard and Noland have suggested that the diversion that occurred was of World Food Program and non-governmental organization aid into illegal markets, where those diverting the aid could sell it at a profit themselves. Of course, those with sufficient money to make such purchases were not the most needy or vulnerable. Haggard and Noland, 24.
[9] See Haggard and Noland, 16–17.
[10] Thucydides, 1.17 *Hellas*, in Strassler, *The Landmark Thucydides*, 13.
[11] See Haggard and Noland, 16–17.
[12] Aristotle, *Politics*, Book IV, chap. X, in Barker, *The Politics of Aristotle*, 179.

drug trafficking, counterfeiting of goods and currency, and banking and insurance fraud. Despite Kim Jong-il's denials, the evidence demonstrates that North Korea engages in drug trafficking—from $500 million to $1 billion per year—as a source of foreign currency to fund its WMD program and other government initiatives.[13]

As Kan, Bechtol, and Collins point out in the superb book on North Korea's state-run criminal enterprises, *Criminal Sovereignty: Understanding North Korea's Illicit International Activities* (Carlisle, PA: U.S. Army War College, 2010), North Korean diplomats have a long history of dealing in contraband. Almost all of North Korea's diplomatic corps in Scandinavia were expelled in 1976 for running a smuggling ring for alcohol and cigarettes through Norway, Denmark, and Finland. Since then, more than 20 North Korean diplomats, agents, and trade officials have been implicated in illicit drug operations in more than 12 countries, including Egypt, Venezuela, India, Germany, Nepal, Sweden, Zambia, Ethiopia, and Laos. Japanese drug officials report that 43 percent of all illegal drugs imported to Japan comes from North Korea, providing a large cash profit for the North Korean government. Raids in Taiwan and Japan have uncovered heroin that was packed in the exact same rice bags that were used to ship donated rice to North Korea as famine relief—thus identifying North Korea as the source of the drugs.[14]

The United States has determined that a definitive connection exists between the North Korean government and the high-quality, counterfeit $100 bills commonly known as "supernotes." According to the most reliable statistics, North Korea has produced between $45 million and $100 million in supernotes since 1989, and estimates of its current yearly production range between $3 million and $25 million per year. Evidence indicating North Korea's involvement includes instances in which North Korean officials were

---

[13] The information on North Korea's illicit activities is taken from a report published by the Committee for Human Rights: DLA Piper et al., *Failure to Protect: A Call for the UN Security Council to Act in North Korea*, (Washington, DC: DLA Piper and HRNK, 2006), which cited "Heroin Busts Point to Source of Funds for North Koreans," *Wall Street Journal*, April 23, 2003 (referencing figures from U.S. military command in South Korea). According to the U.S. State Department, "it is likely, but not certain, that the North Korean government sponsors criminal activities, including narcotics production and trafficking, in order to earn foreign currency for the state and its leaders." *International Narcotics Control Strategy Report 2006* (Washington, DC: U.S. Department of State, 2006).

[14] Jay Solomon and Jason Dean, "Drug Money: Heroin Busts Point to Source of Funds for North Koreans," *Wall Street Journal*, April 23, 2003; Aristotle, *Politics*, Book IV, chap. X, in Barker, *The Politics of Aristotle*, 179; Anthony Spaeth, "Kim's Rackets," *TIME Asia*, June 9, 2003, 14; and Balbina Y. Hwang, "Curtailing North Korea's Illicit Activities," (Heritage Foundation, August 25, 2003), 4.

caught carrying the counterfeit bills. Defectors have identified the buildings in Pyongyang and Pyongsong that contain the counterfeiting equipment.[15]

Though its economic threat to the United States is often described as minimal, producing counterfeit currency has a deleterious effect on the U.S. currency system and harms diplomatic relations between the United States and the rest of the world. Equally important, it should remind us of the kind of government we are dealing with in North Korea. David Asher, a former advisor in the U.S. State Department, observes: "If [North Korea is] going to counterfeit our currency the entire time they're engaged in diplomatic negotiations, what does that say about their sincerity?"[16]

North Korea also uses weapons proliferation, a subject raised in other sessions of the conference, as a way to generate foreign income. There are reliable reports that North Korea provided chemical and biological weapons technology to both Syria and Iran in the early 1990s. However, their export of WMD is dwarfed by North Korea's exports of ballistic missiles; a U.S. government study performed in 2004 estimated that North Korea earned $560 million from missile sales in 2001 alone.[17]

Insurance scams run under the authority of high-level associates of Kim Jong-il in secret offices like Office Number 39 and the Organization and Guidance Department of the Party have netted Kim a huge fortune located in sundry financial institutions in the West, with costs to the international re-insurance industry reportedly reaching $30 million annually in the past decade. As a result of the courageous testimony of a defector named Kim Kwang-jin, who had worked for North Korea's "Korean National Insurance Corporation," the intentions and objectives of the North's undertaking in re-insurance scams are now exposed and explained. His revelations have brought an end to one method the corrupt regime purloined from external sources the funds it needed to maintain its internal oppression. In the long run, his work advances the freedom of the average North Korean, since it weakens the capabilities of the totalitarian regime.

---

[15] Raphael F. Perl and Dick K. Nanto, "North Korean Counterfeiting of U.S. Currency" (Congressional Research Service, March 22, 2006), 8; and Stephen Mihm, "No Ordinary Counterfeit," *New York Times Magazine*, July 23, 2006, 40.

[16] DLA Piper et al., *Failure to Protect*.

[17] Larry A. Niksch, "Korea: U.S.–Korean Relations—Issues for Congress 6" (Congressional Research Service, April 14, 2006), 7, cited in DLA Piper et al., 67. See also Jon Herskovitz, "North Korea's Missiles Find Fewer Buyers," *Gulf Times*, September 6, 2006, cited in DLA Piper et al.

Suppression of Political Dissent

Totalitarian governments' efforts to control the thoughts and expressions of their people have an ancient and terrible history. Aristotle observed that this policy had two components—first, to let the people know nothing of what the government did, but second, to let the government know everything that the people did: "it is part [of the nature of tyranny] to strive to see that all the affairs of the tyrant are secret, but that nothing is kept hidden of what any subject says or does, rather everywhere he will be spied upon."[18]

A vast network of internal spy agencies has been instituted in North Korea, just as it was in the Soviet Union and the Communist bloc. Set up along lines laid out by Soviet advisors, the North's secret security agencies, like those of Stalinist Russia, have operated a system of gulags characterized by false imprisonment, persecution based on political grounds, extermination, enslavement, and torture.

An estimated 200,000 people are now imprisoned in North Korea's various prison camps, and it is believed that as many as 400,000 prisoners have died in these camps over the past 30 years. The situation for political dissenters worsened when Kim Jong-il began to fear that the communist collapse which swept through Eastern Europe in the late 1980s would spread and challenge his rule. As his insecurity increased, so did the number of political prisoners housed in North Korea's political prisons.[19]

In addition to an accused individual, the State Security Department also detains up to three generations of the accused's family members, including the mother, father, sisters, brothers, children, and grandchildren. Like the accused, the family members are not granted a trial. Instead, they are picked up and transported to political prisons without being provided any information as to when, if ever, they will be released. There is a systemic use of torture in interrogations and as punishment in the political prisons. Political prisoners are tortured first in an effort to get them to "confess."

---

[18] Aristotle, *Politics*, Book V, chap. XI, sect. X, in Barker, *The Politics of Aristotle*, 244–45.
[19] A report of the Committee for Human Rights in North Korea: David Hawk, "The Hidden Gulag: Exposing North Korea's Prison Camps" (Washington, DC: HRNK, 2003), 24; Choi Sung-Chol, "The International Community and Human Rights in North Korea" (Center for the Advancement of North Korean Human Rights, 1996), 11. The estimate of deaths in the camps covers the period 1972–95.

Many prisoners report that guards engage in beatings so vicious that prisoners' eyes fall out or bones are exposed. A commonly reported tactic of extracting confessions is to threaten loved ones.[20]

Prisoners are provided only starvation-level food rations despite the fact that they are forced to engage in physically demanding labor. It is this combination that often turns the labor camps into death camps.

The Regime's Control of Public Information

As noted, Aristotle observed that while tyrannical government sought to know everything about what people did, they also sought to guarantee secrecy regarding what the government did. Two thousand years later, Winston Churchill put it in these terms:

> You see these dictators on their pedestals, surrounded by the bayonets of their soldiers and the truncheons of their police. Yet in their hearts there is unspoken—unspeakable!—fear. They are afraid of words and thoughts! Words spoken abroad, thoughts stirring at home, all the more powerful because they are forbidden. These terrify them. A little mouse—a little tiny mouse!—of thought appears in the room, and even the mightiest potentates are thrown into panic.[21]

Americans certainly understand well the need for communications during a period of great political change. During the American struggle for independence, Benjamin Franklin's Philadelphia newspaper was able to tell people in America what they wanted to know from a uniquely American perspective. His newspaper served to disseminate information on proceedings of the Continental Congress, and laid one of the foundation stones for the guarantee of freedom of the press. It also helped to consolidate ideas and galvanize public opinion.

The recent advent of personal communications in North Korea brought on primarily by cell phones and radios, has had a dramatic effect on what is known about the North Korean regime, and has exposed both the regime's brutality and instability. As a *New York Times* article reported on March

---

[20] Hawk, "The Hidden Gulag," 59.
[21] Winston Churchill quoted in "All Great Quotes," available online at http://www.allgreatquotes.com/winston_churchill_quotes11.shtml.

29, 2010, "North Korea, one of the world's most impenetrable nations, is facing a new threat: networks of its own citizens feeding information about life there to South Korea and its Western allies." The article stated that reporters and activists seeking news from inside North Korea go to China to find North Koreans who are allowed to travel there, give them cell phones to take back to the North, and then post their stories on blog sites and news services in South Korea. One Committee for Human Rights in North Korea (HRNK) board member, Nicholas Eberstadt, interviewed for the piece, commented, "In an information vacuum like North Korea, any additional tidbits — even the swamp of rumors — is helpful."[22]

More needs to be known about how to get information into North Korea, especially into the hands of people who will benefit from better informed perspectives on political developments. Significant defectors from the bureaucratic class in Pyongyang are available to explain the official apparatus of information dissemination. HRNK has accordingly taken on a comprehensive study of how information is shared and disseminated within North Korea.

Our study will entail an analysis of the following channels of information:

- Officially-sponsored connections to external media. We know that North Korea pays for a feed from Reuters in particular. We will report on how access to this information is controlled, who gets access, under what circumstances, and what authorized North Korean users are permitted to do with the information. We want to cover the scale of dissemination, contents, censorship, contract procedure and impact;

- Official Democratic People's Republic of Korea (DPRK) government sources of information that are in circulation, comparing the information flow that is made available to the bureaucracy and the general populace;

- The North Korean education system and its role in development of information, dissemination, and control;

---

[22] Choe Sang-hun, "North Koreans Use Cellphones to Bare Secrets," *New York Times*, March 28, 2010.

- The impact of official and unofficial rumors, word of mouth, their different sources and impacts. It is clear that there exists an "elite rumor mill" in Pyongyang that sends signals throughout the party apparatus on important matters that are about to be decided. We want to study how that works and how the regime uses this system to engender support and loyalty.

- The effect of information "leaks" by individuals, fabrication by state security apparatus, its nature and consequences;

- The nature and impact of the increasing inflow of information from outside, for example, balloons from South Korea and their impact;

- The burgeoning impact of external news transmitted through radio or cell phones, and the impact it may be having on the ruling class in Pyongyang.

We hope to understand what types of information are available to different spectra of the population, what are their sources, how strictly the state controls the information flows, what are the informal channels of outside information, how effective the balloon leaflets across the DMZ and U.S.-sponsored broadcasting such as Radio Free Asia and Voice Of America are. This study will provide the international community, human rights activists, and policy makers a clearer picture of what information North Koreans need and how to increase input from outside to promote freedom and democracy in North Korea. Informing North Koreans is critical for promoting their understanding of the nature of the Kim regime and its connection to their misery, as well as to preparing them for the possibility of being free in the future.

What Can Be Done As the Kim Regime Ends?

The record of the United Nations in condemning the Kim regime's human rights abuses is increasingly strong. The human rights situation in North Korea is, the UN Secretary-General stated in Seoul in 2008, "unacceptable."[23] Thailand's Professor Vitit Muntarbhorn was appointed

---

[23] "Ban Urges NK to Improve Human Rights," *Korea Times*, 4 July 2008.

Special Rapporteur for the Situation of Human Rights in North Korea by the Commission on Human Rights in July 2004. In response to his first report to the United Nations issued on January 10, 2005, the General Assembly has passed a number of resolutions concerning the human rights situation in the North. As recently as December 2009, the UN's Human Rights Council convened a "Universal Periodic Review" in Geneva to address the regime's abuses in direct dialogue with the government of North Korea.[24]

Similarly, the Congress of the United States, the National Assembly of South Korea, and the Diet of Japan, and parliaments of Canada, Australia, and the European Union have also either enacted legislation or have provisions under consideration that attempt to support the people of North Korea and influence the regime to adopt more humanitarian policies.

Notwithstanding these actions, policy makers, not just in the United States and other countries as well, tend to focus attention more closely on the regime's military challenges, threats to peace, and nuclear development. Yet there are precedents for integrating human rights concerns into policies toward countries where nuclear weapons have occupied a central point of discussion. For example, both Democratic and Republican administrations found effective bilateral and multilateral means of promoting human rights goals with the Soviet Union even though they were negotiating nuclear weapons agreements with its leaders at the same time. Ideally, broader discussions about political, economic, energy, human rights, and humanitarian concerns have the potential to create a more solid foundation for talks about nuclear issues.

The reality is that the regime's recent actions have become increasingly defiant, even as it totters on the verge of an unstable transition—inevitable because of Kim Jong-il's impending death. The recent sinking of the ROK corvette *Cheonan* raises the specter of war and increased tension, and, if unchecked, the possibility of additional provocative behavior. As Aristotle

---

[24] A professor of law at Chulalongkorn University in Bangkok, Thailand, Muntarbhorn has served in various capacities in the United Nations system, including as Special Rapporteur on the Sale of Children, Child Prostitution and Child Pornography (1990–94) and as expert or adviser to many United Nations organizations. See "Vitit Muntarbhorn Appointed UN Special Rapporteur on Situation of Human Rights in the Democratic People's Republic of Korea," HR/4786, August 6, 2004. See "Special Rapporteur for the Comm'n on Human Rights, Question of the Violation of Human Rights and Fundamental Freedom In Any Part Of the World: Situation of Human Rights in the Democratic People's Republic of Korea," UN Doc. E/CN.4/2005/34 (January 10, 2005), at 2. General Assembly Resolution 60/173.

told us two millennia ago, "the same vein of policy ... makes tyrants warmongers, with the object of keeping their subjects constantly occupied and continually in need of a leader."[25]

As Kim Jong-il attempts to pass his monopoly of power to his youngest son, the international community faces a situation that is even more challenging than that of the past 60 years. The impending change of leadership when Kim dies presents both a fearsome concern and an opportunity for regional peace and security. The implications for the human rights of North Korea's people are profound. Although new leadership may not reverse Kim's policies overnight, it could prove more receptive to addressing some human rights concerns as a means of signaling to the rest of the world that its intentions are not aggressive.

If new leadership comes to power in Pyongyang, and the new leaders seek to develop a different relationship with the rest of the world, human rights concerns could play a major role in testing the new leadership's intentions. Let us assume that even leaders who are predisposed to normalizing North Korea's relationship with its neighbors might be unable for internal political reasons to dispose of the North's nuclear weapons program. The United States could raise human rights concerns and seek North Korean agreement on specific human rights measures that might not undermine the new leadership's standing, such as:

- Accounting for the foreign citizens of 12 nations who are held against their will in North Korea, as a result of the regime's abductions, hostage-taking, and other extenuating circumstances;

- Facilitating reunifications for families who have been separated since the Korean War and for those separated from their families because of famine, extreme poverty, and political persecution in the North. Although the Kim regime has allowed brief visits under closely-supervised family reunions, only 1,600 of the 125,000 South Korean applicants have been able to participate. Some 10 million await information about missing family members;

---

[25] Aristotle, *Politics*, Book V, chap. XI, sect. X, in Barker, *The Politics of Aristotle*, 245.

- Improving international monitoring of food distribution to ensure it reaches the intended recipients;

- Decriminalizing movement within North Korea and across the border, and an end to the persecution of those who return voluntarily or are forced back into North Korea;

- Releasing innocent children and family members of those convicted of political crimes;

- Providing access to prisoners by the International Committee of the Red Cross, the World Food Program, and other international agencies; and

- Reviews of the cases of prisoners of conscience with the Red Cross or Amnesty International with a view to their release.

While these steps do not address the full range of human rights abuses committed by the North Korean regime, they represent human rights issues that could possibly be raised in negotiations with new leadership. While this list is ordered in what is roughly what I would expect the new regime to be able to pursue, any outsider's understanding of the political difficulty of such moves is highly subjective. The range of steps available to new leaders has much to do with their own internal political assessments—indeed, even questions of who is in charge of what function undertaken by the previous regime. The point here is that by engaging in human rights discussions, we will be representing our values well and expanding our comprehension of what can be accomplished with any new group of leaders.

These issues could possibly be discussed without unseating an incoming leader whose power might not be secure enough to allow a more complete reversal of the Kim regime's onerous security policies. Admittedly this is a fragile, complex, and sensitive process, and may lead to the unfortunate conclusion that incoming leaders are not in fact reliable or willing to change, but there is, nevertheless, some hope in the current circumstances.

There are many here who will say that even hoping to address these issues with new leadership in North Korea is overly optimistic. The defector Kim Kwang-jin can certainly attest to the pressures that will be on Chang Sang-taek as he takes over a kind of regency for Kim Jong-eun, and Bruce Bechtol can point out that O Kuk-ryol is a considerable force to be contended with, who will have his own reasons to keep North Korea's tyrannical system going.

But what the classical tradition of Western political development teaches us is that tyrannies, simply because they serve only one individual, do not last. When democracy takes hold, it tends to expand and strengthen. As Washington wrote to Madison, "Liberty, when it begins to take root, is a plant of rapid growth."[26] Tyrannies, on the other hand, topple with their leaders; in spite of their emphasis on security, they are less stable forms of government. If we can take advantage of the pending change in North Korea to advance a freer society there, Aristotle offers a final promise for a positive result: "No freeman, if he can escape from it, will endure such a government."[27]

---

[26] George Washington, letter to James Madison, 2 March 1788.
[27] Aristotle, *Politics*, Book IV, chap. X in Barker, *The Politics of Aristotle*, 179.

Chapter 8

Breaking Barriers: The Media War for North Korea

Ha Tae-keung, president of Open Radio for North Korea, one of several Seoul-based stations aiming broadcasts into North Korea, boasts one piece of evidence of the impact of his broadcasts that none of Open Radio's competitors is likely to match. After the station in April 2010 quoted a North Korean fortune teller as saying that North Korean leader Kim Jong-il would die on May 16, Kim in the six-day period from May 16 to May 22 was reported by the North Korean media to have made 16 field trips to factories, farms, and military units. "He is sensitive to rumors of his death," said Ha. "He would like to be subduing the rumor."[1]

Like many reports of whatever is going on in North Korea, this one is impossible to prove or, for that matter, to disprove. Nobody can be really certain that Kim Jong-il made all those field trips, regardless of the claims of the North Korean reports. There is no way to double-check whether the fortune-teller actually made the forecast, as reported to Open Radio by one of its "Deep Throat" contacts inside North Korea, and of course it is impossible to know if word of the Open Radio broadcast reached Kim Jong-il or his inner circle. Still, what is clear is that the story as told by Ha, fortifies his view that the broadcasts of Open Radio and other more powerful but not necessarily more influential stations—ranging from South Korea's Korean Broadcasting System to the U.S. government's Voice of America and the government-funded Radio Free Asia, set up as a "non-profit corporation"—are definitely heard and, in a sense, heeded inside North Korea.

Whether they're having a very positive impact is another matter. Since many of the broadcasts touch upon the issue of North Korea's appalling record on human rights, the question is how much they can influence policy

---

[1] Ha Tae-keung recounted this story on several occasions, including a seminar on September 28, 2010, at the Seoul Foreign Correspondents' Club. The author attended the seminar on the day of the Workers' Party conference in Pyongyang at which Kim Jong-eun's third son was named vice-chairman of the party's military commission and a member of the party's central committee.

or practice when it comes to human rights abuses. Certainly North Korea in a number of forums, such as meetings of the United Nations Council on Human Rights in Geneva, has shown deep hostility to charges of a wide range of abuses, ranging from unspeakable forms of torture in prison camps to total denial of freedom of speech, freedom of the press, and freedom of religion for all its people. Despite loud public denials, North Korea may have responded to reports on human rights abuses with cosmetic shifts intended to somewhat improve the country's international image.

Beneath that level, however, in terms of the punishment inflicted on citizens suspected of the most heinous of crimes, defiance, or even expression of doubts about the rule of Kim Jong-il, and somewhat lesser offenses, such as theft of vital supplies and materials, it would be difficult to find evidence of any movement toward leniency. The emphasis to date appears to have been an occasional desire to improve appearances while perpetuating the abuses that have characterized North Korea's one-family rule since Kim Jong-il's father, Kim Il-sung, was named premier at the founding of the Democratic People's Republic of Korea (DPRK) in September 1948. (He assumed the title of president in 1972 and—since his death in July 1994—has remained "eternal president.")

Those with the deepest convictions of the influence of the media are likely to cite radio broadcasts as well as leaflets dropped from balloons lofted from sites just below the Demilitarized Zone between the two Koreas. Beyond those efforts at media penetration into North Korea are periodic articles in foreign newspapers and magazines, most of them based on interviews with defectors inside China or in South Korea, as well as books and other studies, notably those by David Hawk, author of *The Hidden Gulag: Exposing North Korea's Prison Camps: Prisoners' Testimonies and Satellite Photographs* (Washington, DC: U.S. Committee for Human Rights in North Korea, 2003), a detailed exposé of conditions at camps inside North Korea, and other works. The impact of any of these reports and studies is difficult if not impossible to ascertain.

The impression, however, is that radio broadcasts have the most immediate and enduring impact, partly because they recur daily, several hours a day. North Koreans are banned by law from listening to them and risk severe penalties if caught in the act. The problem of tuning in is all the more difficult since radios and televisions in North Korea are calibrated for listening or viewing only to North Korean stations. A certain technical skill is required to be able to dial stations in South Korea, China, or elsewhere. The penalties if caught are severe, and jamming is routine. Short-wave radios for listening to foreign broadcasts are available through contacts in China for the equivalent of a few dollars, but those found carrying or listening to them may be punished as traitors. Since there are few power outlets, and scant electrical current, radios and TVs rely on batteries that are often unavailable and too expensive for many people.

Occasionally, however, the media coverage has been so blood-curdling as to elicit a real response from North Korea. One of the most dramatic examples in recent years was videotape shot by a North Korean of executions on two successive days, March 1 and 2, 2005, in Hoeryong city, North Hamgyong Province near the Tumen River border with China in the far northeast of the country. The 12-minute videotape was initially aired by Japan Independent News Net (Jin-net, www.jin-net.co.jp) and then distributed by Life Funds for North Korean Refugees (LFNKR, www.northkoreanrefugees.com), a non-governmental organization (NGO) in Japan that also produced a book, *Are They Telling the Truth—Brutality Beyond Belief*, based on interviews with more than 200 defectors who had escaped to China. The videotape is significant not for revealing anything new, since defectors for years have been telling interviewers about public executions, but as the first documentary image of the actual event.[2]

LFNKR, which distributed copies of the tape with subtitles in English as well as Japanese, has described the contents in consummate detail. "In each case, a large crowd, probably numbering several thousand, watched as verdicts were read aloud," said the description. "The executions by firing squad were then carried out within minutes." In the first case, near a market in central Hoeryong, the chief judge of the province read out his decisions against 11 defendants, most of them charged with "illegal border crossing" and "human trafficking," of whom two were sentenced to death, two received life sentences, and the remaining seven between 10- and 15-years hard labor. In the second trial, in another district of Hoeryong city 10 kilometers to the west near a railroad station, two people were sentenced on the same charges, one to death, the other to 10 years in prison.

---

[2] International Group of Human Rights Volunteers. *Are They Telling the Truth: Is North Korea Practicing Brutality Beyond Belief* (Tokyo: Life Funds for North Korean Refugees, 2004). PDF e-book. Available at http://www.northkoreanrefugees.com.

The LFNKR site describes the procedure with an accuracy corroborated in interviews that the author has had in China across the Tumen River border in the town of Tumen and also in Yanji, capital of the Yanbian Korean Autonomous County and the major center for sub rosa activities on behalf of refugees who have escaped to China. "Defectors from North Korea tell us that when open trials or public executions are scheduled, the people are mobilized by the organizations to which they belong," according to the LFNKR website. "Sometimes, children attend, being led by teachers. Announcement bills are posted throughout the city, and loudspeaker cars drive around announcing the events. All inhabitants are expected to attend the events, although absentees are allegedly not punished."[3]

After the tape was played on television stations in Japan, and to a much lesser extent elsewhere, North Korean authorities conducted a thorough investigation to discover who had shot it and smuggled it into China, but were not able to find the miscreant. "North Korea is not so powerful," according to Kim Sang-hun, chairperson of the North Korea Human Rights Database Center in Seoul. "They were not able to pinpoint anyone." Kim, who said that he knows the person who shot the tape, and Ha Tae-keung are convinced the number of public executions decreased as a result of media publicity surrounding this and other reports. Also North Korean authorities may have decided to conduct executions further from the border to keep incriminating tapes from getting out so easily via would-be defectors and others crossing the border, some not to escape but to do barter trade and see relatives and contacts.

Yet another dividend of such exposés, in the view of Kim Sang-hun, who worked for 20 years for the United Nations' World Food Programme before dedicating himself to efforts on behalf of defectors, is that North Korea has consolidated its gulag system, closing down some of the infamous camps where the worst cases of torture and executions occurred. "The number of PPC [political prison camps] eventually increased to a maximum of eleven at one time," Kim wrote at the conclusion of a lengthy report on the camps. It is now believed that North Korean leaders closed at least three camps near the Chinese border "in response to protests from international human rights NGOs as well as intensified demand for an international human rights inspection team to be fielded in North Korea." After another

---

[3] Ibid.

camp near Pyongyang "was closed for fear of detection by the international community," said Kim, his organization confirmed that prisoners in all camps that were shut down were relocated or released. "It is understood that the shutdown and relocation of some PPC in the 1990s were North Korea's reaction to increasing international concern."

Nonetheless, Kim Sang-hun went on, "North Korea continues to this day to operate five maximum-security camps and one high-security camp." People know a person is detained when he or she "is found to have suddenly gone missing." Kim through his contacts in North Korea and among defectors in South Korea and China concluded that the five remaining camps hold approximately 200,000 prisoners, the same number as when there were 11 camps, a constantly fluctuating mass in which the dead and dying are regularly replaced by new inmates. The only difference, said Kim, is that "changes in social attitudes of North Koreans have increased the cases of confirmation through tips by SSA [state security agency] officers that the missing person was, in fact, sent to the PPC."[4]

Timothy Peters, whose Helping Hands Korea helps brings defectors to South Korea from China, sees any sense of real change as misleading. "Media attention may have caused North Korea to change locations of its prison camps," he said, "but relocating camps is not the same as improving human rights!"[5]

Foreign media reports are not the only reason why attitudes are evolving, however superficially. The North Korean leadership struggle, in which Kim Jong-il, recovering from a stroke that he suffered in August 2008, battling diabetes, on dialysis under the supervision of Chinese doctors and specialists from elsewhere, has been distracted from day-to-day governance. North Korea's endemic economic problems, exacerbated by an ill-considered attempt at currency reform in late 2009 and early 2010, have steadily worsened. Some analysts believe the problem of feeding the populace is approaching the level of the mid-1990s when the country suffered from severe famine in which as many as two million people died from starvation, malnutrition and disease. This time, however, at least some of North Korea's 24 million people are assumed to be better informed, if only slightly, as a result of media reports.

---

[4] Kim Sang-hun, interview, Seoul, August 2010.
[5] Tim Peters, interview, Seoul, 2010.

That factor, said Ha Tae-keung, has impelled the government to act perhaps more quickly than before on pressing issues. As a prime example, he cited the realization of Kim Jong-il that the reform in which the currency was revalued by lopping off two zeroes from the exchange rate, had been a failure. "Kim Jong-il did not watch North Korean TV," he said. "Instead, he pays attention to the South Korean media. We reported a lot about currency reform." One result was that Pak Nam-gi, the finance and planning chief of the ruling Workers' Party, was reported to have been executed in March 2010.[6]

The reports of Pak's demise were originally carried on the websites of Ha's Open Radio and North Korea Reform Radio, another Seoul-based station, as well as those of two South Korean NGOs with contacts in North Korea, Daily NK and Good Friends, neither of which broadcast into the North but are a regular source for North Korea-watchers. Kim Seung-chul, speaking for North Korea Reform Radio in an interview with *The Korea Times*, summarized his view of the impact. The Pyongyang regime "was almost forced to allow the reopening of markets in the wake of the failed currency reform," he said. "They realized that the people are not what they used to be.... Now these people know how the outside world works as they can access uncensored information by secretly tuning into radio programs or reading leaflets."[7]

Websites of these and other organizations disseminate news in English and Korean concerning what their contacts tell them is going on inside North Korea, providing windows into the North that did not exist until several years ago. This kind of reporting is at the forefront of a high-tech information explosion whose impact is not exactly clear. On the one hand, it is far easier now than it was five or ten years ago to broadcast into North Korea and, on the other hand, mobile telephones arm contacts with the means to get through to the South at the risk of being caught and punished severely. Many of the contacts along the Yalu and Tumen River borders with China, use Chinese mobile phone services. A few are deeper inside North Korea; some in southern regions not far from the Demilitarized Zone rely on South Korean services. The information they provide is not uniformly reliable, and reports may be at variance with one another. Still, those North Koreans who dare to tune in know much more about South Korea, the region, and the world, and foreign audiences know much more about North

---

[6] Ha Tae-keung, interview, Seoul, August 2010.
[7] *The Korea Times*, June 1, 2010.

Korea, than was imaginable before 2005 or 2006 when small stations in Seoul began regular broadcasts into the North.

Open Radio competes with three other Seoul-based stations, Radio Free Chosun, North Korea Reform Radio, and Free North Korea Radio. They are all quite different. Open Radio broadcasts four hours daily into North Korea, two hours on shortwave, one on AM and the fourth on FM; Radio Free Chosun broadcasts three hours each day, all shortwave; North Korea Reform Radio broadcasts one hour daily, shortwave; Free North Korea Radio at one stage was broadcasting five hours a day on three shortwave bands. Open Radio offers soap operas and a fictionalized serial that makes much of a potential rivalry between Kim Jong-eun, Kim Jong-il's third son and heir presumptive, and Jang Song-thaek, Kim Jong-il's brother-in-law, who may have visions of ruling as a regent, a power behind the throne, after Kim Jong-il leaves the scene.

Radio Free Chosun, a cooperative operated by activists and defectors, and North Korea Reform Radio and Free North Korea Radio, owned by defectors, are both regarded as more fiercely political than Open Radio. "Stations such as Free North Korea Radio, Radio Free Chosun, Open Radio North Korea and North Korea Reform Radio are the best way to open a breach in Pyongyang's mind-destroying propaganda," said Reporters Without Borders in a ceremony in November 2009 at which Kim Seong-min, founder of Free North Korea Radio, who defected to the South in 1996, won a prize from the anticommunist Taiwan Foundation for Democracy for "courageous defiance" of the North Korean regime.[8]

These stations, distinctive and determined as they are, face different and stronger competition from two U.S. government networks, Voice of America (VOA) and Radio Free Asia (RFA). These focus on North Korea with mounting intensity as a dividend of the North Korea Human Rights Act passed by Congress in 2004 that authorized funding for more programming and more people, mostly Koreans. VOA, broadcasting since 1942, had been slow to penetrate the obstacles to reaching listeners in North Korea. Its Korean service expanded by a half hour from three hours a day in 2006 and in 2007 to five hours a day on four bands, two shortwave and two medium wave. The number of Koreans on the payroll rose from 20 to

---

[8] Reporters Without Borders, "Call for more international support for exile radios after station director wins award," November 6, 2009, http://en.rsf.org/north-korea-call-for-more-international-06-11-2009,34926.

40 in Washington and several more in a newly opened office in Seoul next to the bureau of the American correspondent responsible for filing for VOA in English.[9] In its broadcasts for North Korean listeners, VOA hewed to the factual, dry analytical tone of its reporting in other languages, notably English, for a global audience outside the United States, where it is banned from broadcasting by congressional fiat.

Radio Free Asia, having begun broadcasting to North Korea in 1997, increased broadcast time to five hours a day on eight bands, four shortwave and four medium wave, and opened a bureau in Seoul almost in tandem with VOA. From the outset, however, RFA has differed from VOA in the sometimes outraged tone of its reports and commentary, often picking upon scandals, human rights violations, and other wrongdoing in a muckraking style. The service signaled its crusading approach in a statement of purpose that noted that Freedom House in New York "ranks North Korea dead last in its annual press freedom index and gives it the lowest possible rating for both political rights and civil liberties and Reporters Without Borders ranked the dictatorship 174 out of 175 in their 2009 Media Freedom Index." The statement cited a U.S. State Department human rights report describing North Korea as "a dictatorship under the absolute rule of Kim Jong-il" where "members of the security forces have committed numerous serious human rights abuses" including "extrajudicial killings, disappearances and arbitrary detention" while political prisoners were consigned to "harsh and life-threatening prison conditions" that included "forced abortions and infanticide."[10]

That said, RFA aspires to "offer a faint glimmer of the outside world that is growing somewhat brighter as more citizens take the risk to reset their fixed radios to stations beyond the DPRK," despite the omnipresent fear of 10-year jail terms said to be "common for accessing foreign media." RFA is especially proud of a six-part series produced in 2009 exposing the plight of North Korean refugees in China and "the harsh conditions facing child defectors and the human trafficking of North Korean girls and women." RFA received a David Burke Distinguished Journalism Award from the Broadcasting Board of Governors for a series produced in 2006 in which a

---

[9] VOA, "Voice of America to Expand Korean Service," press release, December 6, 2006; *Kyodo*, "FOCUS: Voice of America boosting programs targeted at N. Korea," Washington, November 30, 2009.
[10] Radio Free Asia, "Radio Free Asia's Korea Operations," March 2010.

defector working for RFA returned to China and "interviewed 14 North Korean women who had fallen victim to criminal gangs of traffickers on both sides of the border." The station had no doubt someone in a high position was listening. Kim Jong-il, it alleged, had "fired a number of officials after RFA exclusively reported on corruption involving the North Korean agency that handles humanitarian aid and South Korean investment in the North," though how RFA knew that Kim had done the firing was not revealed.[11]

Operators of the small stations take pride in their independence and their feisty desire to get through to their brethren in the North on their own terms rather than as mouthpieces for large government-owned organizations. They too, however, depend on American funding for survival. The prime conduits have been the State Department and the National Endowment for Democracy (NED). The endowment calls itself a "private non-profit foundation" but is "funded largely by the U.S. Congress," was "created jointly by Republicans and Democrats," and is "governed by a board balanced between both parties" while enjoying "congressional support across the political spectrum."[12] NED makes a point of transparency, listing precisely how much it gives each year to each beneficiary. The figures for 2009 included $150,000 each for Free North Korea Radio, Open Radio for North Korea, and Radio Free Chosun and $175,000 for NK Communications to produce North Korea Reform Radio.[13]

In keeping with its "belief that freedom is a universal human aspiration that can be realized through the development of democratic institutions, procedures, and values," NED definitely has a monopoly on encouraging the non-governmental flow of information into North Korea. Daily NK received $145,000; Kim Sang-hun's Database Center, $80,000; and *Imjingang* Publishing, publisher of Imjingang, a quarterly journal named for the Imjin River that flows from North to South Korea to the Yellow Sea, garnered $85,000 "for North Korean citizens to share information and opinions about North Korean culture, economics, politics, and other developments."[14] The magazine features reports by North Koreans who have

---

[11] Ibid.

[12] National Endowment for Democracy, "About NED," www.ned.org.

[13] National Endowment for Democracy, "Active North Korea-Related Projects," Washington, March 2010.

[14] Ibid. *Imjingang* broke off in 2009 from its former Japanese partner, *Rimjingang*, based in Osaka, which also publishes articles about North Korean issues. *Rimjingang* is not funded by NED.

smuggled themselves, and their material, out of the country. Given the funding for all these organizations, they're not going to bite the hands that are feeding them; most of them also get funding, not specifically listed but all told about $1 million a year, from the State Department. (Kim Sang-hun denies the CIA is pitching in. "Basically," he said, "the CIA is not interested in human rights in North Korea."[15])

How effective is the media blitzkrieg? For a grant of another $50,000, InterMedia Survey Institute, a research firm located near NED's offices in Washington, surveyed 250 refugees and "legal travelers" from North Korea in the Yanbian region between April 15 and August 31, 2009. Despite "expertise" drawn from former staffers of VOA and Radio Free Europe/Radio Liberty, another U.S. government network, the results were so vague as to raise doubts about the survey's validity. "This year's survey establishes that, even without strict media access selection criteria, North Korean refugees are listening to independent broadcasts inside North Korea," said its slickly packaged report, acknowledging the majority of respondents were from right across the Tumen River. "Starved for information," it went on, "North Koreans are not very discriminating content consumers and seem to have very little brand preference" while "likely to listen to whatever broadcast they can receive most clearly."[16]

One weakness of the survey lies in the use of phrases such as "had access to"—whether to a TV, a cassette with radio, or a simple radio or a cell phone was not clear. "Access" could mean sharing with a friend or neighbor or anywhere else beyond the purview of the law. The survey found what was well known, that "advanced technology is now much more common in North Korea than ever before," that "many North Koreans are now watching VCD and DVDs, including many from South Korea," and that "many defectors to China are able to keep in touch with those inside North Korea via cell phones."[17]

How many people actually are tuning in, for how long and how often, has never been certain despite extravagant claims. VOA in a press release said that "a U.S. private research agency estimates that 36 percent of North

---

[15] Kim Sang-hun, interview, Seoul, August 2010.
[16] Inter-Media, "International Broadcasting in North Korea: North Korea Refugee/Traveler Survey Report," Washington, April-August 2009, 5–6.
[17] Ibid., 4–5.

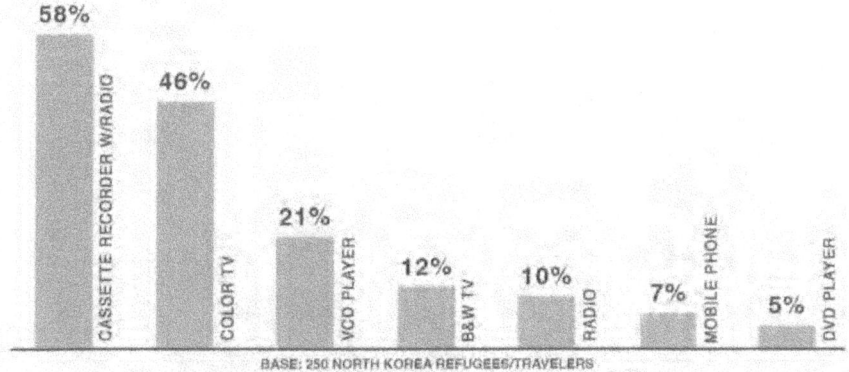

Figure 8.1: Media Access in North Korea

Inter-Media, "North Korean Refugee/Traveler Survey Report, April-August, 2009," 5. (The graphic does not reveal what percent of radios or TV sets pick up broadcasts from outside North Korea.)

Koreans listen to its programmes at least once a week," but did not name the agency or the basis for the estimate.[18] Marcus Noland of the Peterson Institute found that 19 percent of 1,300 North Koreans polled in China and 300 in South Korea wanted to go to the U.S. despite "lifelong unrelenting exposure to anti-U.S. propaganda" and surmised that was due to RFA and others "gradually penetrating North Korea."[19] There is, however, no way to verify this roseate analysis. Nor is it known exactly how or just where the respondents were selected, who interviewed them, and under what conditions. Kim Sang-hun, after years of meeting defectors, attributes desires to go to the United States to stories heard when they got out of North Korea about how it was "the richest country in the world." That poll, he said, showed "how blind and confused they are."[20]

Actually, the most listened-to "foreign" radio station in North Korea has long been an offshoot of the South Korean government, KBS, the Korean Broadcasting System. The station's "global" broadcasts have been targeting North Koreans as well as the large Korean-Chinese community in the Yanbian region of China's Jilin Province and Koreans living in Russia for more than 50 years. Its influence, however, receded after President Kim Dae-jung, propound-

---

[18] VOA, press release, December 6, 2006.
[19] Agence France Presse, April 30, 2009, reporting on survey released on April 29, 2009. RFA also cited Marcus Noland's report in "Radio Free Asia's Korea Operations," March 2010.
[20] Kim Sang-hun, interview, Seoul, August 2010.

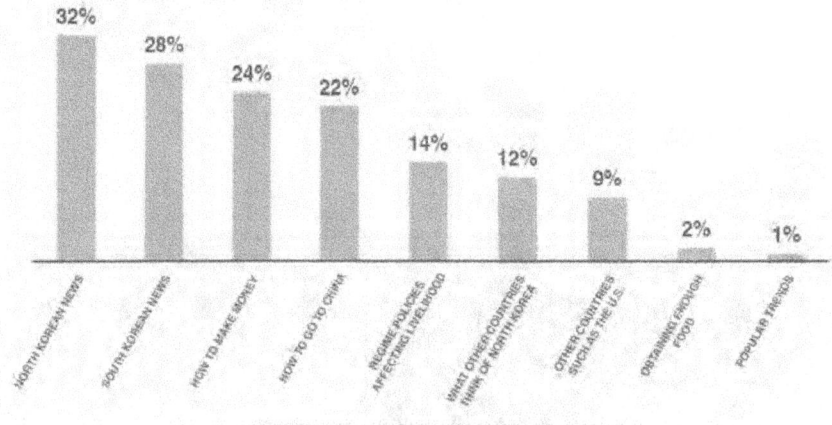

Figure 8.2: What Information Do You Expect to Obtain from International Radio?

Inter-Media, "North Korean Refugee/Traveler Survey Report, April–August, 2009," 7. (The graphic does not give actual numbers of listeners, how often they listened or to what stations.)

ing his Sunshine Policy of reconciliation, had KBS tone down its broadcasts after his inauguration in February 1998 to a five-year term as president. Some KBS broadcasts stopped altogether under the inter-Korean agreement reached between Kim Dae-jung and Kim Jong-il at their June 2000 summit in Pyongyang. Restraints on its broadcasts into North Korea were lifted after the sinking of the South Korean navy corvette *Cheonan* by a torpedo fired by a North Korean midget submarine on March 26, 2010. The allure of traditional Korean drama and popular songs, in addition to informational programs about development in booming South Korea, guarantee a clandestine audience. Defectors also report sharing CDs of popular programs from the South.

In any case, the real listenership of all these stations is debatable. The Ministry of Unification, in one of the surveys that defectors—most often from China or a Southeast Asian nation to which they make their way from China—complete after arriving in South Korea, has found the number of listeners to be quite small. The numbers reported by independent surveys include those who listened to a station briefly, once or twice. Some defectors are suspected, moreover, of seeing it to their advantage to exaggerate on whether or how often they heard foreign broadcasts. Defectors report having received in some cases enormous sums for "interviews," between 200,000 and 300,000 won, that is, nearly $200 to $300, and gifts of 100,000 won, $90, are common. "They know what kind of stories interest interviewers," said a South Korean source. How could they not know how to respond when the questions are as simplistic as, "Do you think your human rights were violated?" and, "Have you ever seen a public execution?" Claims of twenty percent listenership are "high," said one official; still, he believes they had "significant" influence. "Once a (potential) defector listens to a broadcast," he said, "he desires the world outside of North Korea."[21]

In attempting to broadcast to North Korea, however, South Korean stations face one obstacle that would seem improbable considering the North-South confrontation. They all must spend 90 percent of their funding simply on buying the rights to use viable frequencies from foreign companies. "That's because South Korea does not allow them to have shortwave frequencies," said the official. "They buy frequencies from China, Mongolia, and other nations. Regulation on these matters is less strict in China and Mongolia. Frequencies must be allocated. These stations are so small, and they don't have enough money. It costs between five billion and 10 billion won (nearly five million to 10 million dollars) to buy the frequencies." South Korean authorities are concerned about possible conflicts with major South Korean broadcasters. "There might be serious confusion," he said. "It is problematic. We have discussed with government agencies. Right now it is impossible." The government-run KBS carries broadcasts on medium-wave, shortwave, and AM frequencies into North Korea, he explained, and RFA is able to use a frequency previously allocated to KBS.[22]

Access to funding assures the biggest audiences tune in to RFA and VOA, for which the Broadcasting Board of Governors, an independent U.S. federal agency charged with all government-funded international broadcasting, allocated $8.5 million in the 2010 fiscal year and $7.8 million the year before. Those figures are many times the $1 million that the State Department provided in 2010 for South Korean "programs to promote media freedom in North Korea (including, but not limited to, broadcasting)."[23]

As a result, RFA and VOA probably claim 80 percent of the listeners in North Korea, meaning those who might listen as much as two or three time a week for 10 to 20 minutes each time. The duration of listening time is limited not just by the fear of discovery. Equally important, since virtually

---

[21] Interview with Ministry of Unification official, Seoul, August 2010. The official who gave the interview on a background basis asked to remain anonymous.
[22] Ibid.
[23] U.S. Embassy, Seoul, provided these figures, October 5, 2010, in response to the author's query.

all radios run on batteries in a country in which plug-in sockets for electricity are largely nonexistent, people must scrounge for batteries that are costly and hard to find. More often than not, they are smuggled in from China, along with cheap shortwave radios, and sold on the black markets that do business, sometimes quite openly, throughout the country.

The problems of the small stations, moreover, are compounded by allegations of financial misdeeds. Funding for Free North Korea Radio was suspended by both the State Department and NED in an accounting scandal that the station's defenders, including influential American activists, say resulted from misunderstandings and ill-founded gossip, and the station had to broadcast over the internet with a very simple home page. At the same time, the station faced threats made by unidentified individuals against the owner of the building where it had its office and studio.[24]

"There are many other scandals about the other three stations," said a South Korean official. Rumors persist that some bosses enriched themselves while dedicated defectors who worked for them got by on subsistence wages.[25]

There is no doubt, though, that all these stations have one special core listenership: North Korean monitors hanging on their every word. Pyongyang's Korean Central News Agency repeatedly denounces RFA and VOA in verbiage as flattering in a reverse manner from any rave reviews for a book or show. North Korean rhetoricians have come to view RFA with its exposé-type reporting as more odious than the bland VOA. Both, however, have been bestowed with the ultimate accolade, that of "reptile" media, a term not used to describe South Korean stations. After funds for RFA and VOA increased under the North Korea Human Rights Act of 2004, KCNA on January 2, 2008, reported "the U.S. intensified smear broadcasting" as "part of its vicious moves to tarnish the image of the DPRK in the international arena and pull down the socialist system in the DPRK centered on the popular masses." The article also charged "the U.S. has craftily worked hard to introduce transistor radios, CDs of unsavory contents, and other publications through various channels into the DPRK

---

[24] A State Department official and NED confirmed suspension of funding for Free North Korea Radio. A South Korean official, who did not want to be identified, reported the threats.

[25] A South Korean official cited the scandals. An anonymous source at a non-governmental organization cited other anomalies.

in a bid to cause ideological and political vacillation, disintegration, and degeneration among the people in the DPRK and social disorder."[26]

The Seoul-based stations also come in for their share of vituperation. After the inauguration of the conservative Lee Myung-bak as South Korea's president in February 2008, the North's Central Committee of the Democratic Front for the Reunification of the Fatherland blasted the South's "right-wing conservatives" for having "gathered riffraff to set up such smear broadcastings as 'broadcasting for the north,' 'missionary broadcasting for the north,' and 'broadcasting for reform in the north'" as "a shock brigade in the campaign against the DPRK." RFA and VOA, "speaking for the U.S. right-wing conservatives, are joining in," said the tirade, "instigating the south [sic] Korean conservatives to do so." And the rhetoric did not omit Japan, vowing to "never overlook such provocative smear broadcasting launched by the south Korean conservative ruling quarters and the U.S. and Japanese reactionaries to dare to defame the destiny of the DPRK."[27]

North Korean protests are welcomed by yet another potential source of information beyond North Korea's borders, that of defectors whose specialty is to send balloons over the North dropping leaflets printed on waterproof sheets of plastic with stories about the North's ruling Kim dynasty, Kim Jong-il's health, scandals among relatives, their luxurious lifestyle, human rights abuses, the North's true role in the Korean War, and other titillating tidbits. Lee Min-bok, a self-styled "agricultural expert" who claimed to have once been a member of the Science Academy of the DPRK, has led one of three groups launching the balloons. In October 2008, Lee—a defector who had been captured, imprisoned, released, and defected again—was pondering the balloons' impact and considering quitting the project when North Korea called for talks with South Korean officials at the truce village of Panmunjom to protest the balloon-casts. After the unification ministry asked Lee and other balloonists to halt the launches, he renewed his campaign with contributions from donors.[28]

---

[26] Korean Central News Agency, "U.S. Criminal Smear Campaign against DPRK Disclosed," Pyongyang, January 2, 2008.

[27] Korean Central News Agency, "Anti-DPRK Smear Broadcasting Campaign Accused," Pyongyang, March 16, 2008.

[28] Donald Kirk, "North Korea hits back at balloon activism from South," *Christian Science Monitor*, http://www.csmonitor.com, November 13, 2008; Kirk, "Will North Korea cut a nuclear deal before Obama arrives?" *Christian Science Monitor*, December 9, 2008.

Lee Min-bok "was reinvigorated," said Kim Sang-hun. "That angry protest from North Korea gave him fresh strength." A devout Christian who utters a fervent prayer every time he and a cohort let go the string by which they cling to each balloon, Lee described his campaign to me as "psychological warfare" for which he had to write new leaflets every week. "We explain the high standard of living in South Korea, and we bring religious messages," he said.

One rainy afternoon in late November 2008, when the wind was blowing south to north across the ruins of a temple that had been an interrogation center for North Koreans in mountainous Chorwon district, which had been bloodied in some of the Korean War's worst battles, Lee launched 10 balloons bearing 100,000 leaflets. Mingled with the leaflets were South Korean candy bar wrappers and batteries for short-wave radios. The wrappers were to confuse North Korean soldiers and police who might order time-wasting searches for the "traitors" receiving candy smuggled in from the South. The batteries were to enable people to tune in to South Korean broadcasts. Each balloon had an instrument that Lee calibrated on the basis of computerized readings of wind currents to fly a specific distance and direction before letting its load of leaflets flutter down to the target area. The seriousness of government pleas to stop the balloon-casts was belied by the presence of two genial men in sport clothes, either policemen or intelligence operatives, watching discreetly from an unmarked SUV across the parking lot. They said they were there "for safety." So anxious were they to carry out their task properly that they followed Lee's van into Seoul before waving farewells and disappearing.[29]

Balloon-casts, however, are only possible for half a year, generally from June through November, when favorable winds blow from south to north. And meteorological checks notwithstanding, most of the leaflets somehow land fairly near the demilitarized one, falling into the hands of North Korean soldiers rather than civilians. Few ordinary people see them, according to a South Korean official, and fewer still want to pick them up after having heard North Korean propaganda reports that they are actually poisonous to the touch. North Korean soldiers might also be susceptible to propaganda, however, after years of hardship and privation. North Korean authorities have to be sensitive to the impact on troops who might want to know more about the regime they are defending.[30]

---

[29] Donald Kirk, "A change of wind over North Korea," *Asia Times*, December 6, 2008. The author witnessed the balloon launch described in the article.

[30] A South Korean official offered this anonymous view of the impact of balloon-casts.

The real impact of the leaflet drops is if anything more difficult to assess than that of the radio programs. Anecdotal evidence has been quite haphazard. After he was picked up by Chinese police following his first escape from North Korea 1990 and returned to North Korea, Lee Min-bok encountered a prisoner in his cell in a detention center for defectors who had gone to China after reading a leaflet dropped by a balloon. The man had evidently picked up the leaflet just above the Demilitarized Zone. Lee said the prisoner had "walked hundreds of kilometers" before crossing into China, "where he was arrested and repatriated back to North Korea against his will." Kim Sang-hun noted that one defector, formerly "a high-ranking senior member" in the North, had told him he decided to defect "when he saw a cartoon on a leaflet from a balloon." The cartoon was quite graphic. It showed a woman carrying food on her head walking next to a Chinese holding a knife. The caption had him asking the woman, "Are you going to give me your food or your body?" to which the woman answered, "You can have my body."[31]

Lee Min-bok has another personal reason besides his balloon-casts for believing in media exposure. He ascribed his release in February 1991 after three months' detention to the impact of publicity surrounding reports by Amnesty International and others. "There was an internal instruction from Pyongyang, which I overheard from conversations among interrogators, that North Korea had recently told the international community that there are no political prisoners in North Korea," he said in an account for Kim Sang-hun. As a result, authorities were told, "Do not produce too many prisoners" and "keep the number of prisoners to a minimum by sending the less serious offenders to local civil groups for guidance and supervision." It was that word, on top of his previous record as "a recognized scientist and a devoted supporter of the party," he said, that got him his release after having "withstood beatings" while telling interrogators "my objective was scientific observation in the interest of the state." He defected again four months later, in June 1991, first to China, then a year later to Russia and finally, in May 1994, to the office of the UN High Commission for Refugees in Moscow, which got him to South Korea in 1995 through the International Committee of the Red Cross.[32]

---

[31] Kim Sang-hun, interview, Seoul, August 2010.
[32] Lee Min-bok, quoted by Kim Sang-hun, interview, August 2010.

Rajiv Narayan, in charge of investigations in Northeast Asia for Amnesty International in London, is guardedly hopeful despite terrible frustrations: "Most people we get to interview in South Korea or in China are from the border provinces in North Korea." Still, he said, "that is gradually changing" as a result of a certain freedom of movement engendered by "years of food crisis and increased awareness among North Koreans that to survive they have to depend on movement and the private markets." Another problem, however, is "there are so few senior officials from North Korea to interview or willing to testify so we rarely get a view/understanding into the working of the policy-making process." Along with "lack of access," said Narayan, "is the difficulty of actually cross-checking episodes of human rights violations." Sources are "never in North Korea but outside," and there are "rarely two sources to cross-check." And "on the rare occasions when we do get footage of human rights violations they lack further details such as where and when they took place, who were the victims, who were the perpetrators" and, above all, "is the footage credible?" Yes, he said, "I must admit gradually there is more information available, but the above questions on credible, verifiable information, especially in the area of human rights, remain."[33]

Kay Seok, the Korean researcher for Human Rights Watch, is not sure how much is changing. She doubts if many North Koreans have heard foreign broadcasts or, if they have, that they have had much impact. She believes most balloon leaflets fall into the hands of soldiers near the Demilitarized Zone. She views the record on imprisonment and torture as fluctuating, not improving. "North Korea in recent years has even increased punishment for defectors," she said. Nor does Seok see diplomatic pressure as successful. In an article for the Huffington Post, she said the UN Human Rights Council in Geneva in March 2010 had concluded its "universal periodic review," conducted every four years for each member country, of North Korea's human rights record. The North Korean ambassador, besieged for comment by other ambassadors, said only that he had "taken note" of the report, Seok wrote, but a North Korean diplomat stated that his government "categorically rejects" the mandate of the UN special rapporteur on human rights in North Korea as "a despicable, sinister back-door approach" and "a political plot" against his government. "International efforts to engage North

---

[33] Rajiv Narayan, e-mail message to author, August 3, 2010.

Korea on human rights have made strides in raising awareness and building pressure," said Seok, "but there is still a long way to go to achieve fundamental change."[34]

For all the isolated successes, by any standard the war waged by the media—mainly via broadcasts, websites, and leaflets—has had mixed results. "There's no doubt that attacking North Korea on the grounds of human rights violations has had an impact," said Kim Sang-hun, but only to compel authorities to cover up abuses, not to begin to eliminate them. As an example, he pointed to construction in Pyongyang about 20 years ago of two churches, one Protestant, the other Catholic. "These churches are empty except when foreign preachers come," he said. On those occasions about 150 people are given orientations on how to behave in a church service. If any of them seem to believe in the prayers they are repeating, they are admonished and, if they go on attempting to practice Christianity, face the same torture, banishment to a gulag, and possible execution as do those caught with Bibles and holding secret services.[35]

Tom Coyner, a business consultant with a long background in South Korea, believes that "most of the media comment on North Korean human rights" reflects "outside perspectives and indeed values sets." Much as North Koreans might dislike "curtailment of daily freedoms under their local cadre," Coyner wondered how many were "at all aware or concerned with the fundamental concept of 'human rights.'" Any attempt "to tell North Koreans that they lack basic human rights could be viewed as a frontal attack on the core values—mythical or real—of their society." For starters, "one would have to patiently explain just what are human rights and why most people in other nations demand them"— "a most perplexing or inflammatory exercise." Basically, Coyner distrusted "the relevance of what the Western media may be broadcasting vis-à-vis the daily concerns of most North Koreans."[36]

The anger of North Korean authorities over criticism on human rights, however, has convinced activists of the need for unremitting pressure. They are "highly sensitive to international media coverage," said Michael Breen, a Seoul-based writer and consultant who has visited North Korea a number

---

[34] Kay Seok, "Why We Need to Keep the Spotlight on North Korea," *Huffington Post*, March 2010.
[35] Kim Sang-hun, interview, Seoul, August 2010.
[36] Tom Coyner, e-mail message to author, August 4, 2010.

of times and met Kim Il-sung with a delegation of foreign journalists shortly before he died in July 1994. "Critical stories in the South Korean media caused problems for the rapprochement policy of Kim Dae-jung. Sometimes, North Koreans working on visits that were internally sensitive warned overseas counterparts that any media coverage prior to a visit would result in cancellation." Author of a book on Kim Jong-il, Breen believes pressure on human rights abuses has had a certain qualified success. "In the early 1990s when they anticipated imminent ties with the United States and, with it, visits by U.S. congressmen thumping the table about human rights, justice officials in Pyongyang reviewed the possibility of ending the death penalty," he said. "The purpose would be to have something over the U.S.," Breen noted, but Kim Il-sung's death intervened. In any case, there has been no other report of North Korea ever considering giving up executions.[37]

Norbert Vollertsen, a German doctor who spent 18 months in North Korea before his expulsion in early 2001 for revealing the ills of the medical system, credits media reports with having had some effect, albeit unproven, on the lives of those caught up in the gulag system. "Yes, I still think media works when it comes to get a picture about the bad situation in North Korea," said Vollertsen. "I learned from some North Korean refugees the situation in some gulags is improving because the North Koreans know about this watching media eye." In Pyongyang, "I was very often asked by high-ranking officials about the public view in Germany, about their picture in TV, newspapers, etc." For Vollertsen, the reason for such concern was clear: "They do not want to lose their face in the media world. They are very concerned about their dignity, their pride about Korean culture, 'real socialism,' etc. And their only luck so far is that there was not so much interest in tiny North Korea."[38]

---

[37] Michael Breen, e-mail message to author, August 5, 2010.
[38] Norbert Vollertsen, e-mail message to author, August 3, 2010.

Chapter 9

The "Faminist" State

by George Alan Hutchinson

Over the past two decades, the Democratic People's Republic of Korea (DPRK)—North Korea—has faltered at effectively feeding its population. This inefficacy was dramatically manifested during the 1990s when millions suffered and hundreds of thousands died during a protracted famine. The North Korean government refers stoically to the 1990s famine as the "Arduous March," and tends to rationalize its cause by placing primary blame on natural disasters.[1] While it is true that the country suffered due to seasonal flooding during the period—something not out of the ordinary considering the intense period of annual rainfall (known as *Chang-ma*) on the Korean Peninsula—events with far greater implications began unfolding in 1989 that would ultimately expose North Korea's fouled system of providing food to its population. The DPRK declared an end to the Arduous March in 2000 but food shortages have persisted. A cycle of events, strikingly similar to those which started in 1989, has begun to unfold since 2005, and nation appears to be, yet again, hurtling headlong into another disastrous famine. Both periods—one beginning in 1989 and the other in 2005—are characterized by sharp increases in international isolation, precarious succession politics, and overt primacy of the military.

Shaping of the 1990s Famine

For North Korea, the year 1989 marked an epochal plunge into the stark realities of the 1990s. Low on money and credit, the country was caught flat-footed when communism began collapsing that year. Many socialist countries, freed suddenly from the iron grip of the Soviet Union, sprinted toward market economies. Conversely, the DPRK stood still. Dumbfounded by the dramatic swirl of change, the country looked on as the

---

[1] See "DPR Korea FAQ," Official Webpage of The Democratic People's Republic of Korea, http://www.korea-dpr.com/forum/?page_id=39.

system of barter and subsidies it had customarily used to obtain food, fuel, and fertilizer slowly dissolved. As factories went idle, harvest yields declined, and people began to starve, North Korea rapidly slid into crisis. Then, on the heels of communism's collapse, Kim Il-sung died in 1994 and a prolonged succession of power ensued. Although all the mechanisms were in place for Kim Jong-il to take the dynastic reins immediately following his father's death, it took longer than three years for him to gain full authority as the DPRK's leader. It is during this fuzzy period of governance transition that the population may have suffered the most due to chronic food shortages. By the time he was fully positioned, Kim Jong-il had clearly identified the military—an entity with an enormous appetite for food and fuel—as his country's top priority for care and feeding. The *Songun* (military first) ideology officially recognized the needs of the military as the country's most pressing requirement. *Songun* created crass justification to allocate vast resources to the military while other sectors of the country were atrophying.

Shaping of North Korea's Second Famine beginning in 2005

Similar to the cycle that started in 1989, the period beginning in 2005 is characterized by increased international isolation, elevated status of the military, and the murkiness associated with North Korean political succession. However, unlike 1989, when the nation failed to adapt to a world shifting under its feet, it is North Korea that has systematically chosen to shift away from the world since 2005.

In an effort to stem the first famine, the United Nations (UN) World Food Program (WFP) had operated inside the DPRK since 1995, delivering food and attempting, to the extent it could, to ensure it was going where it was intended to go. Efforts by the WFP and other nongovernmental organizations (NGO) were pivotal in eventually making headway against the effects of the famine, and food assistance operations continued there. By 2005, as a result of negotiating, the WFP had increased its footprint, and several staff members were operating out of offices within the country to help monitor food delivery throughout the DPRK. Because of this sizable foreign presence, Pyongyang was suspicious and uncomfortable. Thus, in August 2005, with signs of a bumper harvest on the horizon, North Korea recognized an opportunity to be rid of the "intrusive" WFP and ordered the program to shut down. At the time, in addition to the assistance from the WFP, unconditional food aid had been streaming in from China and South Korea, virtually unmonitored. This gave the North added confidence in its decision to shut down the WFP, and the country reverted to its previously failed public distribution system. From this point on, the DPRK has operated within increasingly thin food supply margins, employing on-again, off-again negotiations with the broader international donor community as it deals with its chronic food shortages. As a result, the international community's fatigue and antipathy toward North Korea has grown.

Since 2005, the world has watched with a mixture of repugnance and bafflement as North Korea scrambles to feed its people, largely through generous international offerings, while it simultaneously pursues an aggressive and expensive agenda to develop nuclear weapons, ballistic missiles, and other asymmetric military capabilities. The North has systematically driven a wedge between itself and most of the international community through its nuclear tests, missile launches, and provocative use of its military. Sanction after sanction, through its own rogue behavior, the North has further isolated itself from the international community, the donor source for WFP food aid. As greater primacy is given to the military and speculation regarding the health of Kim Jong-il increases, large questions loom over how the country would handle another power succession. A cloud of uncertainty is accompanying widespread speculation that Kim is preparing to transfer power to his son. If true, the succession could prove to be intriguing, as it lacks the trappings of the well-orchestrated path previously created for Kim to succeed his father.

As this parallel cycle of events unfolds, North Korea continues to experience catastrophic floods. Particularly devastating floods occurred in 2006, 2007, and 2010.[2] But floods are not the primary cause of the country's food shortages. The nation's floods are highly predictable events that, due to poor policy and fruitless agronomic planning, have only served to exacerbate and call attention to the country's ongoing food shortages.

---

[2] See "North Korea hit by severe floods, state media reports," BBC News, Asia Pacific, http://www.bbc.co.uk/news/world-asia-pacific-10813197.

Pre-built Framework for Disaster—
Bad Agronomics and Big Debt

The WFP ascribes the following reasons for North Korea's food shortage plight: "[A] lack of arable land, poor soil management, insufficient water reservoirs to combat drought, shortages of fuel and fertilizer, outdated economic, transport, and information infrastructure, and a general vulnerability to natural disasters."[3] While this is a reasonable characterization, further clarification is needed. In actuality, as a percentage of its total land area, the North has a fair amount of arable land—about the same as the United Kingdom.[4] In fact, it has more arable land (hectares per person) than either South Korea or China.[5] Thus, more information is required to understand why the country is susceptible to shortages of food.

The process of confiscating privately owned land in North Korea began in 1946 with the Land Reform Act. From 1954–58, the government implemented a phased collectivization of land resulting in cooperative farms at the village level. Seeking to achieve greater output, the village cooperatives were merged to create a single collective made up of about 300 households at the Ri (district) administrative level. This created roughly 3,000 cooperative farms throughout the country. Farm machinery was required in order to operate these larger farms effectively. In turn, fuel and spare parts were needed for the machines to work effectively. To distribute the agricultural products being cultivated, a rationing system was introduced. This system, which began as early as 1946, eventually grew into the Public Distribution System (PDS) which allocated food on a gram-per-day, per-person basis according to occupation. Food collected from the cooperative farms went into the PDS, which did not apply to the farm workers. Rather, as part of the collective farm system, families living on the cooperatives were allotted about 100 square meters of land to use for their private cultivation

---

[3] See "Countries: Korea, Democratic People's Republic (DPRK), World Food Programme, http://www.wfp.org/countries/korea-democratic-peoples-republic-dprk.

[4] See "Agricultural Statistics," NationMaster.com, http://www.nationmaster.com/graph/agr_ara_lan_of_lan_are-agriculture-arable-land-of-area.

[5] See "Arable Land (Hectares per person)," Trading Economics, http://www.tradingeconomics.com/north-korea/arable-land-hectares-per-person-wb-data.html, http://www.tradingeconomics.com/south-korea/arable-land-hectares-per-person-wb-data.html, and http://www.tradingeconomics.com/china/arable-land-hectares-per-person-wb-data.html. For a similar point regarding North Korea's arable land, see John Feffer, "North Korea and the Politics of Famine Part 1: Failure in the Fields," *Asia Times Online*, September 22, 2006, http://www.atimes.com/atimes/Korea/HI22Dg01.html.

"kitchen gardens." Productivity on these private plots tended to be three to five times higher than on the farms, probably because farmers were motivated to care more for them, and frequently skimmed fertilizers and pesticides from the cooperatives for use on them.[6]

By the 1960s, North Korea wasn't satisfied with domestic yields so farmers were ordered to clear mountain slopes of trees in favor of planting corn. This was a temporary answer to increased grain production; but harvesting, transporting and distributing the corn required even more machines and fuel. Also, large-scale cultivation of corn helped deplete the soil of nutrients, rendering it infertile unless additional fertilizer was used. The most damaging aspect of this policy was that as the trees were cleared, the annual heavy rains invariably caused landslides that would wash away the crops and then blanket lowlands with silt and gravel.[7]

Approximately 75 percent of North Korea's total annual precipitation occurs during *Chang-ma*, the rainy season during July and August. Because of this compressed period of heavy rainfall, water had to be stored and then distributed to irrigate crops throughout the year. To reach all of the collective farms, the North had to construct 40,000 kilometers of canals along with thousands of reservoirs and pumping stations. An extensive irrigation network system such as this only works if it is maintained and has sufficient spares and energy input. Other essential elements required for ensuring acceptable grain yields include fertilizer and pesticides, the production of which is energy intensive.[8] Thus, for the North's energy-intensive agricultural system to be sustainable, it would need access to vital

---

[6] See Woon-Keun Kim, "The Agricultural Situation of North Korea," Food and Fertilizer Technology Center for the Asian and Pacific Region, September 1, 1999, http://www.agnet.org/library/eb/475/; Jaewoong Yoo, "Hunger in North Korea: a Challenge for Global Peace," The World Food Prize, http://www.worldfoodprize.org/documents/filelibrary/images/youth_programs/research_papers/2009_papers/CharterSchoolofDE_JYoo_EEAC1ECC35512.pdf; and "Starved of Rights: Human Rights and the Food Crisis in the Democratic People's Republic of Korea (North Korea)," Amnesty International, http://www.amnesty.org/en/library/asset/ASA24/003/2004/en/f5daaf5b-d645-11dd-ab95-a13b602c0642/asa240032004en.pdf.

[7] See Woon-Keun Kim, "The Agricultural Situation of North Korea," Hong Soon-jick, "Environmental Pollution in North Korea: Another South Korean Burden?," Institute for East Asian Studies, Summer 1999, http://www.ieas.or.kr/vol11_2/hongsoonjik.htm.

[8] See Woon-Keun Kim, "The Agricultural Situation of North Korea," and Jaewoong Yoo, "Hunger in North Korea," "(North Korean) Agriculture," Country Studies US, http://countrystudies.us/north-korea/49.htm.

resources—energy supplies, chemicals, fertilizers, pesticides, and spares. Despite the country's proclaimed adherence to the *juche* (self-reliance) ideology, it is doubtful it has ever had the capability of producing enough of these vital resources. This reality was kept out of view during the days of Cold War patronage of China and the Soviet Union.

Sensing the growing reality of its dependency, in the early 1970s, the DPRK attempted to diversify away from its Cold War patrons. It intended on boosting its economy through a program of heavy industrial modernization and made billions in U.S. dollars in purchases of capital goods from Japan and western European countries. By doing so, however, it drastically increased its trade deficit and went into debt. By 1980 North Korea became the first communist country to default on loans from free-market economies. Debts went unpaid and interest continued to mount. By the end of 1989, its total foreign debt was $6.78 billion with $3.13 billion owed to the Soviet Union, $900 million to China, and $530 million to Japan.[9]

1989—North Korea's Steep Decline Begins

The summer of 1989 witnessed North Korea briefly lifting its hermetic seal as 22,000 people from 177 countries poured into Pyongyang to attend the 13th World Festival of Youth and Students.[10] Held during "Anti–United States Month," the week-long festival's theme was apropos: "anti-imperialist solidarity, peace, and friendship." To prepare for the festivities, the country, already wracked with debt, mobilized vast labor resources and spared no expense. Numerous structures were built or refurbished and more than 1,000 Mercedes-Benz automobiles were imported to shuttle guests. Children were mobilized to help prepare for cultural shows and rallies. The North even offered free air travel to the event.[11] This degree of lavishness seemed contrary to North Korea's understanding of its own downward spiraling fiscal situation. Nevertheless, the nation's pride and reputation were on the line. Seoul had just hosted the 1988 Summer Olympics.

---

[9] See "Commanding Heights, North Korea," PBS, http://www.pbs.org/wgbh/commandingheights/lo/countries/kp/kp_overview.html, and "North Korea, Foreign Trade," Country-data.com, http://www.country-data.com/cgi-bin/query/r-9580.html.

[10] See "Festivals," World Federation of Democratic Youth, http://www.wfdy.org/festivals.

[11] See Nicholas D. Kristof, "North Korea Bids Hello to the World," *New York Times*, July 1, 1989, http://www.nytimes.com/1989/07/01/world/north-korea-bids-hello-to-the-world.html?scp=5&sq=north%20korea%20youth%20festival&st=nyt&pagewanted=1.

North Korea's previous demands to co-host the 1988 Olympics were rebuffed by South Korea and the International Olympic Committee. To make matters worse, the Soviet Union, China, and the entire eastern-European bloc refused to go along with Pyongyang's idea to boycott the games.[12] Thus, the Youth Festival provided an opportunity for the North to recover lost face and gain recognition that goes along with hosting a major international event. In the end, Pyongyang trumpeted the festival as a great success, and Kim Jong-il was credited with wisely leading the effort.[13] But success came with a price. According to its own records, North Korea spent almost $9 billion on the festival.[14] Perhaps the best metaphor of the nation's reckless extravagance was (and still is) the Ryu Gyong Hotel. At 105 stories tall the pyramid-shaped building is the most prominent fixture in Pyongyang, but it's not occupied. Construction began in 1987 and was intended to be complete by the start of the festival. All construction, however, stopped in 1992. Sixteen years later in 2008, an Egyptian company resumed construction.[15] A Web site boasts that the building will be finished by 2012, the 100th anniversary of the birth of Kim Il-sung.[16] Thus, from the echoes of the empty Ryu Gyong and the shadows cast by the debt incurred from the youth festival, a growing sense of uneasiness was descending in 1989.

In the same month as the youth festival, Seoul opened a trade office in Moscow.[17] Just weeks before, the People's Republic of China (PRC) was rocked by pro-democracy protests in Tiananmen Square. Meanwhile, Moscow was pulling its troops out of Afghanistan, signaling what would become the end of Soviet expansion and influence. Before the year's end, more psychologically

---

[12] See Michael Janofsky, "Olympics; Village Opens Amid Balloons and Armed Guards," *New York Times*, September 4, 1988, http://www.nytimes.com/1988/09/04/sports/olympics-village-opens-amid-balloons-and-armed-guards.html?scp=2&sq=north+korea+boycott+olympics+&st=nyt.

[13] See *Kim Jong Il: Brief History* (Pyongyang: Foreign Languages Publishing House, 1998), http://libweb.uoregon.edu/ec/e-asia/readb/103.pdf.

[14] See Sheryl WuDunn, "Now, North Korea Would Like to Reach Out," The World, *New York Times*, July 9, 1989, http://www.nytimes.com/1989/07/09/weekinreview/the-world-now-north-korea-would-like-to-reach-out.html.

[15] See David Durbach, "Egypt to Resurrect Pyongyang's Phantom Pyramid," *The Korea Times*, June 9, 2008, http://www.koreatimes.co.kr/www/news/opinon/2008/06/160_25545.html, and "North Korea's Ryugyong Hotel Wakes from its Coma," *Chicago Tribune*, from Reuters, July 18, 2008, http://www.chicagotribune.com/travel/la-trw-north-korea-ryugyong-hotel19-2008jul19,0,23210.story.

[16] See Ryugyong Hotel, North-Korea, http://ryugyonghotel.com/index.html.

[17] See "Relations with the Soviet Union," Country Studies US, http://countrystudies.us/south-korea/77.htm.

disturbing events would play out in front of Kim Il-sung and Kim Jong-il. Communism collapsed in Poland, Hungary, and Czechoslovakia. On November 9, East Germans were given sudden notice that they were free to travel to West Germany. Bulldozers began dismantling the Berlin Wall the following day.[18] Ultimately East and West Germany were reunified—on West German terms. The next month (December), the United States launched an assault on Panama and quickly captured its dictator, General Manuel Noriega, for delivery back to the United States to stand trial for cocaine trafficking, racketeering, and money laundering.[19] Finally, on Christmas Day, 1989, shortly after his communist government was overthrown, Romanian President Nicolae Ceausescu and his wife were executed by firing squad. Video showing their trial and execution were shown on television repeatedly throughout the world.[20] Undoubtedly, Kim Il-sung and Kim Jong-il were watching with discomfort as these events played out.

Money Talks: The Abandonment of North Korea

By 1990, communism was collapsing around the world. On June 4, Soviet President Mikhail Gorbachev met with South Korean President Roh Tae-woo in San Francisco. The historic meeting was the first time since the division of Korea after World War II that Soviet and South Korean heads of state met to speak with one another.[21] Reacting to the meeting, the DPRK reeled and rebuked it as "shameless" and "flunkyist."[22] Making matters worse for Pyongyang, the Soviets served notice that they would soon demand hard currency for their transactions.[23] Possibly even worse, by October, in a move that would pave the way toward eventually establishing diplomatic ties, South

---

[18] See "9 Nov: Berlin Wall Falls," BBC One-minute World News, http://news.bbc.co.uk/2/hi/7934661.stm.

[19] David Jolly, "French Court Sentences Noriega to 7 Years," *New York Times*, July 7, 2010, http://www.nytimes.com/2010/07/08/world/americas/08noriega.html?_r=1.

[20] William Horsley, "Romania's Bloody Revolution," BBC News, December 22, 1999, http://news.bbc.co.uk/2/hi/europe/574200.stm.

[21] Jim Mann, "Gorbachev, Roh Hold Historic Postwar Talks," *Los Angeles Times*, June 5, 1990, http://articles.latimes.com/1990-06-05/news/mn-488_1_south-korean-president.

[22] James Sterngold, "North Korea Faults Roh and Gorbachev," *New York Times*, June 8, 1990, http://www.nytimes.com/1990/06/08/world/north-korea-faults-roh-and-gorbachev.html?scp=6&sq=soviet+north+korea+relations&st=nyt.

[23] Steven R. Weisman, "Increasingly Isolated, North Korea Starts Talking," The World, *New York Times*, September 9, 1990, http://www.nytimes.com/1990/09/09/weekinreview/the-world-increasingly-isolated-north-korea-starts-talking.html?scp=1&sq=soviet+north+korea+demand+hard+currency&st=nyt.

Korea signed an agreement with China to exchange trade offices.[24] Then in 1992, South Korea and China formally established diplomatic relations, and China applied further economic pressure on North Korea by announcing that all trade beginning in 1993 would have to be paid for in cash.[25] In the early 1990s, Seoul and Pyongyang were on markedly divergent paths.

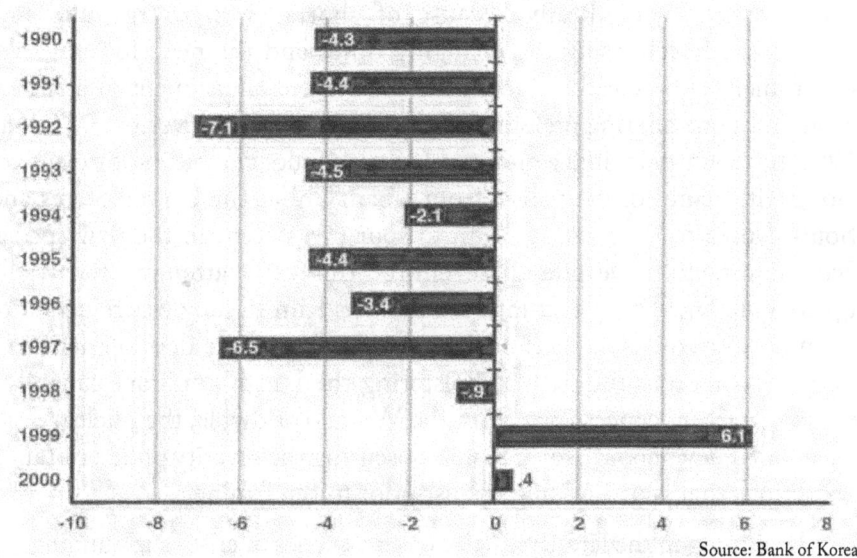

Source: Bank of Korea

Figure 9.1: North Korea's GDP Growth Rate, 1990–2000[26]

Nukes, Jimmy Carter, and the Death of Kim Il-sung

As China and the Soviet Union were forging new ties with South Korea, it appeared North Korea had lost the longtime support of its two major benefactors. Meanwhile, the DPRK's domestic food production was declining and the country was experiencing negative growth in gross domestic product (GDP).

---

[24] Nicholas D. Kristof, "Beijing and Seoul Sign Trade Accord," *New York Times*, October 21, 1990, http://www.nytimes.com/1990/10/21/world/beijing-and-seoul-sign-trade-accord.html?scp=3&sq=china+south+korea+relations+improved&st=nyt.

[25] Nicholas D. Kristof, "Cash Only, No Bartering, China Tells North Koreans," *New York Times*, December 30, 1992, http://www.nytimes.com/1992/12/30/world/cash-only-no-bartering-china-tells-north-koreans.html?scp=2&sq=china+hard+currency+north+korea&st=nyt.

[26] See "Economic Statistics System," Bank of Korea, http://ecos.bok.or.kr/EIndex_en.jsp.

By 1991, credible reports of widespread hunger in North Korea were beginning to surface. To deal with the apparent food shortages, Pyongyang reduced food rations through the PDS and launched a "let's eat two meals a day" campaign. The government was also encouraging citizens to forage for wild foods, such as roots, grasses, stalks, and tree bark.[27] There were claims that one-third of the nation's factories were closed down, with half of the rest operating sporadically because of shortages in energy and raw materials.[28] Recognizing the changing times and the need for cash, the government announced in December 1991 the establishment of a special economic zone offering preferential tax rates for foreign investors.[29] In May 1992, the country invited a group of 145 academics and business executives along with scores of journalists from Japan, China, the United States and South Korea to the Port of Najin to spur investment in the new special economic zone.[30] Despite these efforts, this early attempt at partially opening up failed to attract interest. Perhaps Kim Il-sung was reluctant to open up to trade. Nevertheless, Kim would choose the development of a nuclear weapon as the path to bolstering the North's military capability while extracting concessions from the West. Worldwide, the nuclear issue dominated news about North Korea, obscuring the severity of deteriorating conditions that were building up just prior to the famine.

Beginning in the late 1980s, there were a series of crises surrounding the possibility of the DPRK developing nuclear weapons. The first crisis occurred after North Korea joined the nuclear Nonproliferation Treaty (NPT) in 1985, but refused to sign an accompanying safeguards agreement allowing inspections by the International Atomic Energy Agency (IAEA).

---

[27] See "The Crumbling State of Health Care in North Korea," Amnesty International, http://www.amnesty.org/en/library/asset/ASA24/001/2010/en/13a097fc-4bda-4119-aae5-73e0dd446193/asa240012010en.pdf.

[28] Nicholas D. Kristof, "A Stalinist's Paradise In Korea Flounders," The World, *New York Times*, October 27, 1991, http://www.nytimes.com/1991/10/27/weekinreview/the-world-a-stalinist-s-paradise-in-korea-flounders.html?scp=4&sq=north+korea+food&st=nyt.

[29] Nicholas D. Kristof, "Hunger and Other Hardships Are Said to Deepen North Korean Discontent," *New York Times*, February 18, 1992, http://www.nytimes.com/1992/02/18/world/hunger-and-other-hardships-are-said-to-deepen-north-korean-discontent.html.

[30] David E. Sanger, "North Korea Asks Investors to Look Beyond Bleakness of Communist Decay," *New York Times*, May 21, 1992, http://www.nytimes.com/1992/05/21/world/north-korea-asks-investors-to-look-beyond-bleakness-of-communist-decay.html?scp=1&sq=food economy north korea&st=nyt&pagewanted=1.

The North violated two 18-month deadlines, but the crisis was averted in December 1991 when Pyongyang accepted a South Korean proposal to denuclearize the Korean Peninsula. As a reward, the United States suspended the annual U.S.–South Korean "Team Spirit" military exercise and arranged the first-ever meeting of high-ranking U.S. and North Korean officials in New York.

Having capitalized nicely, the DPRK continued to sharpen its brinkmanship strategy. The next crisis occurred when the IAEA wanted to inspect suspected nuclear facilities in Yongbyon. Wanting to avoid this, the North announced its withdrawal from the NPT in March 1993. A new round of negotiations ensued and when the United States provided it with assurances against the threat of using force, North Korea announced it would unilaterally "suspend" its withdrawal from the NPT. Then in 1994, it caused an uproar when it unloaded spent fuel from its reactor in Yongbyon, giving the country nuclear weapons-grade plutonium. As the United States reviewed war plans and options to punish the DPRK, former President Jimmy Carter traveled to the country in June 1994 and managed to strike a deal with Kim Il-sung. Apparently President Carter gave assurances to the North which in turn, gave Kim room to make vague promises to open nuclear facilities for inspection, pending high-level talks with Washington. The meeting, arguably aimed at saving face and averting war, eventually led to the Agreed Framework on October 21, 1994, whereby the United States and its allies would provide light-water reactors in addition to other forms of compensation.[31] Three weeks later, on July 8, 1994, at age 82, Kim Il-sung suffered a heart attack and died.[32]

Kim Jong-il's Ascendancy and the Preeminence of the Military

As throngs flocked to Pyongyang to mourn the death of Kim, reports were circulating that the North Korean government was dipping into its rice

---

[31] See Bong-Geun Jun, "North Korean Nuclear Crises: An End in Sight?" *Arms Control Association*, Arms Control Today, January/February 2006, http://www.armscontrol.org/act/2006_ 01-02/JAN FEB-NKCover.asp.

[32] David E. Sanger, "Kim Il Sung Dead at Age 82; Led North Korea 5 Decades; Was Near Talks With South," *New York Times*, July 9, 1994, http://www.nytimes.com/1994/07/09/world/kim-il-sung-dead-at-age-82-led-north-korea-5-decades-was-near-talks-with-south.html?scp=4&sq=death+kim+&st=nyt.

reserves to quell unrest and handle the hungry crowds. With a 1.1 million–member army, a dwindling supply of food, and a shrinking economic output, there was speculation as to whether Kim Jong-il would follow his father's path of *juche* or if he would follow liberalization, building upon previous efforts to set up a free trade zone to attract foreign companies near the city of Najin in the northeast.[33] When Kim Jong-il did not appear at the ceremony marking the end of the 100-day mourning period for his father, there was speculation that he was either suffering from health problems or was facing a power struggle.[34] Even after the declared three-year mourning period for Kim Il-sung was officially over, it would be several more months until the younger Kim would step into a clear position of leadership.[35]

Kim Jong-il had previously been appointed supreme commander of the North Korean People's Army (KPA) in 1991 and chairman of the National Defense Commission in 1993.[36] Despite this solid positioning, it wasn't until his election to the position of secretary general of the Korean Workers Party on October 8, 1997, that the Kim Jong-il era of leadership officially began. In a speech given at the time, he indicated that "No matter how difficult the economic situation is, strengthen the military first; labor later." This gave rise to the *Songun* ideology, where military power would be used to shore up the regime. The ideology was described in the *Nodong Sinmun* as "giving all priority to the military and the strengthening thereof," which would then enable "the might of the people's army to push forth with the revolution and other related endeavors."[37] *Songun* would be the means by which Kim Jong-il could guarantee the survival of his regime while increasing the capability of the military, all at the dire expense of the North Korean population writ large.

---

[33] See Andrew Pollack, "North Korea Said to Dip Into Rice Reserves to Bar Unrest," *New York Times*, July 18, 1994, http://www.nytimes.com/1994/07/18/world/north-korea-said-to-dip-into-rice-reserves-to-bar-unrest.html?scp=1&sq=north korea contaminated foreign&st=nyt&pagewanted=1.

[34] See "Absence in North Korea," *New York Times*, October 16, 1994, http://www.nytimes.com/1994/10/16/world/absence-in-north-korea.html?scp=5&sq=north+korea+kim+speculation&st=nyt.

[35] See "North Korea Ends Mourning for Kim Il Sung," CNN Interactive, July 8, 1997, http://www.cnn.com/WORLD/9707/08/north.korea/.

[36] See "North Korea: The Foundations for Military Strength—Update 1995," ch1, "A Post-Kim-Il-song North Korea," Federation of American Scientists, December 1995, http://www.fas.org/irp/dia/product/knfms95/1510-101_chp1.html.

[37] See "The Death of Kim Il-sung and Rule by Legacy," KBS World, http://world.kbs.co.kr/english/event/nkorea_nuclear/general_02d.htm.

The "Arduous March"

In secret meetings in Beijing in June 1995, the North brokered a deal to secure food aid from South Korea and Japan.[38] After one shipment each of rice from Japan (300,000 tons) and South Korea (150,000 tons), tensions erupted and the flow of aid stalled.[39] The DPRK then turned to the UN. By August 1995, the UN's Department of Humanitarian Affairs reported that North Korea was seeking aid to recover from floods which had caused $15 billion in damage.[40] Shortly thereafter, the WFP appealed for $8.8 million in aid and warned of the possibility of a widespread famine in the country.[41] Food shipments began in November 1995.[42] Early on, there were signs that the relief program would not operate unimpeded. In February 1996, apparently because of objections from within the military for seeking "outside help," North Korea indicated that it wanted relief agencies to cease appeals for relief.[43] However, the relief operation continued. By May 1996, the WFP reported that there were some cases of malnutrition, but they were not widespread. The report implied, however, that if food aid did not increase, malnutrition would become widespread.[44]

---

[38] See "North Korea Agrees To Get Rice From South," World News Briefs, *New York Times*, June 22, 1995, http://www.nytimes.com/1995/06/22/world/world-news-briefs-north-korea-agrees-to-get-rice-from-south.html?scp=5&sq=north+korea+aid+&st=nyt.

[39] See "Seoul Still Rules Out Aid for North Korea," *New York Times*, December 28, 1995, http://www.nytimes.com/1995/12/28/world/seoul-still-rules-out-aid-for-north-korea.html?scp=3&sq=150%2C000+tons+of+rice+korea&st=nyt.

[40] See "World News Briefs; Floods Strike 5 Million, North Korea Reports," *New York Times*, August 31, 1995, http://www.nytimes.com/1995/08/31/world/world-news-briefs-floods-strike-5-million-north-korea-reports.html?scp=5&sq=+food++north+korea&st=nyt.

[41] See "U.N. Says North Korea Faces Danger of Famine," *New York Times*, December 14, 1995, http://www.nytimes.com/1995/12/14/world/un-says-north-korea-faces-danger-of-famine.html?scp=1&sq=famine+%248.8+world+food+program+north+korea&st=nyt.

[42] See "U.N. Sends Rice To North Korea," *Washington Post*, November 24, 1995, http://pqasb.pqarchiver.com/washingtonpost/access/19469709.html?FMT=ABS&FMTS=ABS:FT&date=Nov+24%2C+1995&author=&pub=The+Washington+Post+(pre-1997+Fulltext)&edition=&startpage=A.34&desc=U.N.+Sends+Rice+To+North.Korea.

[43] See Nicholas D. Kristof, "North Korea Tells Groups To Halt Drive For Flood Aid," *New York Times*, February 8, 1996, http://www.nytimes.com/1996/02/08/world/north-korea-tells-groups-to-halt-drive-for-flood-aid.html?scp=3&sq=north+korea+famine+aid+&st=nyt.

[44] See Nicholas D. Kristof, "U.N. Says North Korea Will Face Famine as Early as This Summer," *New York Times*, May 14, 1996, http://www.nytimes.com/1996/05/14/world/un-says-north-korea-will-face-famine-as-early-as-this-summer.html?scp=14&sq=aid+north+korea+famine&st=nyt.

During food relief operations, Northern officials did not allow for the monitoring of food aid distribution and it was widely suspected that a good portion of the aid was being diverted to the military.[45] Relief officials acknowledged being unable to move freely about and foreign reporters were barred from entering the country.[46] A 1999 General Accounting Office report found that the WFP was "not able to monitor adequately what happens to food aid donated by the United States to North Korea." The report contended that 90 percent of North Korean institutions (including orphanages, hospitals, and schools) that had received food aid had not been visited by the WFP to observe distribution of food.[47]

Although food aid was getting into the country, it was not being equitably distributed. After operating within North Korea since 1995, Médecins Sans Frontières (MSF, or Doctors without Borders) decided to withdraw in September 1998. Through field teams, MSF attempted to supply medicine and training for workers at more than one thousand health centers and run 60 feeding centers for malnourished children, but eventually the organization became convinced that their aid was not reaching those in need.[48] Other aid groups and North Korean migrants in China reported that grain was being unequally directed to the elite in Pyongyang and others with political connections. Some of the aid was finding its way to the North's black markets. With the relief program not working as intended, the hungry developed coping mechanisms and survival strategies throughout the course of the famine. Some grew food in private gardens for re-sale on quasi-legal gray markets. In the northern provinces, believed to be most severely affected, many crossed the border into China looking for food and money. By 2000, relief groups were

---

[45] See "A Hint the North Korea Army Dines on Food Aid," *New York Times*, August 14, 1997, http://www.nytimes.com/1997/08/14/world/a-hint-the-north-korea-army-dines-on-food-aid.html?scp=6&sq=north+korea+famine+aid&st=nyt.

[46] Barbara Crossette, "Relief Teams Say North Korea Faces Vast Drought Emergency," *New York Times*, August 5, 1997, http://www.nytimes.com/1997/08/05/world/relief-teams-say-north-korea-faces-vast-drought-emergency.html?scp=14&sq=north+korea+famine+aid&st=nyt.

[47] Barbara Crossette, "U.S. Study Finds Lack of Control In U.N. Food Aid to North Korea," *New York Times*, October 12, 1999, http://www.nytimes.com/1999/10/12/world/us-study-finds-lack-of-control-in-un-food-aid-to-north-korea.html?scp=8&sq=north+korea+famine&st=nyt.

[48] See "The Humanitarian Situation and Refugees in North Korea," Médecins Sans Frontières, May 2, 2002, http://www.msf.org/msfinternational/invoke.cfm?objectid=9AC11A91-55C7-4192-BF04DDAB4F25D4F1&component=toolkit.article&method=full_html.

estimating that there were 100,000 to 200,000 North Koreans living illegally in China.[49]

By 1999, it appeared the DPRK was finally emerging from the worst of the famine. It was thought that as many as two to three million people died during the period, although this number has since been scaled down into the hundreds of thousands. It is estimated that due to the famine, more than 65 percent of North Korean children under five had stunted growth while more than 15 percent suffered acute malnutrition.[50] With food supplies accumulating and signs of relief in sight, the government officially declared the end of the "Arduous March" in October 2000 during events coinciding with the 55th anniversary of the Korean Workers Party. The October 3 edition of the *Nodong Simmun* read, "No people or nation in the history of mankind has endured a greater period of peril."[51]

2005—High-stepping Headlong into Crisis

In the same way that 1989 was the precipice from which North Korea would plunge into the first period of famine during the 1990s, 2005 marked the country's abrupt shift away from a path toward food security. Conditions had been improving, largely due to WFP relief operations in place since 1995, help from NGOs, and large bilateral donations from South Korea and China that began in 2000. It appeared the North had found a way to work with the international community to deal with its food shortages. However, the DPRK shifted its tactics and began seeking a way to continue receiving enough food aid while reducing the influence of the WFP.

No conditions had been attached to the aid streaming in from South Korea and China. And by all appearances, China was not monitoring its food assistance at all, and the South, operating under the "Sunshine" policy, had only a small monitoring system in place. South Korean officials conducted

---

[49] Elisabeth Rosenthal, "Famine in North Korea Creates Steady Human Flow Into China," *New York Times*, June 10, 2000, http://www.nytimes.com/2000/06/10/world/famine-in-north-korea-creates-steady-human-flow-into-china.html?scp=1&sq=north+korea+famine&st=nyt; and Nicholas D. Kristof, "U.N. Says North Korea Will Face Famine."

[50] Barbara Crossette, "Korean Famine Toll: More Than 2 Million," *New York Times*, August 20, 1999, http://www.nytimes.com/1999/08/20/world/korean-famine-toll-more-than-2-million.html?scp=5&sq=north korea famine&st=nyt&pagewanted=2.

[51] See "The Death of Kim Il-sung and Rule by Legacy," KBS World, http://world.kbs.co.kr/english/event/nkorea_nuclear/general_02d.htm.

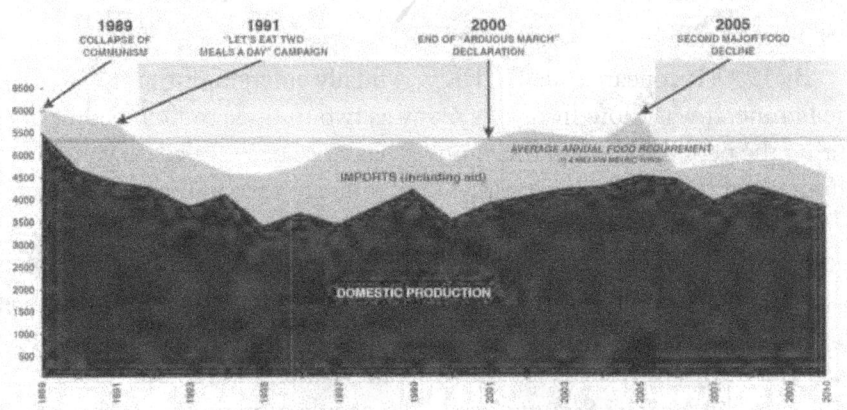

Figure 9.2: The Two Periods of Famine in North Korea[52]

only 20 sampling trips to monitor food distribution centers in 2005. Conversely, by North Korean standards, the WFP's presence was much more intrusive, with more than 40 expatriate staff in six offices conducting thousands of monitoring trips around the country each year.[53] The WFP had negotiated a greater ability to monitor food delivery since 1995, and as a result, monitoring visits had increased substantially. During 2004, the WFP visited 161 of the North's 203 counties to monitor food distribution. However, the DPRK began to clamp down on the WFP's reach. By the fall of that year, it began applying access restrictions to certain areas and refusing a larger number of requests for monitoring visits than it had in previous years.[54]

---

[52] Data for 1989 and 1990, and 2009 and 2010 import data obtained from USDA FAS Production, Supply and Distribution Online (http://www.fas.usda.gov/psdonline/); data for 1991–2001obtained from GAIN Report (Korea, Republic of, Grain and Feed, North Korea Agricultural Situation, 2005); annual food grain requirement is an estimate from the Korea Rural Economic Institute; 2009 production data is from South Korea's Unification Ministry, from "N. Korea Food Crisis to Worsen after Poor Harvest," AFP (Google News), February 9, 2010, http://www.google.com/hostednews/afp/article/ALeqM5g11qy4hB9KWa_GsDHIqbcabW3oCA; 2010 production data is from the Korea Rural Economic Institute: Kim So-Hyun, "North Korea opens port to China, Russia," Asia News Network, September 3, 2010, http://www.asianewsnet.net/news.php?id=10603&sec=2.
[53] See Mark E. Manyin, "U.S. Assistance to North Korea: Fact Sheet," Congressional Research Service, CRS Report for Congress, October 11, 2006, http://fpc.state.gov/documents/organization/76907.pdf.
[54] See "Korea, Democratic People's Republic of," U.S. Department of State, Bureau of Democracy, Human Rights, and Labor, February 28, 2005, http://www.state.gov/g/drl/rls/hrrpt/2004/41646.htm.

With relatively unmonitored food aid flowing in from China and South Korea and signs of an unexpected bumper harvest on the horizon, in August 2005 the DPRK advised that international humanitarian assistance would end by January 1, 2006. UN offices could stay open, but all expatriate staff would have to leave. Any future assistance would have to be "developmental" in nature and implemented entirely by North Korean nationals.[55] In addition to expelling the WFP staff, 12 European aid groups were ordered to leave, apparently due to unhappiness over the European Union's proposed resolution to criticize the North's human rights record.[56] Concurrent with the expulsion of Western aid that August, North Korea introduced bans on private sales of grain throughout the country, and in October, at the 60th anniversary of the Korean Workers Party, announced that the PDS would be restored in full.[57]

Perhaps realizing its miscalculation, within a few months, the North reestablished WFP aid, albeit at a level that was greatly scaled back from previous efforts. Contents of the new program were established by the WFP in February 2006. Its intent was to target children, young women, and the underemployed in 50 of the most vulnerable counties.[58] That May, it agreed to negotiated terms of the deal. The new, scaled down program would reach only 30 counties, unlike the previous program which had extended to more than 160. The number of WFP staff would also be greatly reduced, from more than 40 under the old program to only 10.[59]

As North Korea was fine-tuning a strategy to maintain just enough food supply while reducing dependency and down-sizing foreign presence, a disruptive event with disastrous economic effects occurred on September

---

[55] See "Report on U.S. Humanitarian Assistance to North Koreans," United States House of Representatives, Committee on Foreign Affairs, April 15, 2006, http://internationalrelations.house.gov/archives/109/4-06usaid.pdf.

[56] James Brooke, "By Order of North Korea, U.N. Halts Food Assistance There," *New York Times*, January 7, 2006, http://query.nytimes.com/gst/fullpage.html?res=9D00E0D81E30F934A35752C0A9609C8B63.

[57] See Andrei Lankov, "Pyongyang Strikes Back: North Korean Policies of 2002–8 and Attempts to Reverse 'De-Stalinization from Below,'" The National Bureau of Asian Research, July 2009, http://www.nautilus.org/publications/essays/napsnet/policy-forums-online/security2009-2010/09056Lankov.pdf.

[58] See "WFP Governing Body Approves North Korea Aid Plan," World Food Programme, February 23, 2006, http://www.wfp.org/news/news-release/wfp-governing-body-approves-north-korea-aid-plan.

[59] See Kirit Radia, "North Korea Food Aid Revived, Without U.S.," ABC News International, May 11, 2006, http://abcnews.go.com/International/story?id=1952301&page=2.

15, 2005. Citing the Patriot Act, the U.S. Department of Treasury designated Banco Delta Asia as a "primary money laundering concern."[60] For more than two decades the bank had handled the North's financial transactions. The allegations about the bank's relationship with the North and a warning that the bank could be excluded from future dealings with the U.S. financial system created immediate problems for Pyongyang. About $25 million in North Korean assets were frozen and other financial institutions began shedding ties with the DPRK, making it increasingly difficult for the country to execute international financial transactions.[61]

Floods, Missiles, and More Nukes

On July 4, 2006, North Korea launched seven ballistic missiles, including the long-range Taepodong-2.[62] In a countermove that appeared to take the North by surprise, South Korea suspended humanitarian aid shortly thereafter on July 14, effectively postponing a shipment of 500,000 tons of rice.[63] The next day, the UN Security Council unanimously adopted Resolution 1695 condemning the DPRK for the launches.[64] Almost as if to add to the punishment, within days after the UN Resolution, torrential rains swept through the North, causing landslides and destruction. Entire villages were swept away and thousands of homes were lost.[65] The flooding destroyed hundreds of bridges and thousands of acres of farmland, causing food prices to skyrocket and making food distribution "nearly

---

[60] See "Treasury Designates Banco Delta Asia as Primary Money Laundering Concern under USA Patriot Act," U.S. Department of the Treasury, September 15, 2005, http://www.ustreas.gov/press/releases/js2720.htm.

[61] See David Lague and Donald Greenlees, "Squeeze on Banco Delta Asia hit North Korea where it Hurt," *New York Times*, January 18, 2007, http://www.nytimes.com/2007/01/18/world/asia/18iht-north.4255039.html?pagewanted=1.

[62] See Steven A. Hildreth, "North Korean Ballistic Missile Threat to the United States," Congressional Research Service, CRS Report for Congress, October 18, 2006, http://fpc.state.gov/documents/organization/76930.pdf.

[63] Anthony Faiola, "S. Korea Suspends Food Aid to North," *Washington Post*, July 14, 2006, http://www.washingtonpost.com/wp-dyn/content/article/2006/07/13/AR2006071300751.html.

[64] See "Security Council Condemns Democratic People's Republic of Korea's Missile Launches, Unanimously Adopting Resolution 1695 (2006)," United Nations Security Council, July 15, 2006, http://www.un.org/News/Press/docs/2006/sc8778.doc.htm.

[65] See "'Hundreds Dead' in N Korea Floods," BBC News, July 21, 2006, http://news.bbc.co.uk/2/hi/asia-pacific/5202482.stm.

impossible."[66] Undeterred, on October 3, the Foreign Ministry announced that the country would conduct a test of a nuclear device.[67] Less than a week later, on October 9, North Korea became the eighth country to join the "club" of nuclear weapons states.[68] On October 14, the UN Security Council unanimously adopted UN Resolution 1718 condemning the nuclear test.[69] Humanitarian assistance was exempted from the resolution. While the DPRK showed off its military capabilities, it clearly did so at the expense of its people. In 2006, aid from China was dramatically decreased, with none coming from South Korea. Strapped for cash, hit hard by flooding, and increasingly isolated, things would not improve for the North in 2007.

For five days in August 2007, from the 7th to the 11th, North Korea experienced torrential rains resulting in massive destruction. The Agriculture Ministry issued an extensive report, claiming 11 percent of rice and corn fields in the country were either submerged, buried, or washed away. The level of detail in this and other official reports appeared to indicate desperation and a heightened outcry for help to the outside world.[70] Previously receptive to the North's requests through the "Sunshine" policy, politics were now trending in the opposite direction in South Korea. On August 20, a former Seoul mayor, Lee Myung-bak, won the presidential nomination of South Korea's Grand National Party, making him a clear front-runner to succeed the left-leaning President Roh Moo-hyun.[71] Weeks later in September, an event that underscored the limits of nuclear proliferation occurred when Israeli jets attacked and destroyed a facility in Syria that was believed to be a nuclear

---

[66] See "Floods Claim Huge Toll in North Korea, Group Says," *New York Times*, August 17, 2006, http://www.nytimes.com/2006/08/17/world/asia/17floods.html?_r=1&scp=9&sq=food+aid+north+korea&st=nyt.

[67] See "North Korea Pledges to Test Nuclear Bomb," CNN.com, October 4, 2006, http://www.cnn.com/2006/WORLD/asiapcf/10/03/nkorea.nuclear/index.html.

[68] See David E. Sanger, "North Koreans Say They Tested Nuclear Device," *New York Times*, October 9, 2006, http://www.nytimes.com/2006/10/09/world/asia/09korea.html.

[69] See "Security Council Condemns Nuclear Test by Democratic People's Republic of Korea, Unanimously Adopting Resolution 1718 (2006)," United Nations Security Council, October 14, 2006, http://www.un.org/News/Press/docs/2006/sc8853.doc.htm.

[70] See "Report: North Korea Loses 11 Percent of Crops in Floods," FoxNews.com, August 15, 2007, http://www.foxnews.com/story/0,2933,293310,00.html?sPage=fnc.world/northkorea.

[71] See "NAPSNet Daily Report Monday, August 20, 2007," 6; and "ROK Presidential Race," Nautilus Institute for Security and Sustainability, August 20, 2007, http://www.nautilus.org/mailing-lists/napsnet/dr/2007/20070820.html#item6.

construction project modeled after the North Korean Yongbyon facility. The reactor was being built with possible technical assistance from Pyongyang.[72] That December, Lee easily won the presidential election, restoring conservatives to power with pledges to get tougher on the DPRK and mend relations with the United States.[73] Further exacerbating matters, China implemented a series of grain export reduction measures that month as a reaction to public discontent about rising food prices. One measure eliminated a 13 percent tax rebate on grain exports. This policy change negatively affected food supply in the North and helped to drive up food prices.[74]

By 2008, with food and energy prices soaring throughout the world, there was mounting concern that the DPRK was on the verge of another famine. The WFP warned in April that a potential humanitarian crisis was approaching due to looming food shortages. North Korean food prices were rising rapidly—one third of a month's salary was required to buy a few days worth of rice.[75] There were other, more dire warnings. A *Newsweek* report noted that the margin between the minimum food requirements and existing supply had dwindled to 100,000 metric tons—enough to last approximately two weeks.[76] Responding to the developing crisis, the United States pledged in May to provide the North with 500,000 tons of food. The plan was to begin in June, with the WFP distributing 400,000 tons and the rest to be distributed by nongovernmental organizations. The new agreement was to allow for Korean-speaking aid workers, random monitoring inspections, and access to warehouses and other facilities by monitoring officials. It was expected that 65 monitors would be employed at five sub-offices in a similar construct to that which the WFP used when it operated in the DPRK until 2005.[77] This would be the largest one-year amount of food since 1999, when the United States

---

[72] See David E. Sanger and Mark Mazzetti, "Israel Struck Syrian Nuclear Project, Analysts Say," *New York Times*, October 14, 2007, http://www.nytimes.com/2007/10/14/washington/14weapons.html?hp.

[73] Choe Sang-Hun, "Lee Easily Wins Presidential Election in South Korea," *New York Times*, December 19, 2007, http://www.nytimes.com/2007/12/19/world/asia/19iht-korea.html.

[74] See Bill Powell, "The Next Great North Korean Famine," *Time*, May 6, 2008, http://www.time.com/time/world/article/0,8599,1737780-2,00.html.

[75] See "WFP Warns of Potential Humanitarian Food Crisis in DPRK Following Critically Low Harvest," World Food Programme, April 16, 2008, http://www.wfp.org/node/197.

[76] Stephan Haggard, "Asia's Other Crisis," *Newsweek*, May 17, 2008, http://www.newsweek.com/2008/05/17/asia-s-other-crisis.html.

[77] Glenn Kessler, "U.S. to Send N. Korea 500,000 Tons of Food Aid," May 17, 2008, *Washington Post*, http://www.washingtonpost.com/wp-dyn/content/article/2008/05/16/AR2008051601721.html.

provided close to 700,000 metric tons. As one might reasonably expect, the agreement eventually broke down due to different interpretations by the United States and North Koreans over implementation and shipments to the WFP were suspended in December 2008.[78] In March 2009, the DPRK informed the United States that it no longer wanted additional U.S. food assistance.[79]

Power Succession North Korean Style: The Bumpy Perpetuation of the Kim Dynasty

Kim Jong-il had apparently suffered a stroke sometime in mid-August 2008 and was noticeably absent at the September parade marking the 60th anniversary of the founding of the DPRK. Although his death did not appear imminent and there were no signs of unrest, the event triggered considerable concern. The question of who would take his place should he die or become incapacitated was being raised with great interest.[80] During Kim Jong-il's recovery period, his brother-in-law, Jang Song-taek, effectively ruled North Korea.[81] In April 2009, he was appointed as a National Defense Commission member during at the 12th Supreme People's Assembly (SPA).[82] Days before the assembly, Kim Jong-un, Kim Jong-il's youngest son, was appointed to a low-level post at the National Defense Commission.[83] By June 2009, South Korean newspapers were reporting that Kim Jong-il had named his youngest son as his successor. Apparently, Kim had instructed officials to pledge allegiance to his youngest son and North

---

[78] See Mark E. Manyin and Mary Beth Nikitin, "Foreign Assistance to North Korea," Congressional Research Service, March 12, 2010, http://fas.org/sgp/crs/row/R40095.pdf.

[79] See Kirit Radia, "North Korea Rejects US Food Aid, Kicks Out US NGOs," ABC News, March 17, 2009, http://blogs.abcnews.com/politicalradar/2009/03/north-korea-can.html.

[80] See Mark Mazzetti and Choe Sang-Hun, "Analysts Try to Envision North Korea in Transition," *New York Times*, September 11, 2008, http://query.nytimes.com/gst/fullpage.html?res=9D0CE2D7143 BF932A2575AC0A96E9C8B63&sec=&spon=&pagewanted=1.

[81] Justin McCurry, "Kim Jong-il 'Names Youngest Son' as North Korea's Next Leader," Guardian.co.uk, June 2, 2009, http://www.guardian.co.uk/world/2009/jun/02/north-korea-kim-jong-il.

[82] See "Jang Song Taek Becomes NDC Vice Chairman, Choe Yong Rim Cabinet Premier," North Korea Leadership Watch, July 6, 2010, http://nkleadershipwatch.wordpress.com/2010/06/07/jang-song-taek-becomes-ndc-vice-chairman-choe-yong-rim-cabinet-premier/.

[83] See "N. Korean Leader's Son Appointed to Post in Top Military Body," Yonhap News Agency, April 30, 2009, http://english.yonhapnews.co.kr/northkorea/2009/04/29/88/0401000000AEN2009042900 7600325F.html.

Koreans were learning a new song referring to Kim Jong-un as "the young leader."[84] An aggressive campaign was under way to pump up adulation for the younger Kim, designated at this point as the "brilliant comrade." Mysteriously, however, the campaign stopped abruptly in August 2009 without explanation. It was speculated that Kim Jong-il had recovered and was in good shape, and it was thus politically incorrect to mention the succession issue.[85]

In June 2010, Jang Song-taek was promoted to vice-chairman of the National Defense Commission at a session of the Supreme People's Assembly. His elevation positioned him to act in the capacity of an official guardian for Kim Jong-un, should Kim Jong-il suddenly die.[86] On June 26, the Korean Central News Agency announced that the Political Bureau of the Workers' Party of Korea (WPK) Central Committee would convene in early September 2010. "[A] conference of the WPK for electing its highest leading body reflecting the new requirements of the WPK." This was the first time in decades that the country's political elite had been called to attend a WPK convention. Analysts saw this as a move intended to pave the way for transition to Kim Jong-un. Kim Jong-il officially began to succeed his father by assuming a WPK title at a convention in 1980.[87]

Spitting Venom: The North Korean Military Lashes Out

In 2009, all references to the word "communism" were removed from the DPRK constitution and replaced with the word "*Songun*." By the end of 2009, indications were that the North Korean military had taken complete command of the nation's economy. With missile and weapons sales decreased because of UN sanctions, the army had taken up aggressive management of state trading companies, focusing on increased sales of natural resources such as coal, iron ore, and other minerals to China. Under the army's control of the mines, mineral

---

[84] Justin McCurry, "Kim Jong-il 'Names Youngest Son.'"
[85] See Andrei Lankov, "North Korea's Succession Gets Twisted," *Asia Times Online*, September 11, 2009, http://www.atimes.com/atimes/Korea/KI11Dg01.html.
[86] See "Kim Jong Il Shown on TV, His Relative Promoted," CBS News.com, June 7, 2010, http://www.cbsnews.com/stories/2010/06/07/world/main6556694.shtml.
[87] Jack Kim and Suh Kyung-min, "North Korea Party to Pick New Leadership," Reuters, June 26, 2010, http://www.reuters.com/article/idUSTRE65P0SI20100626.

exports to China increased and larger amounts of revenue began flowing into the military's operating budgets. The army had also deployed soldiers to all of the country's 3,000 cooperative farms to ensure workers were not shortchanging the military. The soldiers also monitored the tens of thousands of city dwellers brought to the farms to help with the fall harvest. The military's haul from the farms is quite substantial. In the northern areas where production and supplies are usually lean, the military takes roughly 25 percent of the total grain production. In other areas of the country, the military skims less, taking about five to seven percent.[88] Growing in power, influence, and perhaps in its confidence, the military was prepared to lash out beginning in 2009.

In April, North Korea launched a Taepodong-2 missile in a purported attempt to put a satellite into orbit. Despite the North's reports to the contrary, the United States Northern Command reported that the payload splashed into the Sea of Japan, essentially making the launch a non-success.[89] Following this, on May 25, the DPRK conducted a second underground nuclear test. The U.S. intelligence community assessed the yield as being approximately a few kilotons, making it larger than the first nuclear test in 2006, which was about one kiloton.[90] The UN Security Council unanimously adopted UN Resolution 1874, which condemned the test and toughened sanctions. Humanitarian assistance was exempted.[91] Bent on pushing the envelope, the North revisited the Northern Limit Line (NLL) dispute.

On March 26, 2010, a South Korean warship, the *Cheonan*, was on routine patrol in the Yellow Sea, not far from the disputed NLL. Without warning, the ship suddenly exploded, broke up and sank, killing 46 of the 104 sailors on board. South Korea assembled an international team that included Australia, Canada, Britain, and Sweden, and presented forensic evidence, which they said proved that a torpedo fired from a DPRK submarine caused the explosion. Included with the forensic evidence was

---

[88] Blaine Harden, "In North Korea, the Military Now Issues Economic Orders," *Washington Post*, November 3, 2009, http://www.washingtonpost.com/wp-dyn/content/article/2009/11/02/AR2009110203603.html?sid=ST2009110203677.

[89] See William J. Broad, "North Korean Missile Launch Was a Failure, Experts Say," *New York Times*, April 5, 2009, http://www.nytimes.com/2009/04/06/world/asia/06korea.html.

[90] See Deborah Charles and Tabassum Zakaria, "North Korea's May Nuclear Test Few Kilotons: U.S.," Reuters, June 15, 2009, http://www.reuters.com/article/idUSTRE55E5BA20090615.

[91] See "Security Council, Acting Unanimously, Condemns in Strongest Terms Democratic People's Republic of Korea Nuclear Test, Toughens Sanctions," United Nations Security Council, June 12, 2009, http://www.un.org/News/Press/docs/2009/sc9679.doc.htm.

part of a torpedo propeller with an apparent North Korean serial number.[92] South Korean President Lee Myung-bak announced that his country "would cut nearly all trade with North Korea, deny North Korean merchant ships use of South Korean sea lanes, and ask the UN Security Council to punish the North."[93] On July 9, the UN Security Council released a statement condemning the attack on the *Cheonan*.[94] While the tone of the statement is stern, it does not contain concrete punitive measures. The statement refrained from directly calling the North out as the perpetrator. Reacting to the statement, North Korean Ambassador Sin Son-ho told reporters the statement was a "diplomatic victory" for Pyongyang.[95]

Knee-jerk Reactions and Band-Aid Solutions: Signs of a Worsening Crisis Appear

In July 2009, the WFP reported that it had received little funding since 2008—only 15 percent of $500 million needed—and the DPRK had imposed new restrictions.[96] Having only received $75 million, the WFP was planning to provide food aid to just 57 of the 131 countries expecting assistance. A joint report from WFP and the UN Food and Agriculture Organization (FAO) warned that nine million people in North Korea could go hungry due to shortages.[97] In the meantime, state controls over the lives of North Koreans were becoming increasingly onerous.

The North was taking tougher than usual measures to crack down on markets, banning small-plot farms, chasing vendors from the streets, and requiring

---

[92] See: "The *Cheonan* (Ship)," Times Topics, *New York Times*, May 20, 2010, http://topics.nytimes.com/top/reference/timestopics/subjects/c/cheonan_ship/index.html.

[93] Choe Sang-Hun, "Korean Tensions Grow as South Curbs Trade to North," *New York Times*, May 23, 2010, http://www.nytimes.com/2010/05/24/world/asia/24korea.html.

[94] See "Security Council Condemns Attack on Republic of Korea Naval Ship '*Cheonan*,' Stresses Need to Prevent Further Attacks, Other Hostilities in Region," United Nations Security Council, July 9, 2010, http://www.un.org/News/Press/docs/2010/sc9975.doc.htm.

[95] See "UN Security Council Condemns '*Cheonan*' Sinking," VOANews.com, July 9, 2010, http://www1.voanews.com/english/news/UN-Council-Draft-Condemns-Sinking-of-South-Korean-Ship-98097064.html.

[96] See "World Food Program Reports Difficulties in North Korea," VOANews.com, July 1, 2009, http://www1.voanews.com/english/news/a-13-2009-07-01-voa10-68819107.html.

[97] See "North Korea Food Aid Slashed," Oneworld.net, July 7, 2009, http://us.oneworld.net/article/365130-lack-food-and-funds-north-korea.

goods to only be sold in state-owned stores.[98] In an apparent attempt by North Korea to reassert control over the economy and curb market activity, it issued a decree on November 30 to revalue banknotes at a rate of 100 to 1. In addition to the revaluation, the allowable amount of currency people could exchange was restricted. Cash kept on hand above that limit would be rendered worthless, the effect of which would effectively wipe out holder savings. Analysts speculated that the main reason for the revaluation was to rein in a newly emerging middle class that was deriving its growing wealth by trading in the markets.[99] The revaluation sparked public outrage and confusion was rampant. There were reports of inflation, increased food shortages, and violence. In one report, agents of the People's Safety Agency, a DPRK government entity conducting a "Fifty Day Battle" against illegal enterprises, were attacked as they investigated market activity in the city of Pyongsung, North Pyongan Province. In another report from the city of Chongjin, a steel worker killed a National Security Agency agent.[100] Due to the huge outcry, the government offered a rare public apology. In February 2010, Prime Minister Kim Yong-il stated, "I offer a sincere apology about the currency reform, as we pushed ahead with it without sufficient preparation and it caused a great pain to the people."[101] The following month, Pak Nam-gi, the official who oversaw the currency revaluation, was executed by firing squad.[102]

Adding to the rapidly deteriorating situation, South Korea's Unification Ministry reported that North Korea produced an estimated 4.11 million tons of grain in 2009, a five percent drop from the 4.3 million tons in 2008. The South's Rural Economic Institute forecasted the North's food grain output to reach 3.84 million tons in 2010, while the UN Food and Agriculture Organization estimated an output of 3.52 million tons. With

---

[98] Blaine Harden, "North Korea Tightening Its Restrictions on Markets, Food Aid," *Washington Post*, July 14, 2009, http://www.washingtonpost.com/wp-dyn/content/article/2009/07/13/AR2009071303293.html.

[99] See "North Korean Official 'Sacked' over Currency Chaos," BBC News, February 3, 2010, http://news.bbc.co.uk/2/hi/asia-pacific/8494978.stm.

[100] Richard Lloyd Parry, "Food Shortages and Violence Mount in North Korea as Utopian Dream Fails," *The Times*, February 4, 2010, http://www.timesonline.co.uk/tol/news/world/asia/article7013254.ece.

[101] Choe Sang-Hun, "N. Korea Said to Apologize Over Currency Changes," February 11, 2010, Asia Pacific, *New York Times*, February 11, 2010, http://www.nytimes.com/2010/02/12/world/asia/12korea.html.

[102] Richard Lloyd Parry, "North Korea executes top official Pak Nam Gi who oversaw currency evaluation," *The Times*, March 19, 2010, http//www.timesonline.co.uk/tol/news/world/asia/article7066576.ece.

annual demand being roughly 5.4 million tons, it is expected that the DPRK's food shortages will grow worse.[103] Worsened by apparent cold-weather damage to winter crops, North Korean authorities began faxing requests to South Korean food aid organizations in the spring of 2010, heightening concerns over its agricultural situation.[104] Running out of options, North Korea turned to China.

On May 3, 2010, Kim Jong-il made his first overseas trip since suffering a stroke in 2008, travelling to China by train.[105] It was thought that he was seeking extraordinary support from China—$10 billion in direct investment, one million tons of food, and 800,000 tons of oil.[106] Three days later at a luncheon with Chinese Premier Wen Jiabao, the Chinese government informed Kim that China would not provide extraordinary aid outside the framework of existing UN Security Council sanctions against Pyongyang.[107] Rebuffed, Kim cut the trip short and returned to Pyongyang. Also in May, the WFP reported that food aid to the North would run out at the end of June due to a drop in international donations.[108] The next month, a South Korean welfare organization with contacts in North Korea reported that Pyongyang had totally stopped supplying food rations to its citizens and private markets were again operating around the clock. The ruling Communist Party apparently issued a directive on May 26 advising work units and individuals to "fend for themselves."[109] As of that date markets are no longer forced to close at 6 or 7 p.m., rules restricting

---

[103] See Kim So-Hyun, "North Korea opens port to China, Russia," Asia News Network, September 3, 2010, http://www.asianewsnet.net/news.php?id=10603&sec=2; and "N. Korea Food Crisis to Worsen after Poor Harvest," AFP (Google News), February 9, 2010, http://www.google.com/hostednews/afp/article/ALeqM5g11qy4hB9KWa_GsDHIqbcabW3oCA.

[104] Hwang Ju Hee, "North Korea Makes Food Aid Request," *DailyNK*, May 7, 2010, http://www.dailynk.com/english/read.php?cataId=nk00100&num=6339.

[105] Jane Macartney, "North Korean Leader Kim Jong Il Travels to China," Times Online, May 3, 2010, http://www.timesonline.co.uk/tol/news/world/asia/article7114797.ece.

[106] Kim Se-jeong, "North Korea Begged China for Food Aid," *The Korea Times*, August 13, 2010, http://www.koreatimes.co.kr/www/news/nation/2010/08/116_71390.html.

[107] Chang Se-jeong and Ser Myo-ja, "Beijing's Rebuff Made Kim Cut China Trip Short," *Korea JoongAng Daily*, May 17, 2010, http://joongangdaily.joins.com/article/view.asp?aid=2920556.

[108] Bomi Lim, "North Korea's Food Aid Will Run Out Next Month, UN Agency Says," *Bloomberg Businessweek*, May 3, 2010, http://www.businessweek.com/news/2010-05-03/north-korea-s-food-aid-will-run-out-next-month-un-agency-says.html.

[109] See "Welfare Group Claims North Korea Has Halted Food Rations to Citizens," VOANews.com, June 14, 2010, http://www1.voanews.com/english/news/Welfare-Group-Claims-North-Korea-Has-Halted-Food-Rations-to-Citizens-96284153.html.

customers to women older than 40 have been dropped, and a ban on allowing certain goods to be sold has been lifted.[110]

For two decades, the Democratic People's Republic of Korea has faltered at providing food for its people. This inability was first manifested quite dramatically during the 1990s, when hundreds of thousands died as a result of famine. North Korea blamed natural disasters, primarily flooding, for the food shortages during the period. However, years of poor agronomic policy, crumbling infrastructure, a lack of strategic resources and the inability to generate currency had already created several extraordinarily vulnerabilities for the North. In 1989, the country was caught off guard as it entered a cycle marked by increased international isolation, a murky and protracted period of political succession, and a growing preeminence of the military. Since 2005, it has entered a similar cycle. As a result, the DPRK is heading into—if not already steeped in—a second, disastrous famine.

Fully recognizing that the only avenue to mitigate the effects of a second famine is through outside support, the North is once again scrambling ineffectively to negotiate on its terms. Pyongyang no longer has the ability to manipulate "Sunshine" concessions from South Korea and has thus lost the leverage it once enjoyed. Rather than focusing on generous aid packages that result in nothing of reciprocal value from North Korea, South Korean President Lee Myung-bak is considering other avenues. He has cut trade with the North and has openly called for a special "reunification tax."[111] The South Korean military has reportedly incorporated scenarios that envision occupying and stabilizing North Korea in a joint military exercise with the United States.[112] Pyongyang's negotiating tactics are being further complicated as aid for the DPRK continues to dry up due to donor nations' growing weariness of the country's on-again, off-again antics, and as the need to increase aid for other disaster-stricken countries, such as Pakistan, increases. Even China appears reluctant to commit to offering much support.

---

[110] See: "Fearing Famine, N. Korea Drops Private-Market Limits," *Columbus Dispatch*, June 19, 2010, http://www.dispatch.com/live/content/national_world/stories/2010/06/19/fearing-famine-n--korea-drops-private-market-limits.html?sid=101.

[111] Bomi Lim and Shinhye Kang, "South Korea Calls for Unity Tax as North Slams Drills," Bloomberg, August 15, 2010, http://www.bloomberg.com/news/2010-08-15/lee-says-south-korea-may-need-extra-tax-to-pay-for-eventual-reunification.html.

[112] See "S. Korea Military Drill Envisions 'Occupying N. Korea,'" Breitbart (AFP), August 24, 2010. http://www.breitbart.com/article.php?id=CNG.60d0175d237b195337baaf43871770ad.491.

Despite its reliance on other countries for support, North Korea continues to defy the international community with its expensive pursuit of nuclear weapons and ballistic missiles, along with its demonstrated willingness to lash out with its military. As a result, it grows increasingly isolated and its options become further limited. Should Kim Jong-il die in the near future and a murky, protracted period of political transition ensue, the effects will be even more dramatic.

It is possible that Pyongyang will work an eleventh-hour deal to increase food aid. However, even if it does, it may be too late, as the wheels of famine have already been put into motion. In the meantime, signs of growing social unrest are evident and Pyongyang appears to be operating in an erratic crisis management mode marked by drastic pendulum swings in policy. Should events play out predictably, the nation will attempt to sustain the military and the Pyongyang elite with existing supplies of food as it negotiates haphazardly for aid for the rest of its people. In the meantime, the government may continue to adjust rations and experiment with radical changes to market and currency policies as it strives to manage its affairs through the second famine. Those poorly positioned or not adequately affiliated will unfairly suffer and many in the outlying areas, including scores of children, will tragically die. The question will be whether North Korea will be able to effectively manage its neighbors and the rest of the international community in time to avoid the full, disastrous brunt of its second great famine.

Symposium Participants

Lieutenant General Raymond P. Ayres Jr., USMC (Retired)

Lieutenant General Raymond P. Ayres Jr., USMC (Retired), served as the Assistant Chief of Staff, Combined/Joint-5, United Nations Command, Combined Forces Command, United States Forces Korea, and as the Commander, U. S. Marine Corps Forces Korea before his retirement in October 2002. A graduate of Iona College, the Naval War College, and Salve Regina College, he received his Marine Corps commission in August 1966 after completing Officer Candidate School. Service with 2d Battalion, 3d Marines in the Republic of Vietnam followed after the Basic School. He later completed Amphibious Warfare School and Marine Corps Command and Staff College. He served as Deputy Commanding General, II Marine Expeditionary Force, Camp Lejeune, North Carolina; Commander, Joint Task Force 160, Guantanamo Bay, Cuba, in support of Operation Sea Signal; and Commanding General, 3d Marine Division, Okinawa, Japan.

Bruce E. Bechtol Jr.

Bruce E. Bechtol Jr., an associate professor of political science at Angelo State University, is a fellow at the Institute for Corean-American Studies and sits on the boards of directors of the International Council on Korean Studies and the Council on U.S.–Korean Security Studies. He was formerly a professor of international relations at the Marine Corps Command and Staff College and an assistant professor of national security studies at the Air Command and Staff College. Bechtol is the author of *Defiant Failed State: The North Korean Threat to International Security* (2010), *Red Rogue: The Persistent Challenge of North Korea* (2007), and the editor of *The Quest for a Unified Korea: Strategies for the Cultural and Interagency Process* (2007).

Joseph S. Bermudez Jr.

Joseph S. Bermudez Jr. is an internationally recognized analyst, author, and lecturer on North Korean defense and intelligence affairs, and ballistic missile development in the Third World. He is concurrently a senior analyst and author for Jane's Information Group and editor of *KPA Journal*. Bermudez has authored five books—including *Shield of the Great Leader: The Armed Forces of North Korea* (2001), and *North Korean Special Forces–2nd Ed.* (1997), which were both translated into Korean and Japanese—and more than 100 articles, reports, and monographs on these subjects. He has lectured extensively in academic and government environments and worked as a consultant, both in the United States and the Republic of Korea.

Cheon Seongwhun

Cheon Seongwhun is a senior research fellow at the Korea Institute for National Unification in Seoul. He is a member of policy advisory committees for the Ministries of Unification and National Defense of the Republic of Korea (ROK) government; a member of the advisory commission for the Foreign Affairs, Trade, and Unification Committee in the ROK parliament; and an editorial consultant for Radio Free Asia. He is the author of numerous books and reports including *ROK–U.S. Strategic Cooperation for Denuclearizing North Korea* (2009); *PSI and the South Korean Position* (2008); and *Cooperatively Enhancing Military Transparency on the Korean Peninsula: A Comprehensive Approach* (1999). Cheon is the recipient of the Commendation of President of the Republic of Korea in 2003, an award for excellent research from the Korea Research Council for Humanities and Social Sciences in 2001, 2002, and 2003.

Robert M. Collins

Robert M. Collins is an adjunct fellow at the Korea Institute for Maritime Strategy in Seoul. He is a 37-year veteran employee of the Department of the Army and served 31 years in various capacities with the U.S. military in Korea, including several liaison positions with the Republic of Korea military. He completed his career in June 2009 as Chief of Strategy, ROKUS Combined Forces Command, Seoul. Collins served the four-star U.S. commander as one of his two senior political analysts on North and

South Korean politics, Northeast Asian security issues, and challenges within the ROK-U.S. alliance. In that capacity he developed strategies and policy and planning concepts in pursuit of U.S. and ROK-U.S. alliance security interests relative to the North Korean threat and regional security challenges.

Chuck Downs

Chuck Downs, executive director of the United States Committee for Human Rights in North Korea, wrote *Over the Line: North Korea's Negotiating Strategy* (1999)—later translated into Korean and Japanese—while serving as associate director of the Asian studies program at the American Enterprise Institute. He was also co-editor with Ambassador James R. Lilley of *Crisis in the Taiwan Strait* (1997). He served as senior defense and foreign policy advisor to the House Republican Policy Committee of the U. S. House of Representatives, and has published numerous articles and testified before Congress on foreign policy and defense issues.

Nicholas Eberstadt

Nicholas Eberstadt holds the Henry Wendt Chair in Political Economy at the American Enterprise Institute. He is the senior adviser to the National Bureau of Asian Research, and serves on the Advisory Council of the Korean Economic Institute of America and the board of directors of the U.S. Committee for Human Rights in North Korea. He has written extensively on issues of demography, development, and international security. His books on Korean affairs include *Policy and Economic Performance in Divided Korea During The Cold War Era: 1945-91* (2010), *The North Korean Economy Between Crisis and Catastrophe* (2009), *Korea's Future and the Great Powers* (co-editor, 2001), *The End of North Korea* (1999), and *The Population of North Korea* (co-author, 1995).

Nicole Finnemann

Nicole Finnemann is the director of research and academic affairs at the Korea Economic Institute and responsible for issues related to North Korea and outreach including KEI's Academic Paper series.

With a focus on negotiation and North Korea, she co-organizes a Human Security in North Korea forum with Greg Scarlatoiu. After meetings with DPRK ministry officials in Pyongyang in 2008 and 2009, she authored "Getting to Normal: A Six Party Talks Simulation," and conducted simulations for more than 2,000 participants around the country, exposing them to the competing interests and needs of the six nations negotiating the denuclearization of North Korea. She has participated in referendum and peace agreement drafting for the Public International Law and Policy Group, and co-founded the American University Negotiation Project.

L. Gordon Flake

L. Gordon Flake is executive director of the Maureen and Mike Mansfield Foundation, which he joined in 1999. He was previously a senior fellow and associate director of the Program on Conflict Resolution at The Atlantic Council of the United States, and director for research and academic affairs at the Korea Economic Institute of America. He is co-editor of both *New Political Realities in Seoul: Working toward a Common Approach to Strengthen U.S.-Korean Relations* (2008) and *Paved with Good Intentions: the NGO Experience in North Korea* (2003), and has published extensively on policy issues in Asia. He is a regular contributor on Korea issues in the U.S. and Asian press and has traveled to North Korea numerous times. He is a member of the London-based International Institute for Strategic Studies and serves on the board of the United States Committee of the Council for Security Cooperation in the Asia-Pacific as well as on that of the U.S. Committee for Human Rights in North Korea, and the Advisory Council of the Korea Economic Institute of America.

Major General Donald R. Gardner, USMC (Retired)

Major General Donald R. Gardner, USMC (Retired), is president emeritus of Marine Corps University, where he served from 2004–9. Prior to that, he was chief executive officer for the Marine Corps University Foundation after his retirement from the U.S. Marine Corps in 1994. A graduate of the Marine Corps Command and Staff College and a distinguished graduate of the Naval War College, his command assignments included: Commanding General, 3d Marine Division (Rein); Commanding

General, III Marine Expeditionary Force; and Commanding General, Marine Corps Bases, Japan. He was awarded the Order of the Rising Sun, Third Class, by the Emperor of Japan for his dedicated service to the security of Japan and the mutual cooperation between Japan and the United States.

George Alan Hutchinson

George Alan Hutchinson is an energy policy consultant for Concurrent Technologies Corporation, who supports the Office of the Deputy Assistant Secretary of the Air Force (Energy, Environment, Safety, and Occupational Health). After Air Force service with expertise in Korean affairs and language, he served as a linguist to the Special United States Liaison, Advisor Korea, and the National Security Agency. He has written articles about U.S.-ROK arms relations for the *Air Force Journal of Logistics*, and contributed papers covering North Korean military doctrine and Republic of Korea energy dependency vulnerabilities.

Doug Joong Kim

Doug Joong Kim is a professor of Russian studies at Kyonggi University and specializes in the U.S.-Russia-China strategic relations in Northeast Asia and North-South Korean affairs. He served as dean of the College of International Studies at Kyonggi, and chairman of the Committee on Central Asian Studies at the Korean Association of International Studies. He is the author of *U.S.-China Relations and Russia and Soviet Forces in the Korean War*, and edited *Foreign Relations of North Korea: During Kim Il Sung's Last Days* (1994) and *U.S. Policies in Northeast Asia*. He also translated *The Kimchi Matters: Global Business and Local Politics in a Crisis-Driven World* (2003) into Korean and is currently working on *Twenty Years of Russia-Korean Relations* and *The Korean War II*.

Helen-Louise Hunter

Helen-Louise Hunter is a founding member of the Committee for Human Rights in North Korea, which has, since its inception in 2001, published a number of significant studies on North Korea's human rights abuses. She was a political analyst at the CIA for 23 years and served as the assistant national intelligence officer for the Far East from 1979–81. She is the author of *Kim Il-song's North Korea* (1999) and coauthor of *North Korea, A Country Study* (2008). Her most recent books are Sukarno and the *Indonesian Coup: The Untold Story* (2007) and *Zanzibar: The Hundred Days Revolution* (2009).

Hugo Wheegook Kim

Hugo Wheegook Kim is president and founder of the East-West Research Institute and editor-in-chief of the *International Journal of Korean Studies*. He has published a number of articles in academic journals and written three books, including *Korean Americans and Inter-Korean Relations* (2003). His current project is *History of Politics and Economy: Theory and Practice*. After active duty in the Korean Army, he retired as a professor of the Korea National Defense University in Seoul.

Sang Joo Kim

Sang Joo Kim is senior fellow and executive vice president of Institute for Corean-American Studies, and chief executive officer of the institute's Liberty Foundation. He also serves on the boards of a number of civic organizations including the Philadelphia Bar Association International Law Committee, and is a member of the American Thoracic Society.

Don Kirk

Don Kirk, journalist and author, has been reporting and writing from Asia since 1962. He first visited Korea as Far East correspondent for the *Chicago Tribune* in 1972, and has published three books about the country—*Korea Betrayed: Kim Dae Jung and Sunshine* (2009), *Korean Crisis: Unraveling of the Miracle in the IMF Era* (2001), and *Korean Dynasty: Hyundai and Chung Ju Yung* (1997)—and written numerous magazine, journal, and newspaper articles on Korea, Japan, and Southeast Asia. He has reported for newspapers and magazines on such topics as the Kwangju revolt, five Korean presidential elections, the 1997–8 economic crisis and the North Korean nuclear issue.

Symposium Participants

Colonel David S. Maxwell, USA

Colonel David S. Maxwell, USA, is Chief, Strategic Initiatives Group, U.S. Army Special Operations Command; a fellow at the Institute of Corean-American Studies; sits on the board of advisors for *Small Wars Journal*, and is a member of the faculty at the National War College. With 21 years service in Asia, his most recent deployed assignment was commander of the Joint Special Operations Task Force Philippines. He served as a planner on the United Nations Command/Combined Forces Command/United States Forces Korea CJ3 staff, and later as the director of Plans, Policy, and Strategy (J5) for Special Operations Command Korea.

John Park

John Park is a senior research associate and director, Northeast Asia Center for Conflict Analysis and Preventions, U.S. Institute of Peace. He is a co-director of the U.S.-China Project on Crisis Avoidance and Cooperation. He is also a co-director of the Trilateral Dialogue in Northeast Asia, which brings together government and military officials from the U.S., ROK, and Japan. He was previously the project leader of the North Korea Analysis Group at the Harvard Kennedy School. His recent publications include, *"North Korea, Inc.: Gaining Insights into North Korean Regime Stability from Recent Commercial Activities"* (2009), and *"North Korea's Nuclear Policy Behavior: Deterrence and Leverage,"* in *Nuclear Weapons and Security in 21st Century Asia* (2008).

Tim Peters

Tim Peters is a Christian activist and founder in 1990 of Helping Hands Korea. His service spans more than three-and-a-half decades, six countries, and the Caribbean and Polynesian islands. He resides with his wife in South Korea where he has lived on three occasions for a total of nearly 20 years since 1975. He has worked as an editor and speechwriter for the Korean Commission of UNESCO, the Korean National Red Cross, and the Federation of Korean Industries in Seoul. He wrote a paper for the World Economic Forum outlining the then-current (2004) predicament of 300,000 North Korean refugees in China, projecting scenarios of the crisis, and recommending practical aid measures.

Ambassador Charles L. (Jack) Pritchard

Ambassador Charles L. (Jack) Pritchard is president of the Korea Economic Institute in Washington. Prior to joining KEI, he was a visiting fellow at the Brookings Institution. He served as ambassador and special envoy for negotiations with the Democratic People's Republic of Korea and United States representative to the Korean Peninsula Energy Development Organization from April 2001 until September 2003. Previously, he was special assistant to the President for National Security Affairs and senior director for Asian Affairs in the President William J. Clinton administration. During that period he was also the director of Asian affairs in the National Security Council and deputy chief negotiator for the Four Party Peace Talks, which aimed at reducing the tensions on the Korean Peninsula.

Alan D. Romberg

Alan D. Romberg is distinguished fellow and director of the East Asia Program at The Henry L. Stimson Center, and a member of the Asia Society Policy Advisory Board, the Korea Economic Institute Advisory Council, the board of directors of the U.S. Council for Security Cooperation in the Asia Pacific, the advisory board of the Public Intellectuals Program of the National Committee on U.S.-China Relations, and the editorial board of *Asian Politics & Policies*. He has written extensively on U.S. policy, focusing on U.S. relations with the People's Republic of China, Taiwan, Korea, and Japan, and is author of *Rein In at the Brink of the Precipice: American Policy Toward Taiwan and U.S.-PRC Relations* (2003), which was published in translation in China (2007). He has served as principal deputy director of the State Department's Policy Planning Staff, senior adviser and director of the Washington office of the U.S. Permanent Representative to the United Nations, and special assistant to the Secretary of the Navy.

Greg Scarlatoiu

Greg Scarlatoiu, director of business issues and public affairs of the Korea Economic Institute, is responsible for managing outreach programs to educate Americans on developments in Korea and U.S.-Korea relations.

He organizes KEI's Opinion Leaders Seminar, Future of Korea, and Ambassadors' Dialogue programs and serves as director of the Korea Club and the Korea-Japan Study Group. He has written extensively on human rights violations in North Korea and the applicability of the Eastern European experience for U.S.-based public broadcasters and the Korean language press, and has lectured on the situation in North Korea for Korean-American organizations. Since 1995, he has been a Korean language broadcaster for stations including the Korea Broadcasting System in South Korea and Radio Free Asia in Washington, DC.

Jude Shea

Jude Shea is the founder and director of the U.S. Forces Korea (USFK) Korea Battle Simulation Center and the ROK-U.S. Combined Forces Command (CFC) Combined Battle Simulation Center. He has been a leader in improving the use of simulations to drive military exercises; particularly in the areas of large scale, full-spectrum operations and the use of wide-area networking to distribute simulations to sites throughout the world. Prior to entering the civil service, Shea served in the U.S. Army for 32 years. His last active duty assignment was as Chief, Command Post Exercise Branch, C/J3 Exercise Division, CFC/USFK.

Scott Snyder

Scott Snyder is director of the Center for U.S.-Korea Policy at The Asia Foundation and a senior associate at Pacific Forum Center for Strategic and International Studies. He is also the adjunct senior fellow for Korean Studies at the Council on Foreign Relations. Among his books are *China's Rise and the Two Koreas: Politics, Economics, Security* (2009), *Negotiating on the Edge: North Korean Negotiating Behavior* (1999), and co-edited with L. Gordon Flake, *Paved With Good Intentions: The NGO Experience in North Korea* (2003). He lived in Seoul as Korea representative of The Asia Foundation during 2000-4. Previously, he served as a program officer in the Research and Studies Program of the U.S. Institute of Peace, and as acting director of The Asia Society's Contemporary Affairs Program.